Tibetan Yoga

Ian A. Baker

Tibetan Yoga

Principles and Practices

With 396 illustrations

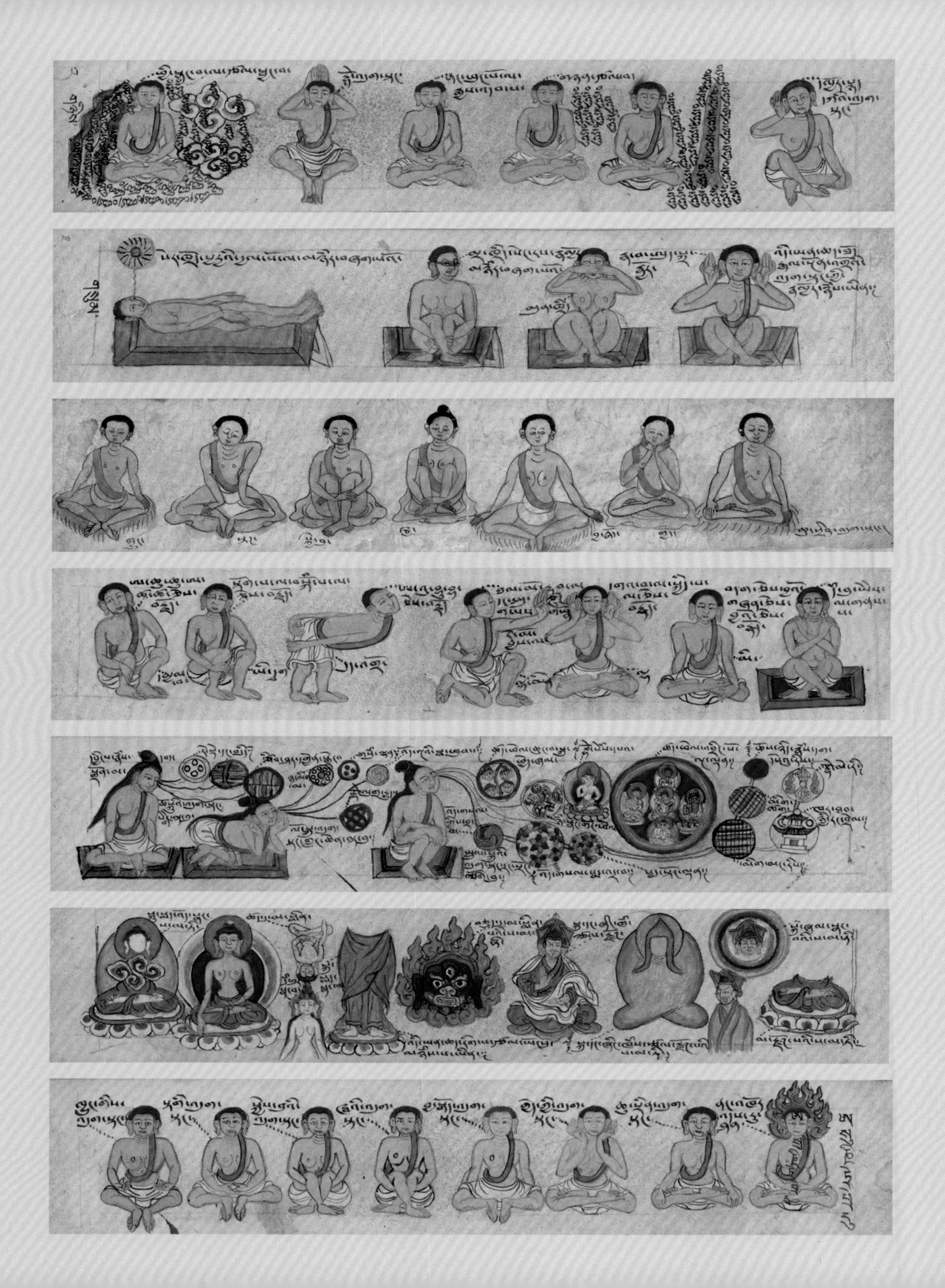

contents

If the body is not mastered, the mind cannot be mastered. If the body is mastered; mind is mastered.

Buddha Sakyamuni, *Majjhima Nikāya Sutrā*

Scholars endlessly expound the scriptures, knowing nothing of the Buddha concealed within their bodies.

Mahāsiddha Saraha, *The Royal Song*, 8th century

Enlightenment arises from within the body or it does not arise at all. Unless the body is realized as the perfect crucible for liberation, freedom from conditioned existence remains only an imaginary dream.

Yeshe Tsogyal, 8th century

Through practising these secret yogas, vitality and wisdom circulate throughout the body and, in this very lifetime, one arises as the primordially awakened Wielder of the Vajra.

Mahāsiddha Nāropā, *Vajra Verses: Instructions of the Wisdom Dākinī*, 11th century

Page 2 **Five elementary processes** inherent in Tantric Buddhist yoga – cohesion, connectivity, thermodynamics, transformation and awareness – are represented in the form of a five-part maṇḍala which, as revealed in this contemporary painting by Rolf Kluenter, shares an analogous geometry with the astrological phenomena of Einstein's Cross.

Page 4 **Illuminated folios from a Tibetan manuscript** at the Royal Danish Library in Copenhagen depict physical postures, breathing practices and gazing techniques used in the Dzogchen practice of *thögal*, or 'leaping over the skull'. As described in the chapter 'Primal radiance', these integral yogic practices alter habitual patterns of perception and lead to a series of visions of enlightening visions.

Opposite **A leaping yogini** by Robert Powell, based on a mural in the former Himalayan Kingdom of Mustang, exemplifies yoga as the art of freedom. Like life itself, yoga expresses the creative impulse to surpass one's current limits and actualize one's fullest capacities. Tibetan yoga encompasses ecstatic rapture as well as rigorous asceticism in its commitment to breaking the bounds of conditioned existence and bringing increased wisdom, joy and delight to the human condition. (See the full painting on page 116.)

Foreword

Bhakha Tulku Pema Rigdzin Rinpoche

In Tibetan language the word yoga, or *naljor*, means to know ourselves in the deepest way possible, beyond the thoughts, emotions, hopes and fears that habitually define our existence and limit our experience as human beings. Many look to the Buddhism of Tibet and the Himalayas for effective methods for expanding awareness and actualizing our interconnectedness with all animate and inanimate existence. Buddhist monasteries in Tibet preserved knowledge of scripture and philosophy, but it is the less well-known non-monastic male and female yogins, or *naljorpa* and *naljorma*, who embody the living spirit of the Buddhist Tantras and their culmination in Mahāmudra and Dzogchen, the realization of humanity's innate enlightened potential. This book reveals a world that has traditionally been kept secret in Tibet, not because knowing one's true nature could ever be considered harmful, but because Buddhist practices that integrate all aspects of life onto the spiritual path can easily be misunderstood unless they are motivated by heartfelt compassion and active concern for the welfare of all beings.

It is well established within the Inner Tantric tradition that texts reveal only the outer meaning and that the inner meaning is conveyed to the practitioner directly by his or her teacher. In old Tibet, this transmission occurred when the teacher whispered the secret oral instructions into a disciple's ear through a hollow bamboo tube. But ultimately it is only through direct experience that the secret, non-conceptual meaning arises in the mindstream of a sincere practitioner. The innermost practices of Tantric or Vajrayāna Buddhism are in this sense *rang sang*, or self-secret. In other words, whatever can be said about them is like giving someone a map to a hidden treasure. The map indicates the way, but unless the map is understood correctly the treasure remains an unattainable dream.

I have known Ian Baker since the 1980s when he undertook meditation retreats in the hiddenland of Yolmo in Nepal, under the supervision of Chatral Sangye Dorje Rinpoche, one of the greatest Dzogchen masters of the 20th century. Baker has also received personal instruction from many other great masters of the Tantric Buddhist tradition and, most importantly, he shares his extensive knowledge and experience in meaningful and insightful ways.

Beyond its outer cultural forms, Tibetan Buddhism expresses a way of life committed to diminishing ignorance, fear, greed and aggression and to maximizing collective wisdom and wellbeing. It is my sincere hope that this book on the hidden world of Tibetan and Tantric Buddhist yoga will inspire its readers to transcend self-preoccupation and to act joyfully, wisely and altruistically within all spheres of human activity. This is the heart of Tibetan Buddhist yoga and the essence of human life, and it transcends all cultural and geographical boundaries. Although the core principles and practices of Tibet's inner Tantric tradition have historically been transmitted secretly, they involve the natural perfection of human existence. Unless such approaches to transforming human experience are effectively revealed and put into practice, they are in danger of being lost. This book contributes directly to their survival.

Bhakha Tulku Rinpoche is a holder of the Tibetan lineage of Tertön Pema Lingpa, one of the Five Great Kingly Tertöns, or spiritual Treasure Revealers, of the Tibetan Buddhist Nyingma tradition. He is also recognized as the incarnation of the great Tertön Dorje Lingpa, and an emanation of the 8th-century scholar, translator and meditation master Vairotsana, one of the first seven monks ordained in Tibet and a heart disciple of Padmasambhava. The present Bhakha Tulku is the tenth incarnation of the Bhakha Tulku line, which has close ties to Bhutan's Wangchuck Dynasty. Bhakha Tulku Rinpoche is shown here performing a fire ceremony at Tamshing Monastery in Bhutan's Bumthang Valley.

Introduction

The hidden nature of the body, breath and mind constitutes an assembly of secrets.

Guhyasamāja Tantra, 6th century

The art of freedom

Despite escalating advances in science and technology, fundamental insight into human existence remains deeply constrained by methods of inquiry that exclude consciousness and the body as viable instruments of research. Tibetan yoga – or more precisely *naljor*, 'unity with the natural state of existence' – overrides this bias and engages the intelligence intrinsic to human embodiment as a means to explore dimensions of experience inaccessible to prevailing modes of neuropsychological and anthropological research. This book introduces fundamental principles and practices of Tibet's Vajrayāna, or Tantric form of Buddhism that have often been obscured within the tradition itself due to historical and sociopolitical constraints as well as Vajrayāna's transformation in Himalayan culture from a yogic technology into a religion privileging ceremonial magic and scriptural study.

The yogic practices at the core of Vajrayāna Buddhism are further endangered by conventions of secrecy that have traditionally made them inaccessible to anyone not in a mentorial relationship with an accomplished master who not only holds the formally conferred right to transmit them, but also embodies the evolved psychophysical capacities that the practices are designed to reveal. This book departs from tradition in expressing a growing consensus that the ideals of Himalayan Buddhism's yogic traditions hold relevance even for those have not been formally initiated into their practice and that the values they assert can enlarge and enliven collective perceptions of the possibilities and opportunities of human life.

Tibetan yoga's core aim is to transform the human condition, freeing it from disempowering struggle and discontent and awakening self-transcendent empathy and compassionate action. Inherent to this worldview is an experience of consciousness that transcends individual preoccupation and expresses the integral, interconnected intelligence of life itself.

Opposite **A contemporary Bhutanese practitioner** – his identity concealed behind a mask representing the legendary Tibetan adept Milarepa – demonstrates strenuous yogic exercises called Trulkhor, or 'magical movements', which include forceful 'drops' (*beb*) that concentrate vital essence and awareness in the body's central channel (*suṣumnā*) to awaken 'fierce heat' (Tummo) as a basis for empowering and illuminating all spheres of human experience.

Open secrets

Tibet's Tantric form of Buddhism arose as a creative convergence of indigenous Tibetan, Indo-Iranian and Chinese practices. This book explores Tibetan yoga's emergence from antecedent traditions and traces its trajectories in diverse philosophical, cultural and scientific spheres. In an age in which languages and consequent forms of knowledge are vanishing at an unprecedented rate, Tibetan yoga offers a vision of human possibility based on autonomous processes within the human body and their correlation with affective states of consciousness that Western models of cognition are only beginning to discern. Tibetan yoga develops these potential human capacities within phases of existence intimately shared by all human beings: namely recurring cycles of waking, sleeping, dreaming, dying and sexual union. Different cultures approach these aspects of life in widely varying ways that reflect the geo-cultural forces that shaped them. Tibetan yoga is no exception in having emerged within specific historical and cultural conditions, yet its sustained genius is its reliance – beneath Himalayan Buddhism's more widely known outer expressions of ritual and iconography – on the uncontrived, natural endowments of the physical body and the consciously extended mind.

Tibetan yoga expresses this ideal of unconditioned consciousness as 'naked awareness'. This state of perpetual becoming is often represented symbolically in Tibetan art as erotically entangled Tantric Buddhist deities. Although sexual practices have always been a component of non-monastic forms of Vajrayāna Buddhism, conjoined divinities more essentially express the non-dual, co-emergent bliss innate to human nature, or what Vajrayāna terms Buddha Nature, a self-transcendent state of wisdom, openness and intrinsic compassion.

Tibetan yoga posits that we are vaster than we consciously acknowledge and that, by expanding awareness beyond its customary range, we can transform not only ourselves but also the world around us. This is the vision expressed in *Tibetan Yoga* and, despite the cultural attribution to Tibet in the book's title, the 'natural state' to which Tibetan yoga refers is an intrinsic endowment of all humanity. This book makes no claim to be anything more than a door opening into an expanse of unrealized human potential. It is no substitute for systematic training with the close guidance of an accomplished master of the tradition, still less for the illuminating insight expressed in the lives and teachings of the Sakyamuni Buddha and the Tantric mahāsiddhas of ancient India, Tibet and neighbouring regions. This book offers instead a visual and anthropological overview of the central practices and insights of the inner Tantric Buddhist tradition, correlating these, where relevant, with contemporary scientific research and revealing how these principles have been encoded in Himalayan Buddhist art. As our world becomes more densely populated and

Below **Chatral Sangye Dorje Rinpoche** (1913–2015), seated on a tiger skin, is widely held to have been one of greatest 20th-century masters of Dzogchen, or Ati Yoga, the culmination of the Tantric Buddhist path. *Bottom* **Dudjom Jigdral Yeshe Dorje** (1904–87), the first appointed supreme head of the Nyingma, or ancient order of Tibetan Buddhism.

Above **Mahāsiddha Padmasambhava** established Tantric Buddhism in Tibet in the 8th century. In this scroll painting, he is depicted in a meditatively transformed state in union with a blue, skull-cup bearing consort. Surrounded by a firewall of pristine awareness and wielding a three-edged dagger and an azure scorpion, Padmasambhava exemplifies Tantric Buddhism's antinomian iconography, each detail of which conceals secret meanings that aid adepts on the path of awakening. Guru Drakpo, *A Wrathful Form of Padmasambhava*, Tibet, 20th century. Pigments on cloth. Rubin Museum of Art, New York, Gift of Shelley and Donald Rubin, C2006.66.3 (HAR 9).

environmentally imperiled by unsustainable models of global development, the principles intrinsic to Tibetan yoga offer a vision of human possibility and positive change that supersedes the practice's cultural origins. At their heart they reveal a model for human flourishing that both embodies and transcends the very nature of culture, humanity's ever-evolving expression of its highest aspirations, capacities and goals. It is with the hope of expanding current transnational models of what constitutes wellness, resilience and ultimate meaning that the historically secret world of Tibetan yoga is introduced in this book.

The opening chapter, 'Outer, inner, secret', situates Tibetan yoga within its historical, cultural and geographical context and addresses the development of Tantric mind–body practices outside the parameters of Buddhist monasticism. Such practices encompass all aspects of human existence within states of waking, dreaming, sleeping and dying. An expanded experience of the human body and its underlying energetic and cognitive potential is thus fundamental to the realization of Tibetan yoga's diverse methods and essential aim. Tibetan yoga develops this capacity, in part, through yogic movements known as Tsalung Trulkhor, 'magical wheel of channels and winds', which amplify innate physiological, respiratory and psychological processes. These practices provide the basis for internal proprioceptive forms of awareness that culminate in Mahāmudra or Dzogchen, otherwise known as Ati Yoga, the spontaneous and naturally radiant non-dual openness of being within which human nature is fulfilled.

The book's following chapters are structured in a traditional sequence that progressively introduces the core principles and practices of Tantric Buddhist yoga. The chapter 'Elemental wisdom' focuses on the variety of contemplative practices within Tibetan Buddhism that establish the basis for more advanced forms of yoga and meditation. Tibetan yoga arises from direct insight into the fundamental 'emptiness', or contingently arising, processional nature of phenomenal existence, including human embodiment. This chapter looks particularly at the Tibetan understanding of five elemental processes that integrate internal and external phenomena and which serve as encompassing metaphors and effective means for experiencing body, mind and breath as an interconnected dimension of bliss, clarity and radiant awareness.

'Immaculate perception' addresses the foundational Creation Phase (Kyerim) practices of Tantric Buddhism that focus on imagining oneself as a Tantric deity, as a support for freeing the mind from habitual, conditioned perceptions. As referenced in Patañjali's *Yoga Sutrās*, the divinities that are invoked have no ontological existence, but they aid the discovery of the liberating, creative powers innate within every individual.

The section 'Enlightened anatomy' introduces Tantric Buddhism's subsequent Completion Phase (Dzogrim), which is based on a visionary physiology of subjectively experienced flows of energy within the human body. Developing this intermediate yogic anatomy through a range of respiration-supported practices called Tsalung Thigle, or 'channels, winds and essences', directs awareness inwards towards a unified and expanded experience of body, breath and mind. These visualization and breathing techniques are further enhanced by dynamic physical exercises called Trulkhor, which are described and illustrated in the subsequent chapter, 'Flowing wholeness'.

A Dzogchen meditation manual depicting visionary phenomena that result from holding prescribed yoga postures combined with fixed gazes and subtle breathing. The apparitional forms reflect subjective yogic experience as well as the ultimately illusory nature of human perceptions. Royal Danish Library, Copenhagen.

In Vajrayāna and Himalayan Buddhism, sequenced physical postures and expansion of the respiratory system are the beginning rather the end of yogic practice. They provide an essential foundation for a set of six internal yogic processes that begin with the cultivation of 'fierce heat' (Tummo) within a meditatively experienced 'illusory body' (*gyülu*). Analogous in concept to Kuṇḍalinī yoga in Hindu Tantrism, the inner fire of Tummo enlivens the neuroendocrine system and metaphorically incinerates inhibiting mental concepts on the path of awakening. This process is described in the chapter 'Incandescence'.

In the Tantric reformulation of Buddhist doctrine, the Buddha's original teachings on universal suffering arising from unmitigated desire are redirected towards the embodiment of self-transcendent bliss. The liberating fire of Tummo induces an experience of 'four joys' that are enhanced through dual cultivation with an appropriate sexual partner. 'Numinous passion' explores the genesis and parameters of sexual yoga in Tantric Buddhism and the ways in which 'blazing and spreading' provides a basis for mutually empowering, non-possessive forms of human relationship.

Clear Light (*ösel*), the third of the Six Yogas, describes a mode of noetic awareness that transcends both waking and sleeping and, though it can be directly cultivated through open presence meditation, it is facilitated by the preceding yogic practices of 'fierce heat' and 'blazing and spreading' as well as by dynamic physiological interventions. This subjective experience of all-pervading luminosity is explored in the chapter 'Noetic light'.

The fourth of the Six Yogas is described in the chapter 'Dreamtime'. Dream yoga (*milam*) is undertaken during rapid eye movement (REM) sleep through conscious control of the normally subconscious process of dreaming. Lucid dreaming allows a practitioner to revise subconscious limbic programming and, when performed consistently, leads to heightened intuition and psychological flexibility during waking states of consciousness.

The fifth yoga, Powa, refers to the transference of consciousness from the physical body at the time of death, whether to a paradisiacal 'Buddha Field' or, in a tradition now reputedly lost in Tibet, into another body. The chapter 'Exit Strategies' explores the origins and development of Tibetan concepts of death and rebirth and outlines the practice of Powa through which a practitioner, at the point of death, bypasses a postmortem realm known as the Bardo and attains 'Buddhahood without meditation'.

The sixth and last of the Six Yogas concerns near-death and after death experiences that were explicated in a visionary 15th-century text translated into English in 1927 as *The Tibetan Book of the Dead*. Six Bardos, or 'intermediary states', are identified and in many respects parallel the sequential phases of the Six Yogas. On an inner level, the six intermediary states refer to psychological transitions that occur

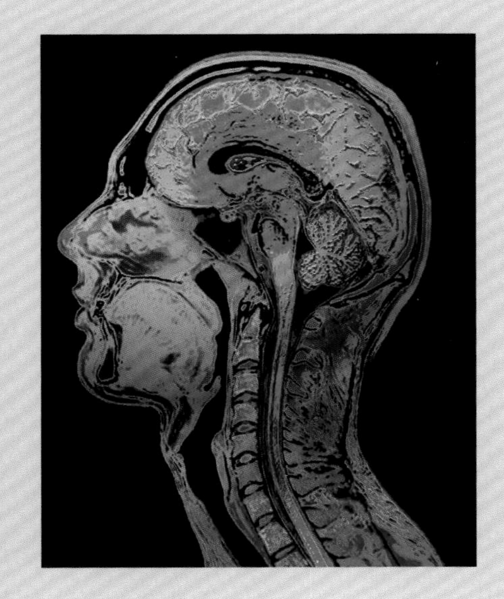

Below right **Magnetic Resonance Imaging of the human brain** reveals how the depths of human consciousness remain an enduring enigma known only by its secondary features. Analogously, 95 per cent or more of the universe is composed of dark energy and matter unobservable by science. Yoga has always been an evolving tradition, drawing deeply from diverse fields of knowledge to expand perception and transform the human condition. Wellcome Library, London.

A detail of a wall painting in the private meditation chamber of Tibet's Sixth Dalai Lama illustrates Tibetan yoga's ultimate goal of awakening radiant, heart-centred and omniscient awareness, symbolized here by the primordial Buddha Samantabhadra in a nimbus of rainbow light.

constantly throughout our lives. The yogic technologies based on these transitional states are directed towards the discovery of a unitary awareness both transcendent of, and immanent within, the emotional vicissitudes of everyday life. Concepts of Bardo Yoga are explored in the chapter 'Liminality'.

Tibetan yogic practices were sometimes enhanced with the use of pharmacologically active substances that point to the biochemical basis of both conscious and subconscious experience. Patañjali's *Yoga Sutrās*, modelled on the eight-fold path to enlightenment outlined by Buddha Sakyamuni, refers specifically to psychoactive plants as potential supports for inner, enstatic experience. The section 'Potent solutions' provides an overview of the controversial use of plant and mineral substances that early Indian and Tibetan texts describe as potential aids to enlightenment.

The book's final chapter, 'Primal radiance', outlines the path of Dzogchen, or Great Perfection, the culmination of the preceding Six Yogas and the unmitigated experience of what is described as the naturally illuminated state of mind and body, also known as Mahāmudra, or 'Great Coalescence'. Dzogchen includes rigorous mental and physical practices that culminate in 'non-dual'

Modern thermal imaging techniques reveal changes in body temperature resulting from specific forms of Tibetan yoga, as shown in this image of Akarpa Rinpoche performing Trulkhor exercises at London's Wellcome Trust. Insights provided by modern science regarding the neurobiological correlates of yoga and meditation are leading to increased understanding of latent capacities of the human mind and body. Wellcome Library, London.

visionary experiences – in environments of total darkness as well as with the support of sunrays and open sky – leading to the attainment, whether figuratively or literally, of a 'rainbow body' (*jalu*). The Afterword concludes with an overview of the induction of Tibetan yoga in the West, its dialogue with science, and the ongoing dialectics of tradition and innovation that have advanced the practice of yoga from its earliest emergence as a means towards realizing humankind's highest physical and metaphysical aspirations.

As a final note, *Tibetan Yoga* omits distracting bibliographic footnotes, although the Notes and Resources section at the end of the book lists extensive textual resources for pursuing additional study as well as practice. Those who are interested in a more academic presentation of yoga and physical cultivation within Vajrāyana Buddhism may also refer to my published articles on the subject, as listed on the website www.ianbaker.com. Lastly, Tibetan words are rendered phonetically in this book so as to make them accessible to a general audience.

Outer, inner, secret

Yoga in Indo-Tibetan tradition

Outer, inner, secret and ultimately hidden (modes of experience and understanding) ... mark the way to perfect Buddhahood through the path of Vajrayāna.

Jamgön Kongtrül Lodrö Thayé, 'Esoteric Instructions', 19th century

Origins of tantric yoga

The word yoga first appears in the Rig Veda (1500–1200 BC), the earliest of India's ancient sacred texts, where it describes a process of 'yoking the mind to its innate luminosity' in conjunction with the rising of the sun. In the earliest Hindu Upaniṣad, the Brihadaranyaka, yoga refers to a state of unification in which 'one sees one's innermost being (*atman*) ... and thus attains the power of the gods'. Practices involving the systematic cultivation of the body, breath and mind towards a transcendent state of freedom continued to develop within ascetic *Śramaṇa* communities in northern India, ultimately leading to the emergence of Jainism and Buddhism in the 5th and 6th centuries BC.

Yoga was further described in Vedic works from the second half of the first millennium BC, culminating in the 3rd-century BC Maitrī Upaniṣad, which refers to a system of six-fold yoga comprised of respiratory expansion (*prāṇāyāma*), introspective withdrawal of the senses (*pratyāhāra*), meditative contemplation (*dhyāna*), mental concentration (*dhāranā*), focused inquiry (*tarka*) and unitive absorbtion (*samādhi*) culminating in 'limitless goodness' in which the practitioner is likened to a blissful 'burning mountain'. This gradual systemization of yoga as a path of emancipation from the entanglements of human existence led in the 4th century AD to the composition of the Yoga Sūtras of Patañjali, which similarly drew on the eight-fold path to Nirvaṇa, or spiritual freedom, outlined centuries earlier by Buddha Sakyamuni. Cross-fertilization between traditions continued with the formulation of the Yogācāra school of Indian Mahāyāna, or 'greater vehicle' Buddhism in the 4th century which presented yoga as a path of insight and engaged compassion leading ultimately to universal enlightenment.

Mahāsiddha Dārikapa was an Indian king who attained enlightenment as a slave to a courtesan, signifying Tantric Buddhism's freedom from more constraining models of emancipation. Darikapa's haloed consort sits in lotus posture with her hands pressed against the 'wind gates' on her upper thighs, intensifying the flow of psychophysical energy through her subtle anatomy. Darikapa demonstrates the result of this internal yoga, rising in dance and twirling a double-headed skull drum signifying awakened consciousness. The fiercely aroused, multi-armed and multi-headed Tantric deity in the upper right-hand corner indicates the power and intensity of Vajrāyana Buddhism's approach to existential freedom. Xylograph painted on cloth, Tibet, 17th century, Musée Guimet, Paris.

Below **The 11th-century female mahāsiddha Niguma** developed a doctrine of Six Yogas for realizing the awakened mind within all phases of life and death. 'Outer, inner and secret' refer in Tantric Buddhist yoga to increasingly subtle forms of practice based on the 'three doors' of body, speech and mind through which reality is experienced, expressed and transformed.

With its distinctive emphasis on the primacy of consciousness, Yogācāra – the 'Way of Yoga' – deeply influenced the emergence of the Vajrayāna, or Tantric form of Buddhism that flourished in India between the 6th and 12th centuries AD and continues to thrive throughout the Himalayan region and beyond. Vajrayāna arose within the larger socio-cultural context of Tantra, a philosophical movement within Indian culture that valorized sensory experience as the source of self-liberating knowledge. Vajrayāna scriptures known as Tantras drew in part from contemporaneous Hindu Śaivite sources to establish a richly syncretic tradition of spiritual practice, firmly rooted in Mahāyāna Buddhism's ideology of universal compassion, but unconstrained by its monastic conventions. In embracing the full range of human experience Vajrayāna extended Buddhism's relevancy beyond its then declining monastic institutions that, often by their own estimation, had become immured in sterile scholasticism. Vajrayāna built on its Mahāyāna Buddhist foundations to develop yogic technologies for freeing human nature from chronic discontent and actively cultivating its innate capacities for altruistic joy. The Vajrayāna model for transcending egocentric preoccupation and embodying wisdom and compassion was initiation into one or another Tantric Buddhist lineage, based on psychological and ritual identification with a designated Tantric Buddhist deity.

The 8th-century Hevajra Tantra, based in part on pre-existing Śaivite practices connected to an intermediate subtle anatomy of interconnected energy channels, famously proclaimed that what can bring confusion and distress to ordinary beings brings grace and illumination to the practitioner of Tantra. Within a liberating programme focused on cultivating an imperishable 'vajra body', the Hevajra Tantra further asserts that the yogi or yogini must dance and sing as well as engage in the 'yoga of passion', thus advocating sensual and emotive practices on the Buddhist path of self-transcendence.

Opposite above left **A rock-carved yogini** in an 9th-century temple in Orissa, India, holds her arms in the position of drawing a bow, a movement that became a standard feature of Tibetan Trulkhor, or 'magical movement', for opening energy flows within the yogic body. This stone figure comprises one of sixty-four yoginis representing, on an esoteric level, energetic phases within nature and the human body.

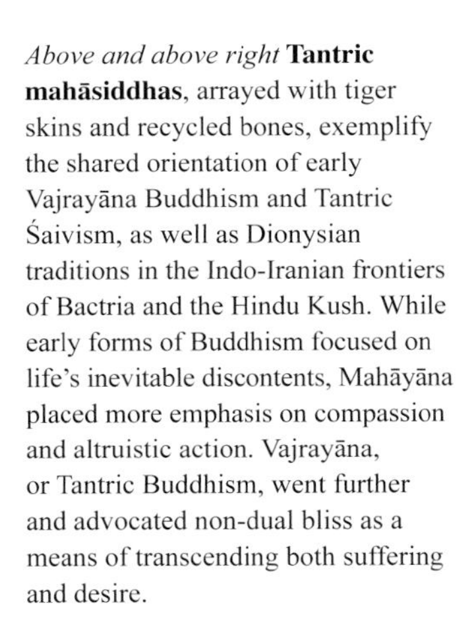

Above and above right **Tantric mahāsiddhas**, arrayed with tiger skins and recycled bones, exemplify the shared orientation of early Vajrayāna Buddhism and Tantric Śaivism, as well as Dionysian traditions in the Indo-Iranian frontiers of Bactria and the Hindu Kush. While early forms of Buddhism focused on life's inevitable discontents, Mahāyāna placed more emphasis on compassion and altruistic action. Vajrayāna, or Tantric Buddhism, went further and advocated non-dual bliss as a means of transcending both suffering and desire.

Vajrayāna's foundational texts were often interpreted symbolically in order to adapt their seemingly radical practices to monastic environments, but it was among peripatetic male and female yogins and householders unconstrained by institutional vows that Tantric yoga flourished in accordance with its view of integration, rather than abnegation, of potentially enthralling activities. The greatest expounders of Vajrayāna's expansive approach to Buddhist practice were the mahāsiddhas, or realized adepts through whom the Vajrayāna Buddhist teachings ultimately reached Tibet. The mahāsiddhas' view of life, largely expressed through ecstatic 'songs of realization' (*doha*), represent the original emancipatory and existential ethos of Tantric Buddhist practice, which transformed in monasteries into symbolic ritualized performances and scriptural incantation. The core teachings of the mahāsiddhas were generally dismissive of such observances and advocated in their place a more inclusive, and, at times, socially transgressive approach to spiritual liberation.

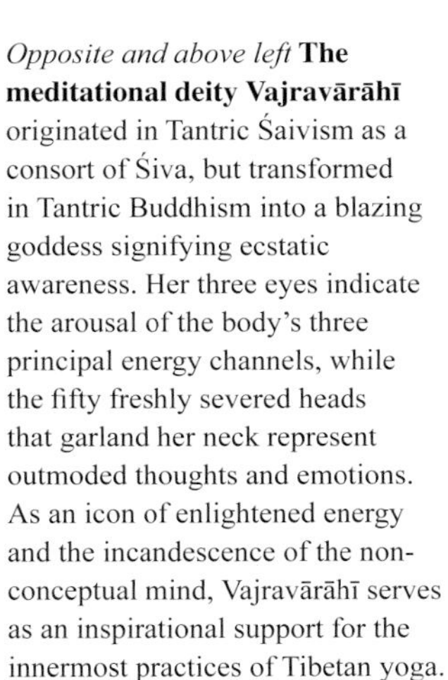

Opposite and above left **The meditational deity Vajravārāhī** originated in Tantric Śaivism as a consort of Śiva, but transformed in Tantric Buddhism into a blazing goddess signifying ecstatic awareness. Her three eyes indicate the arousal of the body's three principal energy channels, while the fifty freshly severed heads that garland her neck represent outmoded thoughts and emotions. As an icon of enlightened energy and the incandescence of the non-conceptual mind, Vajravārāhī serves as an inspirational support for the innermost practices of Tibetan yoga.

Above **The Indian mahāsiddha Nāropā**, who lived in the 11th century, is the figure most closely associated with the Six Yogas that comprise the Completion Phase of Tantric Buddhist yoga. In this image from the Piyang caves in western Tibet he is depicted with a meditation belt and an antelope horn trumpet as well as a skull bowl that associates him with the Kāpālika, or 'skull bearing', tradition of Indian Tantrism from which much Tibetan Buddhist yogic iconography and practice derive. Other prominent mahāsiddhas surround Vajravārāhī in the painting opposite.

Above **The ancient kingdom of Gugé**, located amidst rock walled canyons in western Tibet, was central to Buddhism's revival in Tibet in the 10th and 11th centuries. Although little remains of Gugé's former palaces, Toling Monastery – founded by Richen Zangpo in 996 AD – preserves some of Tibet's oldest and most impressive murals.

One of the earliest mahāsiddhas, Saraha, left his duties as a high-caste Brahmin priest and took up residence with the daughter of an arrowsmith, paradoxically proclaiming in one of his songs of realization that only then had he become a perfect monk. A later mahāsiddha, Tilopā (988–1069 AD), was also a royal cleric who, according to his biography, abandoned his initial profession to produce sesame oil during the day, while at night serving as the procurer for a courtesan. Tilopā transmitted his core teachings on Mahāmudra – the innately liberated nature of mind and body – in the form of six yogic principles derived from the prevailing Buddhist Tantras of his time; instructions that, by some accounts, he is said to have received from Sukhasiddhi, a female mahāsiddha from Kashmir.

Differing in its structure from the six-fold vajra yoga presented in the contemporaneous Buddhist Kālacakra Tantra, or 'Wheel of Time', and the six yogas

Left **A mural at Tsaparang**, the mountaintop capital of the Gugé kingdom until the 17th century, shows artistic influences from neighbouring Kashmir. This detail from the Red Temple depicts a skeleton, assorted goddesses and a multi-armed manifestation of the elephant-headed deity Gaṇapati demonstrating yogic poses.

A yogini meditates in regal ease amidst animals and birds, shown on the eastern wall of the White Temple at Toling Monastery, Tibet. Sitting on a mat of leaves and supported by a meditation belt and with flowers adorning her hair, she holds her right hand in *varada mudrā*, a gesture signifying supreme generosity. Yogic lineages in Tibet originating from female teachers include the Shangpa Kagyu order founded in the 11th century by Khyungpo Naljor, based on teachings that he received from the female mahāsiddhas Niguma and Sukhasiddhi who were reputedly close associates of the male mahāsiddhas Tilopā and Nāropā.

of the earlier Maitrī Upaniṣad, Tilopā's Six Yogas focused on inner heat, radiant bliss, clear light, lucid dreaming, transference of consciousness and navigational instructions for end of life and postmortem experiences. Tilopā transmitted these Six Yogas to his foremost disciple, Nāropā (1016–1100), an illustrious Bengali scholar who had left the Buddhist monastery of Nalanda in search of more inclusive forms of knowledge. The Six Yogas and their culmination as Mahāmudra – an openness and luminosity of being expressed within all activity and beyond conventional distinctions of Saṃsāra and Nirvāṇa – subsequently became the foundation for the Kagyu, or 'whispered lineage', that was brought to Tibet by Nāropā's foremost disciple, a Tibetan layman named Marpa Chökyi Lodrö (1012–97), who carried the teachings of the Six Yogas from the jungles of eastern India across the Himalayas to Tibet.

Tantra in Tibet

Opposite **The dismounted nāga king, Nele Tokan**, pictured in this mural painting in the private meditation chamber of Tibet's Sixth Dalai Lama, is shown taking an oath to Padmasambhava to protect the Tantric Buddhist path of wisdom and compassion. The three prongs of Padmasambhava's skull-embellished Tantric staff (*khaṭvāṅga*) signify his power over ignorance, greed and aggression – the primary obstacles to enlightenment – while, esoterically, they represent the three principal energy channels of the yogic body.

Below **Chatral Sangye Dorje Rinpoche,** 'Enlightened Indestructible Freedom From Activity', was widely regarded as one of the most highly realized Dzogchen yogis of the 20th century and a living embodiment of Padmasambhava. Prior to his departure from Tibet, he instructed the regent of the Dalai Lama in the view and practice of Dzogchen.

Mahāyāna, or 'Great Vehicle', Buddhism entered Tibet from India and China from the 7th century onwards and remained largely distinct from indigenous shamanic and spiritual traditions. The central figure credited with having established Tantric, or Vajrayāna, Buddhism in Tibet was Padmasambhava, a charismatic mahāsiddha who arrived in the 8th century and converted local nature deities into protectors of the Buddhist path of wisdom, compassion and skilful means. Padmasambhava's exposition of Vajrayāna Buddhism was codified within Tibet's Nyingma, or 'ancient' Tantric Buddhist tradition, into a system of nine vehicles for realizing the ultimate nature of mind and reality. Emphasis was placed on the three culminating 'Inner Tantras' of Mahā Yoga, Anu Yoga and Ati Yoga that represented increasingly integral stages of awakening to one's posited Buddha Nature. Mahā Yoga, or 'great union', focuses on Creation Phase (Kyerim) processes in which the creative imagination is ritually engaged to transform oneself existentially into a Tantric deity at the centre of an all-encompassing maṇḍala. Anu Yoga, or 'unexcelled union', cultivates self-transcendent bliss and insight within the 'inner maṇḍala' of one's own body through so-called Completion Phase (Dzogrim) practices, while Ati Yoga, or 'supreme union', represents the Great Perfection (Dzogchen) in which Buddhahood is accomplished effortlessly. Padmasambhava described the culminating non-dual view of Ati Yoga to Tibet's 8th-century reigning monarch as 'the mind awakening to its innermost nature, transcending conceptual views and taking the result [or fruition of Tantric practice] as the means of realization'.

In traditional accounts, Padmasmabhava is said to have brought the teachings of Tantric Buddhism from Uḍḍiyāna, a legendary realm in the foothills of the Hindu Kush mountain range where Asian, Middle Eastern and Hellenic traditions traditions had converged for more than a millennia. The enigma of Padmasmabhava's origins increased with later accounts of his having been born, as his name 'Lotus Born' implies, from a *Nelumbo nucifera* flower in a sacred lake. But, as with other elements of magical realism in the life stories of the Tantric mahāsiddhas, Padmasambhava's biography offers a less literal account of his origins than a timeless narrative of spiritual awakening. In this respect, Padmasambhava's mytho-poetic undertakings outline a path of fearlessness, integration and adaptability culminating in eight designated manifestations of enlightened activity – ranging from scholar, ascetic, lover and king, to tiger-riding sorcerer. Revered throughout the Himalayan region as the 'second Buddha', Padmasambhava embodies, on an esoteric level, the Tantric ideal of spontaneous responsiveness in the service of unconditional altruism and spiritual freedom. His influence continues to evolve in Tibet, Bhutan and Nepal through the subsequent discovery of *terma*, spiritual 'treasure teachings' that have been revealed by his followers from the 11th century onwards and are said

to have been concealed during Padmasambhava's lifetime by his enlightened consort Yeshe Tsogyal (777–837), 'Royal Lake of Primordial Wisdom', for the benefit of future generations.

It was during the second wave of transmission of Vajrayāna Buddhism from India to Tibet in the 11th century that distinctively yogic practices associated with the subtle body appeared in the Land of Snows in written form. Marpa Chökyi Lodrö's transmission of the Six Yogas of Nāropā derive from so-called Completion Phase practices explicated in Tantric Buddhist texts known as 'Yoginī Tantras'. Analogous renditions of the Six Yogas in Tibetan Buddhism originated with the female mahāsiddhas Sukhasiddhi and Niguma in Kashmir. Marpa's primary Tibetan disciple, the celebrated yogin Milarepa (1040–1123), had been introduced to the non-dual teachings of Dzogchen, but found the 'Path of Skilful Methods' of the Six Yogas to be, for him, a more efficacious means to enlightenment. Yogic practices such as Tummo, literally meaning 'fierce feminine', which amplify psychophysiological processes through the cultivation and transformation of metabolic heat became the basis of a so-called 'whispered lineage' that was also described as the 'warm breath of the ḍākinīs', in reference to the practices' interior iconographical association with female Tantric deities and associated lines of doctrinal transmission.

Yogic practices continued to develop in Tibet through Tantric lineages connected with other legendary Indian mahāsiddhas such as Virūpā, whose revelation of the innermost essence of the Hevajra Tantra in the form of Lamdré, or 'Path of Fruition', forms the basis of the 11th-century Sakya school of Tibetan Buddhism and its elaborated Completion Phase practices of Trulkhor, or 'magical movements', for opening the body's inner maṇḍala of subtle energy currents and revealing the

Tibet's celebrated yogi Milarepa was a major figure in the non-monastic transmission of Tantric Buddhism. His long hair, conch shell earrings and meditation belt signify his yogic orientation, as do the snow-capped mountains where he perfected his practice of Inner Fire.

Opposite above **Tibet's sacred Mount Kailash** was one of Milarepa's favoured places for meditation. In traditional accounts, he is said to have reached the summit on a sunray, defeating a sorcerer of Tibet's pre-Buddhist Bön faith, who was attempting the ascent by riding on his shamanic drum.

Opposite below **The cave monastery of Gurugyem** in the Khyunglung Valley in western Tibet lies at the heart of the once flourishing pre-Buddhist civilization of Shang Shung, which practised Bön.

A mahāsiddha and a monk depicted on a mural in Ogyen Choling Manor in Bhutan exemplify the contrast between yogic and clerical traditions within Himalayan Buddhism. The non-celibate yogic adept wears his long hair tied above his head, while a meditation belt across his knee and shoulder signifies his mastery of Tantric yoga. The monk wears his hair short, redirecting his libidinal energies towards study and inner illumination.

mind's non-dual 'brilliance' (*prabhāsvara*), or Clear Light. Despite the mahāsiddhas' foundational role in defining Tantric Buddhist traditions, their teachings were not always well received in monastic contexts. Translations of Saraha's revelatory 'Treasury of Verses' on the uncontrived nature of Mahāmudra were abruptly stopped at Tibet's Samye Monastery in the 8th century for fear the verses' overt critique of monastic conventions would be taken too literally by Tibet's first ordained monks. Similarly, when the Indian master Atisha (982–1054) arrived in Tibet two centuries later and helped establish the Kadampa tradition of Tibetan Buddhism, the instructional verses of the mahāsiddhas were intentionally omitted from the curriculum due to his sponsor's concern for their potentially negative impact on monastic life. The renowned 14th-century scholar Je Tsongkhapa (1357–1419), whose activities led to the formation of the latest school of Tibetan Buddhism, the Geluk, wrote commentaries on the Six Yogas that placed the practices within a graduated approach to enlightenment emphasizing monastic discipline and scholastic study, the very conventions that the mahāsiddhas largely rejected. The Six Yogas' core stated purpose – gathering and dissolving the inner winds, or *prāṇa*, in the body's central channel through the power of meditation – nonetheless remained a central component of Tibetan Buddhism, albeit within renewed emphases on secrecy and monastic protocol.

Above **Dancing mahāsiddhas** on a mural in Pelkhor Chöde Monastery in Gyantse, Tibet, exemplify the strength, flexibility and joy at the heart of genuine yogic practice. To the right, two female figures pay obeisance to a monk. In all its forms, Tibetan yoga seeks liberation from the vicissitudes of existence by bringing forth latent human capacities.

Right **Mahāsiddha Lawapa** was an Indian king who renounced his throne to become a wandering ascetic. This detail of a Tibetan scroll painting shows him meditating with the support of a meditation stick (*gom shing*). The shaft symbolizes the body's central energy channel, while the crescent-shaped 'horns of the moon' at the top of the pole represent the bifurcation of a subtle energy current connecting the eyes and the heart. (See full image on page 287.) Rubin Museum of Art, New York.

Modes of transmission

In order to assimilate Vajrayāna Buddhism's largely heterodox practices, Tibetans developed a heuristic model of outer, inner and secret interpretations that could be applied in varying contexts within an overriding philosophical view of intrinsic 'emptiness' (Śūnyatā) in which all phenomena, whether physical or mental, are devoid of ultimate reality. On an outer level, the Buddhist Tantras themselves were explained as having been taught secretly by Sakyamuni Buddha during his own lifetime, most often to monarchs who had requested means for attaining enlightenment without having to forgo worldly prerogatives and responsibilities. On an inner level, Vajrayāna teachings were understood as historically and culturally determined extensions of Buddha Sakyamuni's core insights into the nature of human consciousness and the latent potential for spiritual awakening. Secretly, the Tantric Buddhist teachings were understood as creative expressions of the liberated mind itself, a seamless continuum beyond any sustainable division between spiritual and worldly phenomena, emptiness and matter, truth and illusion. As mahāsiddha Nāropā explained, 'The innermost secret of the mind is that it neither exists nor doesn't exist, an indissoluble union of emptiness and appearance.'

The outer, inner, secret heuristic was also applied to the Buddhist tradition as a whole, with the secret Vajrayāna teachings representing the highest insight into the nature of human experience while firmly based on Mahāyāna ideals of universal compassion and the foundational ethical precepts of the Buddha's earliest recorded teachings. Tibet's first order of Tantric Buddhism, the Nyingma, applied the same three-part model in their elucidation of the so-called 'Inner Tantras' of Mahā Yoga, Anu Yoga and Ati Yoga, characterized, respectively, as being exoteric, esoteric and 'self-secret'. At the highest levels of Ati Yoga (Dzogchen), outer and inner practices are transcended through effortless abiding in the intrinsic radiance of one's Buddha Nature. The three phases of the Higher Yoga Tantras were further associated with psychological orientations of renunciation, transformation and integration while subtleties of understanding were primarily transmitted individually according to a disciple's disposition and capacity to receive them. In an 11th-century work entitled *Means for Attaining the Real*, mahāsiddha Nāropā clearly defined the approach to be taken in the culminating phase of Essence Mahāmudra and Dzogchen: 'In the nucleus of perfect pristine cognition, the goal is achieved without following any sequential path.'

Opposite below **A folio from a Tibetan manuscript** at the Beijing Palace Museum depicts a series of thirty-two yogic exercises associated with the Completion Phase of the Hevajra and Cakrasaṃvara Tantras.

Below left **A dancing mahāsiddha** on the walls of Tibet's Lukhang temple reflects exhortations in the Hevajra Tantra and other early Tantric Buddhist texts that 'the yogin must always dance and sing'.

Below right **A yogini in Tibet** merges her awareness with the sky in a posture associated with both Dzogchen and Essence Mahāmudra. Her blue-lined meditation belt and red and white Tantric shawl symbolize the internal merging of 'solar' energy, associated with the feminine, and 'lunar' energy, associated with the masculine.

The yoga of pilgrimage

Below **Tibetan pilgrims** in specially padded clothing circle Tibet's sacred Mount Kailash by prostrating the length of their bodies along the ground, rising again to repeat the process from the furthest point that they reach with their outstretched hands.

Opposite above **The Inner Sanctuary of Mount Kailash** is traditionally visited only after completing thirteen circuits around the 21,778-foot-high holy mountain. The pilgrims here are headed towards the 'Cave of the Thirteen Golden Stupas', above the snowline on the southern face.

Opposite below **A prayerful pilgrim**, measuring the length of his body along the earth, begins a 32-mile circuit around Mount Kailash.

Tibet's evocative, high-altitude landscape inspired its spiritual traditions long before the arrival of Buddhism. Pilgrimages to sacred mountains remain a strong aspect of Tibetan Buddhism that unifies individuals with the larger community and environment. As a yogic practice, pilgrimage is described as having outer, inner and secret aspects. In its most rigorous form, pilgrims journey to and around sacred sites making full-length prostrations with their bodies, as pictured in the images below of pilgrims circling Tibet's sacred Mount Kailash. On an outer level, the practice of prostration focuses the mind on fundamental Buddhist values and develops stamina and resilience. On an inner level, the practice is said to open a subtle energy channel paralleling the spine, thus making the body a conduit for elemental awareness. On a secret level, the surrendered repetitive movements recalibrate the mind, opening it to whatever arises and revealing consciousness's ultimate transcendence of both external and internal circumstances. This spirit of pilgrimage is expressed powerfully in the Tibetan adage of unconditionally bringing whatever arises in the body, mind, or field of experience onto the spiritual path.

Another indigenous methodology for cultivating extraordinary physical and mental capacities is the now almost entirely lost tradition of *kyang gyap*, literally 'swift footedness', in which mantras and ointments are inscribed on

Right **A wandering, dreadlocked yogini** on pilgrimage in Tibet's sacred land of Pemakö gazes into the great bend of the Tibet's Tsangpo River as it arcs around a sacred mountain. Tibetan texts liken the river's powerful current to the central energy channel of the Tantric meditational deity Vajravārāhī, whose additional attributes are described on page 23.

Opposite **A Tibetan lama** stands at the edge of a cataract in the depths of Tibet's Tsangpo Gorges after completing a ritual offering to local protector deities. See pages 80–82 for a description of the Tibetan Buddhist practice of Chöd.

the feet to empower one to move rapidly across Tibet's open landscapes when combined with esoteric breathing practices, internal recitation of sacred syllables and visualization. As described by one of its few contemporary practitioners, Akarpa Lobsang Rinpoche, 'yogic running' is undertaken in the absence of food or drink and is based on channelling the energy of the earth through the feet and directly to the brain through the body's central meridian.

On its innermost level, pilgrimage is undertaken as a spiritual exercise that integrates movement with inner contemplation. Rather than seeking solace and comfort at sacred sites, the practitioner of Dzogchen, or Great Perfection, is encouraged to seek out places that 'make the mind waver' and to embrace whatever is experienced. The 11th-century mahāsiddha Padampa Sangye expressed this rarefied approach to pilgrimage succinctly: 'To realize the essence of consciousness … approach whatever you find repulsive. Anything you are attracted to, let go of it! Visit cemeteries and places that scare you. Find the Buddha within yourself!'

By embracing whatever arises, the pilgrim on the path of Great Perfection transcends default patterns of perception and cognition. In response, the world returns transfigured. The Fifth Lelung Shepai Dorje Rinpoche powerfully evoked this 'pure seeing' (*danang*) while travelling through the hiddenland of Pemakö in Tibet's Tsangpo Gorges in 1729: 'When journeying to these sacred places, fear naturally transforms into great splendour and one remains perfectly at ease. A new spiritual awareness flares up in one's stream of consciousness: a conception-free unity of bliss and emptiness.'

The supreme yoga

The culminating phase of all Tibetan yoga is called Dzogchen, or Great Perfection and is upheld as revealing the ultimate unconditioned nature of human consciousness, without recourse to the transformational rites and psychophysical practices that characterize much of the Tantric, or Vajrayāna, form of Buddhism from which Dzogchen emerged. While commonly perceived, and presented, as pertaining principally to the reflexive 'self-liberating' potential of the mind, the practice of Dzogchen is nonetheless traditionally infused with physical exercises that push the body – and thereby consciousness and perception – beyond accustomed limits in order to facilitate the arising of a primordial unitary awareness called *rigpa* or, in Sanskrit, *vidyā.*

As described in this book's final chapter, 'Primal radiance', physical cultivation in Dzogchen ranges from demanding preliminary practices to rigorous yogic exercises that balance and amplify psychosomatic processes. These are undertaken prior to Dzogchen's more widely known contemplative techniques of Kadak Trekchö, or 'cutting through to primordial purity', and the more rarely transmitted visionary practices of Lhündrup Tögal, or 'leaping over the skull into spontaneous presence', involving precise body postures, breathing techniques and methods of gazing.

Luminescent spheres in the sky above Gurugyem Monastery in West Tibet reflect visionary phenomena that occur in the Dzogchen practice of Tögal, or 'leaping over the skull'. In Dzogchen, subjective visions are viewed as 'non-dual' appearances that illuminate perception and cognition. Practitioners pass through four visionary phases that ideally culminate in the attainment of a photic 'rainbow body'.

Sunbeams reflecting through a crystal symbolizes the Dzogchen view of consciousness as a unity of emptiness and luminous appearance. In this detail from a mural in Tibet's Lukhang temple, rays of light reflect off a copper vessel filled with agitated water and strike a transparent crystal which, in turn, displays flickering five-coloured rainbow lights. The sequence introduces the nature of mind as primordially empty yet infinitely expressive.

In all aspects of Dzogchen practice, the body is cultivated and its natural processes enhanced in order to facilitate effortless abiding in the self-liberated radiance of intrinsic awareness, equated in Dzogchen to the Buddha Nature held to be the essence of human consciousness. As the renowned Tibetan master Rigdzin Jigme Lingpa (1730–98) summarized, 'The pith essence of the Great Perfection is to dwell in the natural radiance of all that occurs, at one with actions, energies and thoughts and beyond all contrived boundaries of view and meditation; at ease in the naked clarity of the present moment.'

Based on present moment awareness of the mind's intrinsic freedom from discursive thought processes and conditioned behaviour, the 'pure and perfect presence' of Dzogchen is pointed out as the innate human potential to live beyond dualizing beliefs, reactive patterning and psychological distress. When integrated into all aspects of one's experience, this naturally perfected openness and compassion is upheld as the culmination of the spiritual path in which mind and body, reason and intuition, intention and application, cohere in enlightened awareness and altruistic action. Although physical yoga, breathing practices and mindfulness training can help to align one with one's fundamental nature, Dzogchen lies beyond all secondary methods. Padmasambhava described Dzogchen as 'the mind directly recognizing its own essence', an effortlessly distributed attention to the seamless field of the perceiver and the perceived and the act of perception.

Yoga in Tibet today

Yoga existed at the core of Tibetan identity long before the arrival of Buddhism in the 7th century. The vision of the fundamental unity of the individual and the cosmos was equally part of Tibet's pre-Buddhist Shang Shung civilization, centred on the 'precious snow peak' of Mount Kailash, where practitioners of various forms of yoga and meditation have converged for millennia, exchanging both ideas and techniques. Much changed in Tibet after 1959 when the Lhasa Uprising against Chinese occupation led to an ensuing Tibetan diaspora and a comprehensive prohibition of religious activity in Tibet for nearly two decades. These changes led to the dissemination of Tibetan Buddhism throughout the world, but the dynamic 'secret' practices of Tibetan yoga that 'take the body as the path' and forgo monastic convention continue to remain little known, even within the tradition.

Political conditions in much of what was historically Tibet are no longer conducive to the transmission of the inner Tantric teachings. The situation in eastern Tibet is more open, however, and Tibetan yoga is being actively revived in remote areas, such as at Gebchak Nunnery, where female practitioners of Dzogchen train in Tummo, or 'fierce heat', as well as in the visionary practices of Lhündrup Tögal, 'leaping over the skull into pure presence'. Active areas

Opposite and above left **Terdrom, 'Trove of Treasures'**, is associated with the yogini princess Yeshe Tsogyal. She reached enlightenment in a cave near the summit of the mountain in this photograph and, until recently, her successive emanations, the Drigung Khandromas, lived in the hermitage visible to the right. Yeshe Tsogyal's yogic practices focused on Tummo, the Yoga of Inner Fire, leading her to proclaim: 'My body has become the deity, my speech mantra, and my mind Buddha!'

Above right **Naljorma Ani Rigsang** instructs a young disciple at her hermitage in Terdrom. Although renowned for its healing hot springs and active nunnery, Terdrom is a thriving centre for the transmission of esoteric yogic practices such as the 'Heart Essence of the Ḍākinīs' (Khandro Nyingthik).

of yogic practice in central Tibet include a retreat centre above Drigung Til Monastery and a community of yoginis in Terdrom, presided over by a reputed reincarnation of the 8th-century female Buddha, Yeshe Tsogyal. These practices also continue actively in Nepal, and with royal patronage, in the Himalayan Buddhist Kingdom of Bhutan.

Unlike many religions, yoga, at heart, has never been a doctrinal, political, or coercive tradition, but represents an integral psychology and pragmatic means for awakening a subjective experience of self-transcendence and unity with both noumenal and phenomenal reality. Tantric yoga has thus remained, as one contemporary lama has described it, the 'hidden treasure' at the heart of the Himalayan Buddhist tradition. It intersects with the post-modern Western quest for spiritual meaning beyond religious dogma as well as with formative philosophical currents (*phileo* meaning 'love' and *sophia* 'wisdom') of Western civilization.

The perennial individual and collective challenge of embodying wisdom and love within all aspects of our interconnected lives can only be realized when the pursuit of insight is undertaken with one's entire being, with affectionate and effortless attention to the minutiae of moment to moment occurrence. In the hidden ravines of Terdrom in Central Tibet, a renowned lama took refuge in a cave in 1959, when Communist armies were overrunning the nation.

Opposite and below **A remote temple** on the pilgrimage circuit around Terdrom, in central Tibet, lies amidst caves and limestone cliffs. Its former caretaker dances at the threshold in front of a woven yak wool curtain embellished with four 'endless knots', Buddhist symbols of the interweaving of timelessness and time as well as the continuum of enlightened awareness.

Lama Lobsang Karma remained in the cave for more than twenty years, intensifying his practice and living largely on lichen and flowers. He emerged long after the Cultural Revolution was over and discovered that his monastery had been destroyed – but not his spirit. As he recounted, 'The Buddha reveals how love and understanding overcome all obstacles. The highest yoga is not to sit silently on one's buttocks, but to dance, to let the Buddha's wisdom flow through your mind and body and into the world.'

I learned that Lobsang Karma had once been the dance master of the remote and partly restored hermitage where we had met and, as we spoke, he demonstrated the swirling movements of the sacred Cham dances in the stone courtyard, lit with high-altitude light. What was the secret, I asked him, to his obvious vitality and radiance after nearly a quarter century in a cave. 'I danced every day', he said, and then quickly qualified by saying that it wasn't he who danced, but the deities who danced through him, referring to the foundational Tibetan 'deity yoga' in which the adept imaginatively identifies with a conjured divinity in order to transcend limiting beliefs in an independent and autonomous self: the ultimate purpose of all forms of Tantric Buddhist meditation.

Elemental wisdom

The varieties of meditative experience

If Enlightenment exists apart from meditation,
how can meditation reveal it?
If it is ineffable, how may it be discussed? ...
The whole world is enslaved by concepts,
And no one recognizes their essential nature.

Mahāsiddha Saraha, 8th century

The art of contemplation

Opposite **Contemplative practices** in Tibetan Buddhism range from rigorous asceticism to ecstatic rapture and share a common aim of expanding the capacities of mind and body and cultivating empathy with all existence, as indicated in these details from a mural in the Lukhang temple in Lhasa, Tibet.

Below **A dread-locked yogin** at the Lukhang temple forms symbolic hand gestures called *mudrās* to shift his state of awareness.

The Tibetan word for meditation is *gom*, and infers 'familiarization' or mindfulness of one's inherent Buddha Nature, a transpersonal state of empathy, insight and spontaneous altruism. Early Buddhist scriptures refer to meditation as a process of progressively awakening to deepening states of Infinitude (*anantya*), culminating in exalted self-transcendent awareness infused with clarity and compassion. Such descriptions influenced the development of classical yoga, as evidenced in Patañjali's *Yoga Sutrās*, which borrow from Buddhist doctrine to define yoga as an eight-fold path leading to the cessation of afflictive mental states and the attainment of existential freedom.

Tibetan Buddhism encompasses a vast range of contemplative techniques that traditionally begin with meditation on the 'Four Immeasurables' (*apramāṇa*) of loving kindness, compassion, sympathetic joy and freedom from attachment and aversion. Embracing these sublime attitudes is the basis for all subsequent meditation practices in the Tibetan tradition – from the mindfulness-based disciplines of focused attention and uncensored awareness that have been adapted in contemporary clinical contexts to alleviate stress, anxiety and depression to the dynamic methods of Tantric yoga that stimulate, rather than relax, the central nervous system so as to arouse dormant capacities of the mind and body.

In Tibet's Vajrayāna form of Buddhism, meditative practices progress from preparatory reflections on the nature of existence and the cultivation of unconditional compassion to creative reorientations of subjective experience (Kyerim or Creation Phase), to transformative engagement with the flows of energy through the body's subtle interstitial circulatory system (Dzogrim or Completion Phase). The resultant experiences of bliss, clarity and conception-free insight culminate in Dzogchen, the Great Perfection, also known as Ati Yoga, in which consciousness awakens to its spontaneously present Buddha Nature.

The elements of experience

By traditional accounts, the Buddha's enlightenment was precipitated by his recollection of a moment in childhood when he rested in perfect repose under a rose-apple tree. As recounted in Buddhist scripture, recalling that moment of primal harmony amidst the elements of nature led directly to Prince Gautama's ultimate attainment of Nirvāṇa.

Contemplation of the cycles of nature is foundational to Buddhist meditation, and the elements of the natural world entrain consciousness towards more unitary states of awareness. Long before the emergence of palatial monasteries, Buddhist practice centred on peripatetic forms of contemplation in which processes in the natural world paralleled insight into the shimmering transience of mental states, ultimately revealing an emancipatory continuum of being beyond emotional reactivity.

Foundational Buddhist meditation practices often involve contemplation of Earth, Water, Fire, Air and Space as universal processes correlated with body, breath and consciousness. As described in the chapter 'Enlightened anatomy', these elemental phases are encoded in the body as a system of bioenergetic nodes (*cakras*) that provide a basis for Tantric contemplative techniques that harmonize cohesion (Earth), fluidity (Water), creativity (Fire), motility (Air) and awareness (Space) both within and beyond the human bodymind.

The Five Elements are further correlated in Buddhist contemplative practices with five interrelated constituents of physical and mental existence – namely form, sensation, perception, volition and consciousness. In Buddhist terms, none of these factors constitute an independently existing 'self', and reflection on these five interconnected phases thus leads, in Buddhist analysis, to the emergence of Five Wisdoms in which thoughts and emotions are experienced as interactive processes absent of any abiding reality. At the level

Below left **The Five Elements** comprising phenomenal reality are depicted in this seminal *bija* maṇḍala as coloured orbs within an all-encompassing sphere of rainbow light. The contemplative diagram represents the enlightened qualities of Five Transcendental Buddhas, signifying the spectrum of fully awakened transpersonal awareness.

Below right **A yogin points to a crystal** that signifies the pure, unconditioned nature of consciousness. The Five Elements manifest around him as rock, water, fire, air and a luminous sun disk representing the mind's radiant, all-encompassing clarity.

Arboreal symbolism infuses Buddhist thought. An early Buddhist scripture compares spiritual practice to a tree, 'the fibres of which are patience, the flowers virtue, the boughs awareness and wisdom, and the fruits teachings'. Although the Buddha attained enlightenment sheltered by a ficus tree, monasteries often cut down forests to build virtual replicas of the palace that Prince Gautama abandoned, supplanting 'the roots of trees, mountains, glens, caves, cemeteries, and forest groves' that the Buddha indicated as being the most conducive environments for meditation, as depicted in this wall painting in Toling Monastery in western Tibet.

of Dzogchen, or Great Perfection, the Five Wisdoms are presented analogically as Five Lamps, which – coextensive with the element of Space – symbolize the radiant multidimensionality of enlightened awareness. As the 11th-century mahāsiddha Maitrīpa stated in his essential instructions on Mahāmudra: 'Recognizing everything as space, like a magical apparition, neither meditating nor not meditating, neither attached nor not attached, such is a yogin's realization ... Who then needs to run to a monastery to meditate?'

As Maitrīpa's words make clear, meditation in Tantric Buddhism is less about specific techniques than self-transcendent identification with universal processes, such as the Buddha experienced at the age of nine beneath the boughs of a rose-apple tree. Such shifts in awareness, however they are occasioned, represent emergence from egocentric into ecocentric existence – a unitary field of body, mind and nature in which the known and unknown constituents of reality express themselves ever more consciously, joyously and instructively through the vehicle of the human bodymind.

The wisdom of emptiness

The element of Space, as an analogue of enlightened awareness, is fundamental to all forms of Tibetan yoga and meditation. In early Indian and Tibetan thought, Space signifies the limitless, unreified nature of reality as well as the consciousness that perceives that reality. Mahāyāna and Vajrayāna Buddhism both refer to this open indeterminate potentiality as Śūnyatā, or 'emptiness', and all forms of Tibetan meditation are based on experientially realizing this intangible informational dimension. Just as quantum field theory points out that what appears as empty space is in actuality a flux of elementary particles, Mahāyāna Buddhism describes Śūnyatā as being coextensive with the realm of form, reflecting quantum physics' view of reality as existing only when it is perceived.

Buddhism's doctrine of universal emptiness maintains the absence of any self-existing reality and, since all apparent substances, including the self, are thus purely relational, early schools of Buddhism present emptiness as a basis for detachment. But just as contemporary science reveals the phenomenal world, including the cells of our bodies, to be ephemeral photonic transactions of sub-atomic particles, emptiness is equally a cause for wonder and delight. This perspective is embodied in Great Perfection contemplative techniques, described in the chapter 'Primal radiance', in which being itself is experienced as all-pervading luminescence and the five elemental phases as an interplay of informational photons and somatic light.

Dzogchen's representation of emptiness as a primordial conjunction of luminosity and awareness reflects the 'empty forms' that serve as objects of contemplation in more elaborated forms of Tantric Buddhism, illuminating the simultaneity of absence and appearance expressed equally in quantum physics' recognition that only when an object's wave function collapses as a result of observation does it assume a particular place or motion, and thus provisional existence. This numinous ambiguity in which things are not as they appear is reflected in Vajrayāna Buddhism's creative forms of meditation involving visualization, mantra and amplified states of awareness that are described more extensively in the following chapter, 'Immaculate perception'. But for such practices to be undertaken without delusion – or falsely concluding that because things are illusory they don't actually exist – necessitates prior realization of the unbounded luminescent nature of existence, attained through a diverse range of foundational meditative exercises.

Opposite above **The primordial Buddha Samantabhadra** emanating as a radiant sphere of light represents the pure and perfect presence of intrinsic enlightenment, as espoused in Dzogchen. Samantabhadra, the 'All Good', is invariably depicted as blue to signify the all-encompassing spaciousness of pure awareness.

Opposite below **Four meditating yogis** with spheres of elemental light radiating above their heads illustrate four of the Five Lamps of intrinsic wisdom that illuminate in-dwelling Buddha Nature. Experienced within a numinous state of emptiness, the Lamps of the Five Wisdoms signify the spontaneous liberation of inhibiting emotional corollaries of the Five Elements.

Left **An inverted yogi** on a mural in Tibet's western region of Ngari illustrates the reversal of habitual patterns of consciousness intrinsic to contemplative practice.

ཀུན་བཟང་།

Opposite **A 12th-century maṇḍala of Cakrasaṃvara and Vajravārāhī** in union presents an implicate order of bliss and emptiness, signified by the maṇḍala's outer ring of charnel grounds in which adepts consume intoxicants and engage in sexual rites in order to transcend inhibitory thoughts and emotions. Such mental events obscure the maṇḍala's palatial interior, where the deities' erotic display signifies the non-duality of emptiness and appearance, emptiness and bliss, and emptiness and all-illuminating clarity. Metropolitan Museum of Art, New York.

Above **Contemplation of impermanence** is foundational to all forms of Buddhist meditation and is dramatically illustrated in this mural detail of a yogin gazing into the eyes of a jackal who is devouring a human corpse. The entropy of all relative phenomena supports the philosophical view of Śūnyatā, including the emptiness of thoughts, emotions, and self-conceptions. Yet, Śūnyatā itself is also empty and, in the words of the poet Wallace Stevens, is simultaneously 'a nothing that is not there and the nothing that is'. Awakening experientially to this paradoxical reality is described as actualizing one's inherent Buddha Nature, as vividly expressed in Tantric Buddhist art.

Moving inwards

Withdrawing sensory awareness from external objects (*pratyāhāra*) is described in Patañjali's *Yoga Sutrās* as the foundational stage in meditative practices leading to deepening states of concentration (*dhāraṇā*), contemplation (*dhyāna*) and unitary absorption (*samādhi*). Sensory withdrawal is foundational to meditation practices across traditions, lessening distracting emotions, promoting mental tranquility and insight, and heightening awareness of internal sources of sensation, perception and awareness.

In Buddhist Tantras, such as the Kālacakra, or 'Wheel of Time', *pratyāhāra* refers to the transformation of the five sense faculties of sight, hearing, smell, taste and touch into the mentally generated sensorium of an enlightened deity that is simultaneously viewed as an insubstantial manifestation of universal emptiness. The Kālacakra's exposition of sensory interiorization closely parallels the phase of physical isolation (*kāyaviveka*) in the Guhyasamāja, the Tantra of the Secret Assembly, and is undertaken in total darkness until non-conceptualized 'empty forms' arise in one's field of vision. These visions, which in Buddhist analysis are neither existent nor non-existent, provide the basis for the ensuing meditative stage of *dhyāna*, or contemplation, through which consciousness is stabilized prior to being energized through dynamic breathing exercises (*prāṇāyāma*) that, in the context of the Kālacakra Tantra, concentrate vital energy in the pelvic cavity below the navel. This deeply embodied approach to meditation continues with the subsequent phase of *dhāraṇā*, in which subtle elemental substances (*bindu*, Tib. *tiglé*) are cultivated within psycho-energetic

Below left **Introversion of the senses**, as illustrated in this mural detail, awakens dormant psychophysical capacities. Described as the 'magical movement of the liberating lion' (Senge Namdrol Trulkhor), the posture is combined with holding the breath beneath the navel. The eyes are covered with the two index fingers, the ears are blocked with the thumbs, the nostrils with the two middle fingers, the lips with the ring and little fingers, while the head is circled three times to the right and three times to the left. Afterwards, the body and limbs are vigorously shaken while exhaling forcefully.

nodes (*cakra*) that parallel the spine. In the fifth phase of 'recollection' (*anusmṛti*), these cultivated essences give rise to four successive states of meditative bliss within the core of the body, echoing early Buddhist accounts of four *jhānas*, or sequential stages of proprioceptive rapture. The Wheel of Time's six-fold Vajra Yoga coalesces in *samādhi*, or supreme absorption in the conjoined bliss and emptiness represented by the deity Kālacakra as the innate freedom, spontaneity and unbounded consciousness inherent within all beings and attainable through progressive 'familiarization'.

Meditation postures vary depending on their specific intention, but whether focused inwards in a crouching pose to awaken the heart *cakra* or vertically aligned in the classic lotus position, their common objective is to bring mind and body into a natural state of unity, easing tensions and, as expressed in early Buddhist Sutrās, allowing awareness to merge naturally with Infinitude. In most postures, the spine is lengthened to expand the lungs, reduce wandering thoughts, and facilitate the free flow of somatic energy. The head typically rests effortlessly on top of the seven cervical vertebrae while the pelvis drops and attention is concentrated below the navel where, according to Tantric physiology, the body's three principal energetic channels join together. Buddhist texts describe the ideal meditation posture as one that balances the five elementary qualities of Earth, Water, Fire, Air and Space, as expressed within the human body, its sensory extensions, and the outer environment of minerals, water, sunlight and ethereal winds.

Opposite right **A crouching posture** assists in withdrawing the senses from external objects and attaining an interior state of mental concentration focused at the heart *cakra*, thus aligning consciousness with its innate numinosity and freeing it from what neuroscience describes as its default mode network. Beijing Palace Museum.

Above **The classic seven-pointed meditation posture** of the Buddha Vairocana – the embodiment of Supreme Enlightenment – involves crossing one's legs in lotus posture and turning one's feet upwards on one's thighs. The arms are relaxed with one hand held on top of the other four finger-widths beneath the navel with the palms upwards and the thumbs gently touching in a gesture of equipoise. (According to some traditions, if desire is predominant in one's mind, the right hand is placed over the left. If aggression is predominant, the left hand is placed over the right.) The spine is held erect, like a stack of golden coins. The shoulders are opened, like an eagle drying its wings in the sun. The head balances effortlessly on top of the spine, like a lotus bud on its stalk. The eyes rest on the ground an oxen yoke's length in front of the body. The breath is allowed to come and go without manipulation. The lips, teeth and tongue rest comfortably, with the tip of the tongue lightly touching the roof of the mouth.

Entering the flow

In Tibetan yoga, each of the Five Elements provides a meditative means for awakening to the mind's limitless nature and the larger flow of life. Turning inwards, beyond the persona, and attuning to the inner archetype of Water, practitioners enter figuratively into the fluid depths of somatic consciousness, transcending habitual boundaries of perception and discovering an expanded, processual reality. In the Great Perfection *Tantra of the Illuminating Lamp*, adepts are instructed to crouch above a turbulent waterfall and, with 'the gaze of an elephant', to penetrate the essence of water. 'When you listen uninterruptedly to the sound of water', the Tantra states, 'the supreme unborn essence will fully emerge ... You will come to understand the flow of consciousness in future, present, and past.'

Opposite and right **The Yoga of the Five Elements** consists of meditating successively on the primal sounds of Earth, Water, Fire, Wind and Space and allowing their resonances to permeate one's consciousness. By cultivating more inclusive forms of sensory awareness, practitioners recognize the reverberations of the Five Elements as analogues of their psychophysical aggregates. Awakening to one's Buddha Nature in the roar of falling water, the mind no longer grasps at either external or internal phenomena; and thoughts and emotions pass through consciousness unimpeded in a flow of pure and perfect presence.

Dynamic stillness

The English word meditation stems from the Latin *meditatum*, 'to ponder', but refers more generally to contemplative techniques for bringing the mind to a state of sustained attention, freeing consciousness from disturbing thoughts and emotions, and cultivating fluent presence and expanded capacities of mind and body. The ultimate aim of the physical and mental disciplines of Tibetan yoga is to transcend the dualistic habits of ordinary consciousness that obstruct awareness of what is referred to in Dzogchen as the Natural State (*nelug*), the self-liberated unity of primordial emptiness and radiant awareness. Training often begins with meditative concentration on the breath in order to stabilize consciousness and progresses to more expansive forms of meditation in which the mind transcends disquieting thoughts and emotions through open presence awareness. Insight develops naturally with the pacification of discursive mental activity and the gradual emergence of lucid, thought-free presence. Neural imaging of brain activity during various forms of meditation increasingly reveals meditation's positive influence on the human immune system, healing

A monk in Chumphug, a sacred valley in Bhutan, sits in open-eyed presence. Meditation cultivates emotional clarity and contentment and is often described in natural similes. As the Hevajra Tantra states: 'Like the continuous flow of water and the flaming tip of an oil lamp, day and night the practitioner always remains in meditative equipoise.'

The cliff-side ḍākinī temple of Khandro Lhakhang at Kunzangdrak in Bhutan exemplifies the isolated settings that lessen distractions and support awareness of the luminous continuum of mind and phenomenal reality. Kunzangdrak was the principal seat of the renowned 15th-century Bhutanese treasure-revealer Tertön Pema Lingpa.

and psychophysical wellbeing. In Tibetan tradition, the mind's progression from subliminal turbulence to increasing lucidity and dynamic stillness is often described analogically as its transformation from a waterfall to a fast-flowing stream to a calm river that merges with a boundless ocean. The 11th-century mahāsiddha Padampa Sangye defined meditation succinctly as 'the door into the innermost treasury of the heart.'

Return to the source

The Pearl Garland Tantra states, 'I have no path to travel. I have gone to the other shore … I am all alone, but I am connected to everything.' This passage from an early Dzogchen text expresses the creative power of tactical withdrawal within the Tibetan Buddhist tradition of meditative retreat. Although meditation motivated by compassion ultimately implies creative engagement with all of life, it is often practised initially in remote settings to attune to what ordinarily eludes attention. Solitary retreat allows one to temporarily disidentify with social roles and obligations, so that one's inner nature may more readily shine forth. In this sense, solitude becomes an incubational space in which world and self cohere in more integral states of consciousness, alone and at one with all things. Yet as expressed in Tibetan analogies, the ultimate meditation caves are the cavities of the body within which inner perception arises as clarity and bliss. Outer retreat can facilitate such emergence, but so can seamless and unconditional immersion in the world. As the 18th-century Dzogchen master Jigme Lingpa stated, 'If the meditator uses whatever occurs in life as the path [to realization], the body itself becomes a retreat hut', implying that there is ultimately no need to seek one elsewhere.

Below and opposite **Contemplative isolation,** in absence of any social context, activates the unconscious and expands inner awareness, resulting in enriching forms of cognition. Tibet's hiddenland of Pemakö, pictured below left, is considered an optimal location for meditative retreat, as are caves in the inner sanctuary of Mount Kailash, shown opposite.

Meditating on the secret oral instructions
I had no use for didactic books.
Having discovered a sanctuary within my own body
I had no need for a monastery.
Having embraced the spirit rather than the words of the scriptures
I abandoned all misleading concepts.

Milarepa, 11th century

Open presence

Focused meditation disengages the mind from mental and physical processes and facilitates a natural state of clarity and ease. Open presence meditation furthers this state of calm abiding while deepening the mind's perceptual range and expanding mental qualities of tranquility and non-referential joy, as a basis for insight into the nature of reality and consciousness. In the tradition of Great Perfection, this merging of one-pointed attention and circumferential awareness is described as the integral union of *śamatha* and *vipaśyanā* that arises in formal meditation practice as well as within all circumstances that are engaged with open attention. The 19th-century polymath and meditation master Jamgön Kongtrül Lodrö Thayé described this state of illuminated awareness as 'open luminous presence … neither a substratum nor its absence, empty yet perfectly aware'. This awakened state of being has been correlated scientifically with the paradoxical absence of measurable neurological activity beyond the hypothalamus and insular cortex at the core of the brain suggesting, as Buddhist tradition maintains, that consciousness is more than an emergent property of neuroelectrical activity.

As an integral expansion of awareness, meditation within the tradition of Great Perfection is based on recognition of the fundamental unity of

Lion's Cave hermitage in Bhutan is renowned as the place where the 8th-century female Tibetan adept Yeshe Tsogyal practised advanced Tantric meditation with her Nepalese consort Atsara Sahle. Traditionally, practices of noetic bliss are only engaged once a practitioner has fully recognized the selfless nature of all phenomena, thus freeing the mind from debilitating attachments.

A Bhutanese yogini rests in open presence meditation. Core meditation instructions within Dzogchen advise maintaining the body like a mountain, the mind like the sky and the breath and eyes like a boundless ocean, disengaging from the flow of thoughts and sustaining an open, receptive and naturally radiant state of awareness.

consciousness and its field of awareness. As the great 20th-century female adept Sera Khandro expressed it, 'In my isolated mountain retreat of self-luminous detachment, resting in luminosity without fixation, I sustained the essential nature of self-emergent simplicity. Gazing upon my original face of carefree openness, I embody the truth of the self-liberation of divisive emotions.'

Effective meditation is often contrasted with states of conceptual and emotional distraction. But from the point of view of Dzogchen, distraction is not a defect of the mind, but a natural re-prioritizing of attention. Tibetan teachers point out that if our meditations, and lives, are habitually 'distracted', it may simply be that we aren't devoting ourselves to what matters most. In matters of sex and death, focus is spontaneous (thus the iconography of Tantric deities) and distractions are rare. When our occupational and spiritual pursuits are absent of joy and passion, afflictive emotions readily take us off course and obscure the active expression of innate wisdom and compassion. On the other hand, when viewed with discernment, distractions can become practitioners' most powerful allies in assessing whether or not they are aligned with their highest intentions and the most effective means for achieving them. They then become, as Nietzsche invoked them, 'divine distractions'.

Beyond meditation

The knowledge and experience that derive from meditation are often described as being inconceivable by the mind. The mahāsiddha Tilopā conveyed this truth to his disciple Nāropā in six yogic principles that, in elaborated form, underlie all practices of Tibetan yoga. Tilopā pointed out that the wisdom that results from contemplative experience is ultimately self-disclosing. He nonetheless imparted to Nāropā a culminating six-point teaching on non-dual realization beyond formal meditation, as the essence of non-conceptual awareness. As Tilopā instructed, 'Don't imagine; don't think; don't deliberate; don't meditate; and don't analyse. Remain in the mind's natural state.' The scholar and meditation master Gyalwa Yangönpa (1213–87) clarified the meaning of these six instructions in his *Hidden Description of the Vajra Body*: 'Thoughts related to subject and object are mental projections. The essence of mind is non-objectified natural clarity. The nature of that clarity is emptiness, the radiance of which is boundless. The mind's ultimate essence is totally beyond all concepts!'

The non-conceptual radiant clarity that is the essence of mind is the base, path and result of all forms of Tibetan yoga. The practical methods through which that natural endowment is realized are elaborated in the Six Yogas that Tilopā transmitted to Nāropā on the banks of the Ganges River in India and which subsequently became the foundation of Tibet's Inner Tantric tradition. To summarize what will be covered in detail in subsequent chapters, the six interconnected yogic practices consist of perceiving the body as 'empty', and thus mutable; cultivating incandescent vitality; abiding in intrinsic luminescence; approaching all experiences as negotiable dreams; and recognizing the triune maṇḍala of body, breath and mind as what the *Tantra of the Secret Assembly* refers to as a 'union of secrets', and which Yangönpa invoked as a 'playground of enlightened beings ... shimmering in blazing splendour'.

Opposite **A Tibetan lama** performs a ritual offering to local spirits while climbing to the enlightenment cave of Yeshe Tsogyal, the 8th-century Tibetan princess who renounced courtly life to meditate in remote mountains with her teacher and consort Padmasambhava, the Tantric master credited with establishing Vajrayāna Buddhism throughout the Himalayas.

Right **Yeshe Tsogyal's enlightenment cave** is located 17,075 ft (5,200 m) above sea level on a mountain ridge in Terdrom, in central Tibet. The isolated cavern is reached by a precipitous track across cliffs and cascading scree slopes. Yeshe Tsogyal and Padmasambhava found refuge here after being persecuted by hostile ministers opposed to the introduction of Buddhism in Tibet.

In ultimate truth,
there are neither hindrances nor Buddhas.
There is no meditator or meditation.
There is no practice or experience.
Neither is there any Buddha Body or Buddha Mind
Therefore there is no Nirvāṇa.
All such terms are just names and concepts.

Milarepa, 11th century

Above **Naljorma Tseyang Ösel** holds up a crimson rhododendron flower after completing two consecutive three-year meditation retreats in the mountains of Bhutan.

Right **Lama Lhundrup Dorje,** an adept from eastern Tibet, meditates in Khandro Sangpuk, 'Secret Cave of the Ḍākinīs', where Yeshe Tsogyal attained enlightenment practising Tummo, the Yoga of Inner Fire. The cave is accessed via two sets of wooden ladders lashed together with yak hide, and its circuitous passageways are likened to the energy channels of the subtle body.

Opposite **The Tibetan yogi Milarepa** was renowned for his mastery of the Yoga of Inner Fire. In this 18th-century sculpture of clay, wood and pigment, he meditates in a mountain cave, surrounded by animals such as tigers, deer and snow lions. He holds his hand to his ear, signifying his fame for having composed 100,000 songs revealing the joys and challenges of the Tantric Buddhist path. Newark Museum of Art, New Jersey.

Don't sit at home
Don't meditate in the forest,
But recognize the essence of mind
Wherever you find yourself.
When one abides in complete and perfect enlightenment,
Where then is Saṃsāra and where is Nirvāṇa? ...
Everything is Buddha without exception ...
Consciousness is pure in its original nature.

Mahāsiddha Saraha, *Dohākośa*, 8th century

Opposite **Lama Lhundrup Dorje** holds out the ends of his red and white robe in a simulation of yogic flight, while standing below the limestone cave where Yeshe Tsogyal attained enlightenment. In a treasure text entitled *Refined Essence of Oral Instructions*, Padmasambhava instructs Yeshe Tsogyal to 'Rest freely and relaxed. Everything is included in this!' In regard to the key points of speech, he dismissed mantra recitation and breath control and emphasized remaining silent like a mute. Regarding the mind, his final advice was to rest consciousness 'in its natural state, free, easy and without fabrication … beyond concentration, relaxation, projecting, dissolving and inward focus.'

Right **A circular rainbow** forms around the sun in Terdrom. As stated in the 12th-century *The Turquoise Heart Essence*: 'There is nothing in Saṃsāra and Nirvāṇa that isn't encapsulated by outer, inner, and secret aspects of the Five Elements … In the same way, everything is wholly and completely contained in the yogin's body.'

Immaculate perception

Freeing the imagination

As long as you do not recognize the supreme Buddha within yourself, how can you attain your true form? ... When false perceptions cease, you will know yourself as you truly are.

Mahāsiddha Saraha, 8th century

Entering the maṇḍala

Opposite and below **The meditational deity Dorje Drolo** represents one of eight manifestations of Padmasambhava, each of which expresses an existential orientation ranging from scholar, king and ascetic to Tantric lover. Signifying the multidimensionality of being espoused in Vajrayāna Buddhism, Dorje Drolo – riding on a pregnant tigress and with eyes bulging in all directions – embodies the activity of 'crazy wisdom', a viable stance when logic and reason fail to yield satisfactory results. Dorje Drolo's gaze recalls the words of Wallace Stevens who wrote of the 'visibility of thought / In which hundreds of eyes, in one mind, see at once.'

Yoga practices within Vajrayāna Buddhism developed within the larger context of Indian Tantrism, and especially within the Yoginī Tantra class of Tantric Buddhist texts that emerged in India between the 8th and 10th centuries. The crowning literary development of Indian Buddhism's Vajrayāna, or 'Adamantine Way', the Yoginī, or 'Mother' Tantras share common features with Tantric Śaivism and involve imaginative identification with ecstatic, multi-limbed Tantric deities that signify the dynamic unity of emptiness, bliss and radiant compassion at the heart of enlightened existence. Transforming early Buddhism's ascetic disposition into passionate engagement, Vajrayāna extended Buddhism's influence and applicability beyond conservative monastic institutions. As the 8th-century Hevajra Tantra famously proclaims, 'One must rise by that by which one falls ... By whatever binds the world, by that it must be freed.' Central to this endeavour was a revalorization of both the body and the imagination as essential vehicles, rather than obstacles, to existential and spiritual freedom.

Yogic practice in Vajrayāna Buddhism traditionally begins with initiation into one of several Buddhist maṇḍalas, visionary realms presided over by erotically entwined Tantric divinities symbolizing the numinous play and expanded perception of self-transcendent awareness. In accordance with the Buddhist view of reality as a projection of consciousness, altering perception of seemingly objective phenomena changes reality's manifestations; just as perception in quantum physics inherently determines what is observed. To overcome static, self-limiting beliefs and conceptions, the initial Creation Phase (*utpattikrama*, Tib. *Kyerim*) of Tantric Buddhist practice involves imaginatively transforming oneself into a radiant, omniscient deity in a radical form of *imitatio Dei* in which one emulates divinity in order to become the object of one's attention and affection. Based on the view that all beings are inherently Buddhas – emanations of wisdom, power and compassion – Deity Yoga (devata yoga) underlies all subsequent forms of Tibetan Buddhist yoga.

Seeing the buddha within

In the earliest Buddhist Sutrās, the Pali word *saddha*, commonly translated as faith, refers more precisely to 'confidence', in reference to an inner quality of being rather than devotion towards any externally projected source of salvation. Deity Yoga, as practised in Tantric Buddhism, actively cultivates this attitude of fearless humility by envisioning oneself as a wrathful, peaceful or ecstatic Tantric deity, corresponding with one's karmic affinity and as determined formally through ritual initiation into the deity's maṇḍala, or sacred abode. If engaged with openness and understanding of the relativity of all phenomena, Deity Yoga engenders flexibility of mind and reinforces the recognition that perceptions of self and reality are, in essence, alterable mental fabrications. The process is ideologically related to Theosis, or 'deification' as taught in Eastern Orthodox Christianity, a transformative process for attaining union with the Godhead. In Tantric Buddhism, ultimate reality assumes innumerable provisional forms, empowering a view of self and reality that, rooted in emptiness, is ever mutable and unconfined by any single mode of existence. This perspective is not unlike Ludwig Wittgenstein's philosophical dictum that 'all could be otherwise ... the eyes say only either.'

Above and opposite **Deities in amorous embrace** signify inner qualities that the practitioner cultivates through visualization and imaginative identification. The scroll painting opposite of a dancing form of Avalokiteśvara, the Bodhisattva of universal compassion, serves as an iconographical support for the ecstatic, self-transcendent state of Buddhahood.

Right **A practitioner of Deity Yoga** contemplates five wisdom manifestations of the Bodhisattva Vajrasattva that signify transfigured expressions of the five afflictive human emotions of ignorance, greed, aggression, jealousy and pride. Tantric Buddhism's pantheon of meditational deities supports self-transformation, while faith is described as a skilful means for freeing the mind from subconscious conditioning and objectifying beliefs.

The bliss that arises from Deity Yoga
Is a Buddha that is neither tangible nor intangible ...
Its limbs and faces signify the supreme immutable bliss
That dwells within all beings.

Hevajra Tantra, 8th century

Right **A Caryā dancer** at the Sankhu Vajrayoginī temple in Nepal invokes the Tantric meditational deity Vajravārāhī with the support of ritual accoutrements that include a gilded crown, a necklace of ivory skulls and a silver-lined human cranium. The Caryā dance form developed within the Newar tradition of Tantric Buddhism as a fully embodied approach to Deity Yoga in which divinity is enacted through dynamic choreography and consecrated states of ritual possession (*āveśa*).

Opposite **Maṇḍalas are portals** into Tantric Buddhist practice. Contemplating or visualizing their fractal symmetries and complex symbolism supports a transfigured, multi-dimensional experience of reality and human nature, as revealed in this Tibetan maṇḍala of Vajrayoginī and its central configuration of five intersecting triangles symbolizing the five elemental processes fundamental to Tantric Buddhist psychology and practice, 19th-century Tibetan scroll painting (*thangka*), Wellcome Library, London.

Primal syntax

Visualizing oneself as an enlightened Buddha in the Creation Phase of Vajrayāna Buddhism is traditionally supported through the recitation of a corresponding mantra, a Sanskrit word or phrase that entrains the mind towards its object of concentration. All mantras arise from 'seed-syllables' of the Sanskrit alphabet. Tantric texts proclaim these one-syllable *bija* mantras as the causal source of material phenomena, and describe them as pervading the human body as syllabic streams of vowels and consonants. In Tantric Buddhist practice, these somatic phonemes, or minimal units of sound, reference the mastery of grammar that was a prerequisite for undertaking any advanced discipline described in Sanskrit texts. In the practice of Deity Yoga, embryonic seed-syllables constitute a grammar of awakening and are envisioned and intoned to engender Tantric deities, through which practitioners symbolically identify with a self-transcendent reality.

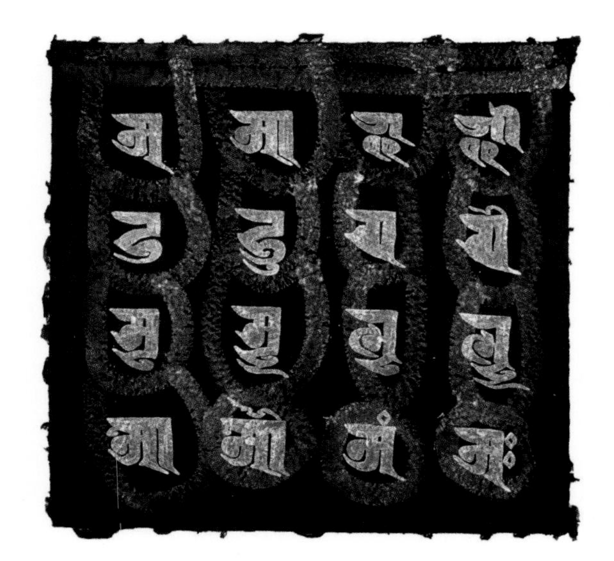

Creation Phase processes of Tantric Buddhism transform constraining beliefs in a single and inherently existing self into a pantheon of expanded possibilities, akin to the observation of poet and philosopher Fernando Pessoa that, 'Each of us is several, is many, a profusion of selves.' Deity Yoga begins and ends, however, with meditation on Śūnyatā, in which all provisional forms and identities, as well as language itself, arise from and dissolve into primordial emptiness, a dynamic field of relational occurrences and interactive events. In contemporary terms, the professed mutability of emptiness and form reflects quantum physics' view of the ultimate identity of energy and matter. Recognition of the fundamental equivalence of emptiness and apparent form – or ultimate and relative reality – is the starting point of all Tantric Buddhist practice. As the *King of Empowerment Tantra* states, 'If you did not already possess the supreme power of reality within yourself, how could you obtain it through an external rite of empowerment?'

Opposite above **The sixteen vowels of the Sanskrit language** begin with the phoneme *āli* and correspond with flows of subtle energy within the human body. Deity Yoga engages these female vibrations so as to imaginatively transform oneself into an archetypal Tantric divinity. The sixteen vowels, here depicted in a painting by Robert Powell, are associated cosmologically with the sixteen phases of the lunar cycle. In union with 'solar' consonants, associated with the male principle, they signify a primal syntax through which somatic energy communicates as conscious thought and awareness.

Opposite below **Sanskrit's thirty-six consonants** – beginning with the phoneme *kāli* – correspond with energy currents in the human body, signifying an internal grammar of experience that echoes the view of Pythagoras that language and numbers hold sway over universal flux. In this contemporary painting by Rolf Kluenter, sound manifests as visible syllables that resonate within the embodied cosmos of the yogic body.

Left **Seed-syllables pervade the human body** as vibratory phonemes, as illustrated in this detail from an 18th-century Tibetan manuscript. Mantras evolve from these embodied sounds and, combined with visualization, support the transformation of habitual mental patterning into realization of transpersonal divinity. The Guhyagarbha Tantra describes enlightenment as *āli-kāli*, the union of the body's in-dwelling female and male syllables.

Above **Vajrayāna Buddhism views internal experience as a language** in which vibrating syllables signify informational streams within the adept's body. As depicted in this manuscript folio, the Hevajra Tantra associates vowels with the moon and wisdom and consonants with the sun and skilful means. The novelist Ursula LeGuin wrote analogously in *Wave in the Mind* that, 'That constant, delicate, complex throbbing is the process of life made visible.' Beijing Palace Museum.

Ecstatic contemplation

The Perfect Buddha cannot be found

In any of the ten directions or the four times.

Other than the perfect Buddha

That is the mind's inner radiance

Do not seek the Buddha elsewhere.

Guhyagarbha Tantra, 8th century

Tantric Buddhism defines Buddhahood as a state of freedom from deluded thoughts regarding the nature of reality. As expressions of human nature unbound by conventional limits, Tantric Buddhist deities offer anthropomorphic support for self-transcendence. Deity Yoga is prefigured in the *Yoga Sūtras* of Patañjali, in which contemplation of Īśvara, an omniscient being invoked by the seed-syllable Oṃ, is indicated as one of five provisional means for attaining the liberated state of yoga. As stated in verses 2:44–45 of the *Yoga Sūtras*, 'From recitation arises union with one's chosen deity. From contemplation of Īśvara comes perfection of *samādhi*.'

Whether visualized as peaceful, wrathful, or ecstatic, divine forms envisioned in the Creation Phase of Deity Yoga reflect the intrinsic mutability of self-perception, as opposed to an idealized alter ego. Tibetan Yoga begins with an essential abandonment of singularizing identity and corresponding fixations. Arising as one's 'chosen deity' (*iṣṭadevatā*, Tib. *yidam*), the practitioner of

Opposite **Tantric deities in erotic embrace** facilitate internal states of sympathetic bliss when contemplated through Deity Yoga. When expansively engaged, the human imagination becomes a powerful force that can liberate mundane perception and transform both inner and outer phenomena, as depicted in this image from the walls of Devikota temple in Tibet's hiddenland of Pemakö.

Right **The lion-faced ḍākinī Simhamukha**, garlanded in skulls, embodies the ever-present mutability of consciousness as well as a dynamic means for discarding limiting self-perceptions. By embracing the ecstatic potential of the human imagination, practitioners of Deity Yoga gain insight into the ways in which the mind continuously re-creates itself according to both consciously and subconsciously held attitudes and beliefs.

Deity Yoga recognizes that, in Wittgenstein's terms, 'all can be otherwise.' Deity Yoga thus actively cultivates a creative revisioning of ordinary experience as well as radical transcendence of inhibiting self-conceptions. As Chögyam Trungpa cautioned, however, as the ultimate deity is one's own mind, there is no need to conjure one with multiple heads and arms. 'Truth' in Tantra, as in alchemy and magic, is the harnessed power of the imagination, rather than the objects or ideas to which the imagination gives shape.

The female Buddha Tārā is depicted sensuously to emphasize her immanence within the human female form. In Tantric Buddhism, it is not a supreme, transcendent Deity with which a practitioner identifies, but rather with any number of beatific, fierce or ecstatic divinities representing potentialities of the human mind. Imagination is fundamental to religious practice. As Wallace Stevens wrote in *Opus Posthumous*, 'God and the imagination are one. The thing imagined is the imaginer. Hence, I suppose, the imaginer is God.'

Opposite **Tārā represents the active power of the Buddhas,** and she manifests in varying forms. In this detail of a fresco in the Piyang caves in western Tibet, her left hand holds a blossoming *utpala* lotus. Her right hand forms *karana mudrā*, a gesture of dispelling negativity. The image recalls the primeval Khadiravaṇi Tārā, or 'Saviouress of the Acacia Forest', who appeared in South India to the siddha-alchemist Nāgārjuna. The Acacia Forest where Tārā first appeared is also referred to as 'The Holy Realm of Turquoise Leaves'. The leaves and bark of various species of acacia contain strong concentrations of Dimenthyltryptamine (DMT), a powerful hallucinogen that has been described as 'lifting consciousness into other worlds' and which may have been an early ingredient in *amṛta*, the nectar of immortality. Aphrodisiacal effects of acacia catechu preparations are also described in the Kāma Sūtra.

The Tibetan practice of Chöd, or 'severing', consists of ritually imagining one's own death and dismemberment, thereby inverting the mind's normative, but ultimately self-limiting, instincts for self-preservation. Traditionally undertaken in wild and frightening settings, Chöd invokes the terror of self-annihilation in order to attain a self-transcendent, unitary state of consciousness, as demonstrated by this Chöd practitioner in Tibet's Tsangpo Gorges.

Opposite below **A Chöd practitioner invokes chthonic forces** of the subconscious mind, as depicted in this image of a yogin in a snake-infested charnel ground. The practice relates to Chögyam Trungpa's comment that, 'It is with our emotions that we create demons and gods. Those things we don't want in our lives and world are the demons; those things that we would draw to us are the gods and goddesses. The rest is just scenery.' Ogyen Choling Manor.

Transforming appearances

Practitioners of Deity Yoga visualize both Tantric deities and themselves as unities of emptiness and appearance. The ultimately formless nature of Tantric deities is anticipated in the Maitrī Upaniṣad (4:5), which states that deities should be meditated on, but ultimately denied, so as to attain 'ultimate union within one's innermost being.' In Deity Yoga, the practitioner recognizes the meditation deity as an intrinsic expression of their innate Buddha Nature and ultimately dissolves their self-visualization into boundless luminosity. Some Tantric texts strongly state, however, that practices based solely on ritually altering perception are insufficient for realizing a divinized state. The Vajra Bhairava Tantra, for example, emphasizes the limitations of meditating upon conjured deities: 'The embodied forms of the Divine as taught in the scriptures are not the true essence … they are like sleights of hand, dreams and illusions, and palaces in the sky. Such practices are taught to support the meditations of those impaired by dualistic thought, whose minds are confused and entangled in the details of ritual procedures … They are taught to help unawakened people make progress on the path.' The text further indicates authentic divinity as a joyous state of plentitude, 'beyond space and time, without direction or locality and ultimately indescribable … When this is the ultimate reality, what is there to be worshipped or propitiated?'

A similar aniconic view is expressed in the *Perfection of Immortal Elixir*, which teaches that visualizing oneself as a deity is ineffective for producing enlightenment, likening the practice to 'deludedly chewing on a rock and, when thirsty, drinking the sky.' Similar cautions regarding literal conceptions

Right **The female Tibetan adept Machik Labdron** is pictured here in her customary ecstatic dance posture with hand bell and drum. Machik Labdron formulated Chöd, or 'severance', in the 11th century as a means of subverting subconscious mental programming and realizing a liberated, self-transcendent state. She stated that Chöd 'is not deity empowerment bestowed on the body; it is the ultimate empowerment bestowed on the mind'.

of Deity Yoga are also expressed in the 4th-century Vajracchedikā, or 'Diamond Cutter', Sūtra: 'Those who perceive me as form, those who perceive me as sound, those committed to false paths, do not perceive me. The true body of the Buddha is the infinite expanse of reality (Dharmakāya).'

Deity Yoga does not consist solely in envisioning one's body and mind as a Tantric Buddha. The Creation Phase of Vajrayāna Buddhism, to which Deity Yoga is central, is further distinguished by conceiving of one's environment as the deity's maṇḍala, or idealized abode, and perceiving one's enjoyments as the deity's intrinsic, unconditional bliss. The fourth component of Creation Phase Deity Yoga is performing all actions with the altruistic disposition of a Bodhisattva, for the benefit of all beings. This self-transcendent orientation is radically expressed in ritual enactments of death and self-sacrifice undertaken in the Tibetan Buddhist practice of Chöd, or 'severing' attachment to mind and body, a multi-sensorial form of Deity Yoga that fuses Creation Phase and Completion Phase practices in self-transcendent, ecstatic awareness.

Severing hindrances

Yoga represents an embodied inquiry into the sources of existence and is thus deeply linked with the physical and intangible processes of the natural world. The Tibetan Buddhist practice of Chöd, or 'severing' of the conceptual mind, combines indigenous shamanistic ritual with the existential and ontological orientation of Buddhism so as to dissolve distinctions between life and death. In the spirit of universal emptiness, the practitioner of Chöd conjures entities of the unseen world and enacts a symbolic rite of death and renewal that frees the mind from physical and mental attachments and directly induces a state of lucid, concept-free awareness, identified as the mind's original nature. Often begun with a ritual dance to subjugate egoic distractions of hope and fear and to tame the ground where the rite is to be performed, Chöd progresses to a radical form of Deity Yoga in which the practitioner projects their consciousness as a wrathful and luminous goddess who cuts off their head with a flaying knife and stews their dismembered body parts in a cauldron as offerings to local spirits. Supported by the rhythmic pounding of a snakeskin drum and the piercing wails of an instrument fashioned from a human thighbone, the meditative ritual of Chöd severs obstacles to self-transcendent awareness by cutting through hindering attachments to physical appearances.

Chöd draws on funereal practices described in the late 4th-century Laṅkāvatāra Sūtra that refers to Buddhist ascetics dwelling amidst charnel grounds and transcending conventional boundaries of the sacred and profane. As the Laṅkāvatāra Sūtra states, 'As all things are unreal, there is neither defilement nor purity.' The Hevajra Tantra similarly advocates meditation in cemeteries where 'having offered the body as a gift to the 'fearful mother' (*mātr*), the yogin can begin to practice.' Chapter six of the Hevajra Tantra further claims that the experiential consequence of such direct engagement with the subconscious depths of the psyche confers 'courage equal to that of a lion.' Machik Labdron, Chöd's 11th-century female founder, evocatively described the practice of Chöd as 'Utter Mystery! It can't be named. Supple and free; all sense of "I" is gone! Totally transparent; emotional reactions can't take hold. Radiantly clear awareness, free from any fixation, inside or out. Vividly present, direct knowing, perfectly unencumbered.' In its various forms, Chöd represents the total engagement of the human imagination in service of a radically transformed experience of human embodiment in which 'adversities are taken as the path' to supreme spiritual awakening.

Below **A ritual thigh-bone trumpet** and a double-headed, snake-skin drum are principal supports for the practice of Chöd.

Opposite **A cave-dwelling Tibetan yogin** displays ritual objects central to the transformational rite of Chöd that severs the ego's hold on human experience. The female adept Machik Labdron spread the teachings of Chöd throughout Tibet in the 11th and 12th centuries. Her teachings combined internalized rites of shamanic dismemberment with the Buddhist view of the inherent emptiness of material reality, including the physical body.

Imagining enlightenment

The Creation Phase of Tantric Buddhism reveals the mentally constructed nature of phenomenal reality through elaborate techniques of creative imagination focused on identification with the divine form and embodied wisdom of a chosen Tantric deity, representing one's essential nature. The word 'imagine' derives from the Latin *imaginare*, 'to form an image of' and *imaginari*, 'to picture to oneself'. In the Creation Phase, the mundane world is imaginatively overridden and replaced by a divine reality, pictured as an all-encompassing maṇḍala of concentrically expanding perception, presided over by a Tantric deity. The culmination of Deity Yoga, however, is to embody the qualities of the deity within the maṇḍala of one's psychic anatomy. This second phase of Deity Yoga is referred to as the Completion Phase in which one dissolves one's visualization of the deity in the direct realization of Śūnyatā, or universal emptiness, in which all appearances arise as the radiance of a luminous insubstantial reality. The process of internal divinization central to the Completion Phase is the basis for the subtle body energy practices of the Six Yogas that 'take the body as the path'. The yogas based on the body's energy channels no longer rely on mental transformation into an imaginary other, but on the direct realization of one's intrinsic Buddha Nature. As stated in the Guhyagarbha Tantra, 'From any of the four times and ten directions the perfect Buddha will not be found. Mind, in its essence, is the perfect Buddha. Do not search for the Buddha elsewhere.'

A stream of neurons in the human brain reflects the heightened activity in the cerebral cortex brought about by mental visualization. Mentally imagined imagery activates the same areas of the brain as visual perception and can profoundly influence neural processes and functions, as well as thoughts and emotions. Science Photo Library, London.

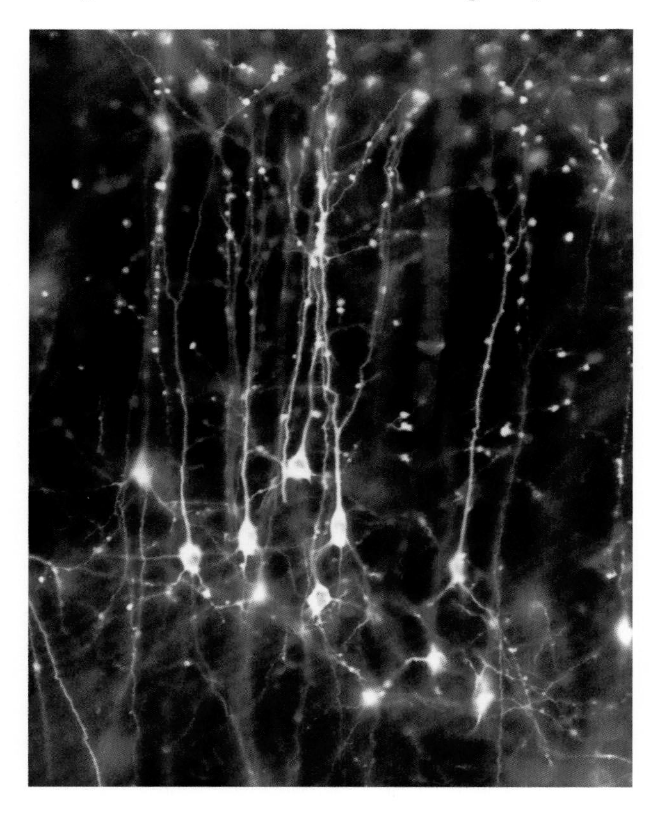

Tibetan Buddhist and related yogic practices based on internally generated mental imagery-have been investigated scientifically, leading to recognition of the creative imagination as a tool for positively influencing the subconscious mind, beyond the mechanics of image formation and memory retrieval. The practice of maṇḍala visualization, in particular, has been shown to cultivate what is known as eidetic imagination, the ability to externally project internal visual impressions as precisely rendered visual replicas. Deriving from the Greek word *eidos*, a 'lucidly visible form', eidetic images refer to vivid mental imagery that is not derivative of memory or external events and which, combined with concentrative meditative absorption, can lead to expanded perception and cognition. In its substitution of transpersonal imagery in place of ordinary appearances, the Creation Phase of

A 'yak eye' manifests within pellucid space in response to a recursive Dzogchen gazing technique called Lhündrup Tögal, 'leaping over the skull into spontaneous presence', as illustrated in an image from the upper chamber of the Lukhang temple in Lhasa, Tibet. In the culminating phases of Tantric Buddhist practice, mental imagery is no longer consciously produced, but spontaneously and vividly perceived.

Vajrayāna Buddhism addresses what the philosopher of science Alfred North Whitehead referred to as the 'fallacy of misplaced concreteness', thus enlarging the scope and capacity of human consciousness and perception. Tibetan Buddhism refers to this process as 'overthrowing the tyranny of ordinary appearances', as well as other limitations to a comprehensive perception of self and reality. The yogic phases in this process consist, sequentially, of dissolving the ordinary sense of self through meditation on emptiness; substituting divine for ordinary appearances through the Creation Phase practices of Deity Yoga; and internalizing the qualities of the deity through Completion Phase practices based on the transpersonal anatomy of the yogic body, the subject of the following chapter.

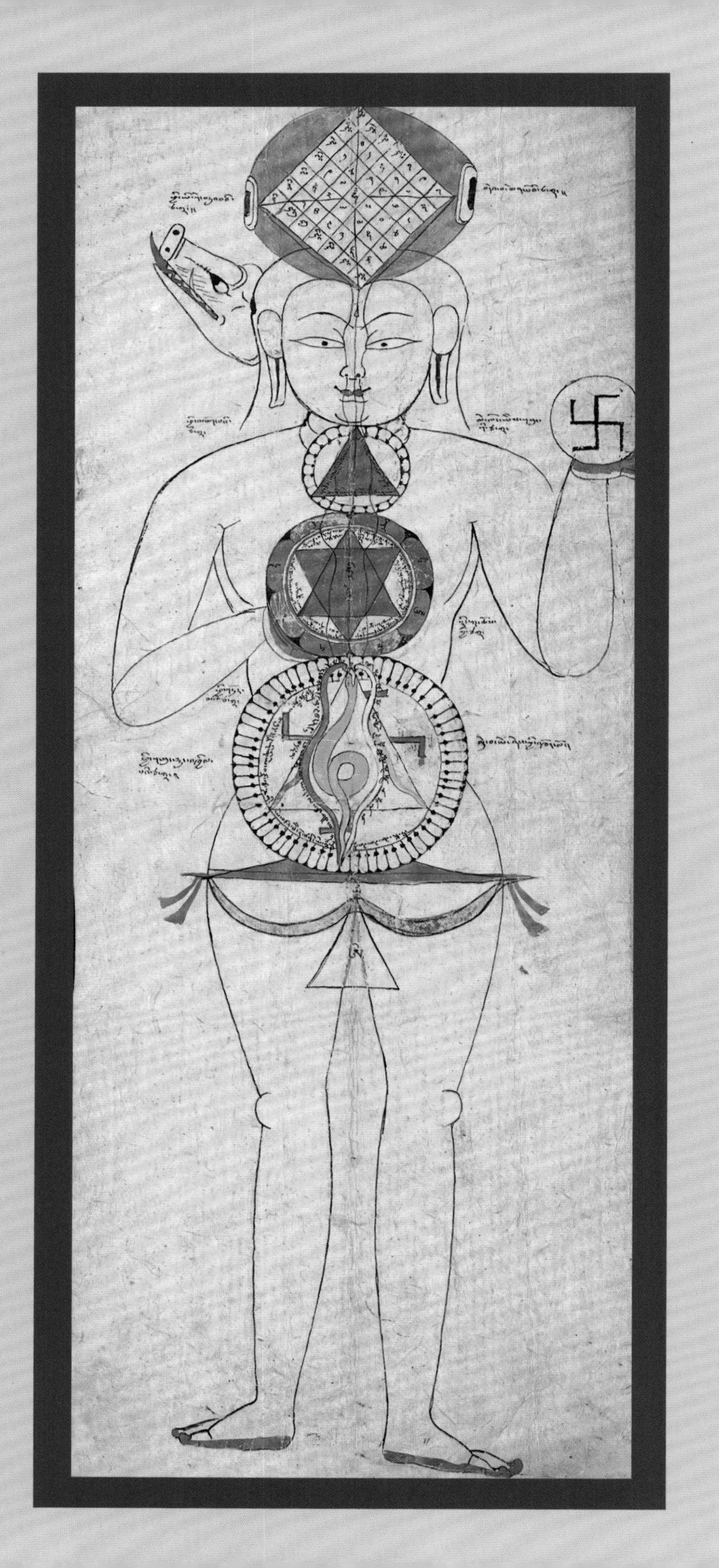

Enlightened anatomy

The yoga of channels, winds and essences

Mastering the path of channels and winds,
The Buddha was in the palm of my hands.

Marpa Chökyi Lodrö, 11th century

Awakening the three bodies

While the Creation Phase practices of Vajrayāna Buddhism actively engage imagination, intellect and emotion in liberating reified perceptions of reality, subtler yogic practices of the Completion Phase (*saṃpannakrama*, Dzogrim) extend the process through an envisioned metaphysical anatomy activated through mental focus, breath control and dynamic physical disciplines. As the female adept Siddharājñī proclaimed, 'Don't look for another source of refuge. The body itself is a sacred maṇḍala. Don't look elsewhere for the deity. The mind itself, unborn and unperishing, is the ultimate Buddha and teacher.' The so-called Six Yogas of the Completion Phase entrain natural psycho-physiological processes towards realization of an illuminated condition of body, speech and mind. The resultant Coalescent Seal (Mahāmudra) or Great Perfection (*mahāsanti,* Tib. Dzogchen) represents an embodied realization of the Buddhist Yogācāra doctrine of the 'three bodies' (Trikāyavāda), consisting of the Nirmāṇakāya, or 'emanation body', the Saṃbhogakāya, or 'beatific body', and the primordial Dharmakāya, or dimension of total reality. Although described as three inseparable 'bodies' (*kāya*) of progressive subtlety, the terms ultimately transcend any somatic reference while serving as 'supports' (*āśraya*) for internal yogic experience. In one expressive metaphor, the Dharmakāya is likened to an infinite, waveless ocean, from which arise mists and rainbows, symbolizing the Saṃbhogakāya. Enhaloed clouds condense and fall as rain, symbolizing the naturally manifesting Nirmāṇakāya. The Completion Phase of Tantric Buddhism, on which the practices of the Six Yogas are based, specifically refers to 'taking the three *kāyas* as the path' (*ku sum lam khyer*) as a process of transformation in which the bodymind is ultimately experienced as co-extensive with the universe at all stages of waking, dreaming, sleeping and dying. In his *Hidden Description of the Vajra Body*, the Tibetan adept Gyalwa Yangönpa refers to the conventionally experienced body, speech and mind as gateways for realizing the three bodies (*trikāya*) of absolute reality as one's own innermost, self-transcendent anatomy.

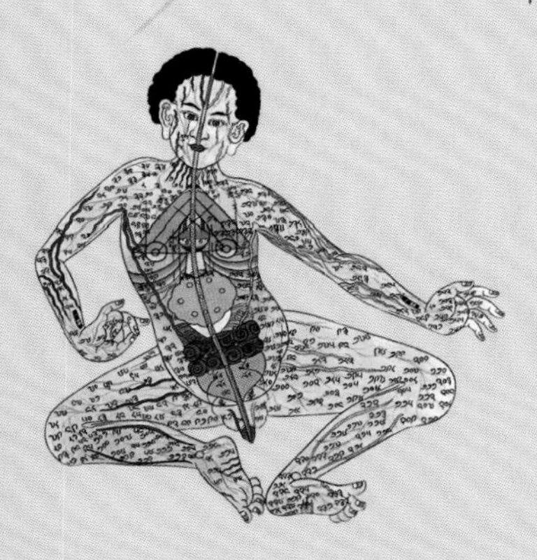

Opposite **An 11th-century meditation diagram** based on the female deity Vajravārāhī integrates Buddhist, Hindu and Bön conceptions of the yogic body as a network of interconnected energy channels concentrated at specific focal points, called *cakras*, along the body's central axis. The golden snake rising from the figure's pelvis symbolizes the awakening of *kuṇḍalinī*, the 'serpent power' associated with self-transcendent awakening. The figure holds a swastika, a universal symbol of creative change. Pritzker Collection.

Above **A figure from a Tibetan medical chart** reveals the *vajranāḍi*, the innermost energy current at the midline of the yogic body.

The anatomy of bliss

Tantric Buddhist accounts of the human body as encoding universal, subatomic processes pre-figure the observations of quantum physics that matter is ultimately energy. While Creation Phase practices actively engage imagined Tantric deities to transfigure conventional perceptions of self and reality, Completion Phase practices magnify innate psycho-energetic processes in order to reveal transpersonal dimensions of mind and body. In yogic practice, the body's innermost structure is described as a network of 72,000 substantive and intangible pathways referred to in Sanskrit as *nāḍi*, or in Tibetan as *tsa*. This para-physiological circulatory system encompasses the flow of blood and pre-lymphatic fluids as well as subtle energy 'winds' known as *prāṇa*, or in Tibetan *lung*, that, when consciously engaged, function as vehicles of amplified awareness and information. Tibetan tradition likens the integration of consciousness with these subtle energy currents to a rider mastering an otherwise unruly 'wind horse', leading to the realization of non-referential joy, represented as the Mahāsukhakāya, or 'body of great bliss', an experiential extension of the trinity of Dharmakāya, Saṃbhogakāya and Nirmāṇakāya. In Tantric Buddhist tradition, meditation instruction on the body's internal maṇḍala of energy channels, winds and subtle essences is traditionally conferred in conjunction with the second of four successive empowerments (*abhiṣeka*), culminating in the realization of the innate enlightenment of human embodiment. As described in the Hevajra Tantra, the body is a 'shimmering jewel' endowed with ambrosial nectars. Mahāsiddha Virūpā's influential *Vajra Lines* further designates the body as a Tantric text that, when fully comprehended, purifies impediments to the realization of Great Bliss (*mahāsukha*), a synonym for enlightened existence.

The human body as a maṇḍala of energy channels, winds and vital essences radiating from a luminous central axis (*madhyamā*) is depicted in this Shangpa Kagyu diagram. A blue column flanked by white and red channels – the *lalanā* (Tib. *kyangma*) and *rasanā* (Tib. *roma*) – and transected by energetic focal points called *cakras* (Tib. *korlo*) is crowned by a blue vajra, extending beyond the top of the head and symbolizing the self-transcendent, indestructible nature of the 'vajra body' (*vajrakāya*). Drawing by Lama Tinley.

Below left **The central channel** (*madhyanāḍi*, Tib. *tsa uma*) of the yogic body, depicted in this Tibetan diagram, is also referred to as the *suṣumnā* or *avadūti nāḍi.* Tantric texts describe the central channel as originating in the *muladhara cakra* at the base of the spine and ascending the body's central axis to the crown of the head. The central channel may be energetically related to the embryonic notochord, a flexible mesodermal structure that develops during human gestation and is later replaced by the vertebral column. All forms of Tantric yoga involve drawing vital energies into the central channel at the innermost core of the human body.

Below right **Three principal energy channels** of the yogic body, as shown in this mural detail from Tibet's Lukhang temple, parallel the hypothalamic (pituitary) gonadal axis of the human endocrine system. Tantric texts describe an infinite number of channels, all of which originate from these three primary *nāḍis*. The red and white side channels represent polarized psychosomatic energies that are unified within the ultimately dimensionless central channel through yogic practice. Tantric Śaivism refers to the central channel as the 'channel of consciousness' (*cinnānāḍi*) and likens it to 'a line without thickness', symbolizing both infinity and non-duality. It is further described as 'beautiful like a chain of lightening and fine like a lotus fibre'. The seed-syllable *āḥ* depicted on a lotus at the centre of the yogin's body signifies transpersonal, heart-centred awareness, or Great Perfection.

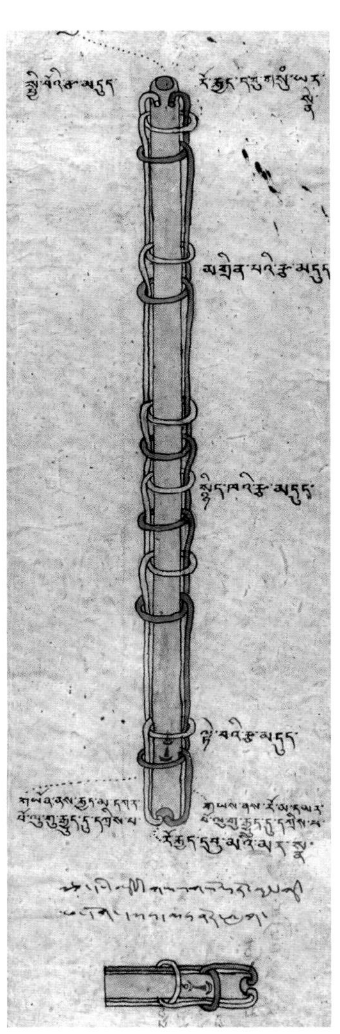

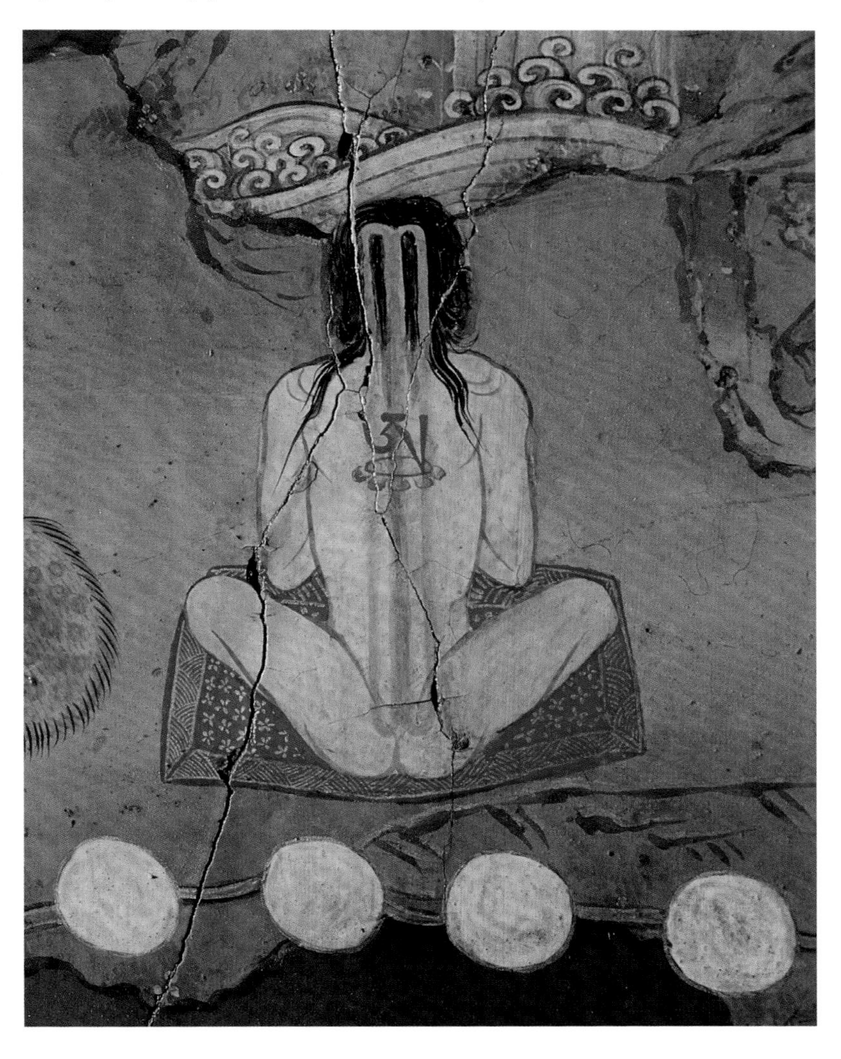

An 18th-century cosmological scroll illustrates correspondences between the universe and the human body, as described in the 10th-century Kālacakra Tantra. The central figure displays six microcosmic energy nodes (*cakra*) within the human body, pictured as coloured spheres that correspond with intersecting astronomical models of the universe shown at the right. Red and white side channels parallel a blue-green central channel at the body's axis, a conduit for 'unaltering present moment awareness' (*aksaraksanam*). In his 16th-century commentary on the Kālacakra Tantra, the Tibetan adept Tāranātha wrote that, 'The nature of mind, free from artifice, abides as great bliss and emptiness, possessed of all ultimate qualities.' Rubin Museum of Art, New York. (Item No. 61201).

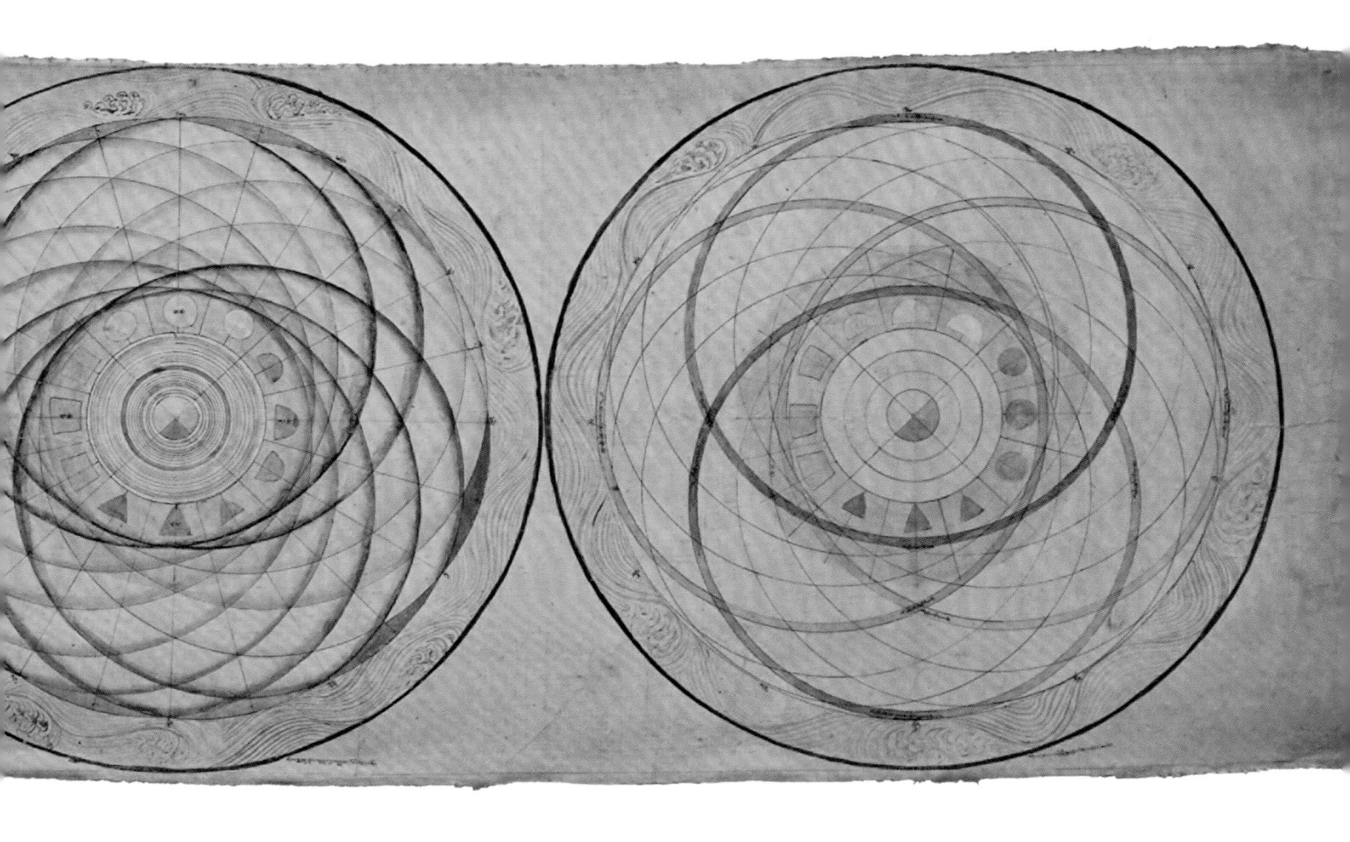

On the basis of the human body, all phenomena of Saṃsāra and Nirvāṇa are fully revealed.

Gyalwa Yangönpa, *Hidden Description of the Vajra Body*, 13th century

Wheels of energy

The subtle channels that form the energetic substructure of the yogic body intersect at *cakras*, or 'wheels' along the body's central meridian, which extends downwards as well as upwards from the navel, or '*cakra* of emanation'. *Cakras* vary in number between traditions. The Cakrasaṃvara Tantra denotes five *cakras*, including the '*cakra* that sustains bliss' in the genital region. The Kālacakra Tantra enumerates six *cakras*, including the '*cakra* of immortality' at the forehead that correlates with neuroendocrinal processes in the brain. The Sakya Lamdré, or 'Fruitional Path', connected to the Hevajra Tantra, delineates eighteen *cakras*, including twelve at the body's principal joints. Other Tantric traditions describe the whirls of energy at the interstices of the body as ḍākas and ḍākinīs, the animating energies of enlightened consciousness. *Cakras* are also fundamental to Kuṇḍalinī yoga, which channels psychic energy through a system of seven energy plexuses along the body's central axis. In Buddhist Tantra, five principal *cakras* are denoted at the head, throat, heart, navel and genitals. The *cakras* are typically represented as lotuses with varying numbers of petals signifying radiating energy channels called *nāḍis*. Each *cakra* is further associated with a Sanskrit seed-syllable and often with a Tantric deity within an encompassing maṇḍala circle. As symbols of subtle psychophysical processes connected with the flow of energy and consciousness through the human body, *cakras* support the attainment of Buddhahood through realization of embodied existence as a unity of emptiness, bliss, and compassion – the subjectively experienced essence of body, breath and mind.

Unless you know the hidden nature of the body, none of the 84,000 methods (of the Tantras) will yield any fruit.

Samputā Tantra, 10th century

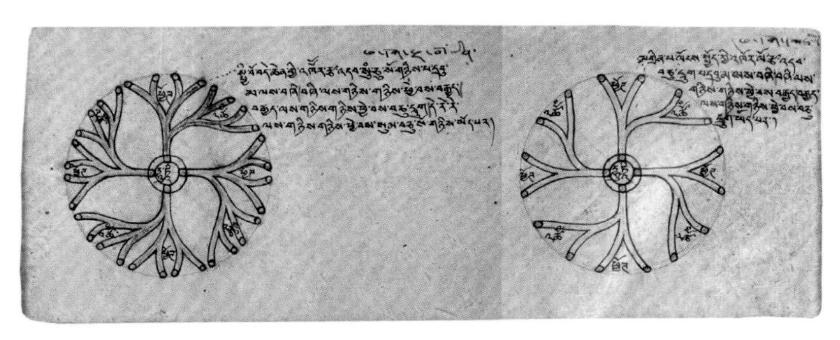

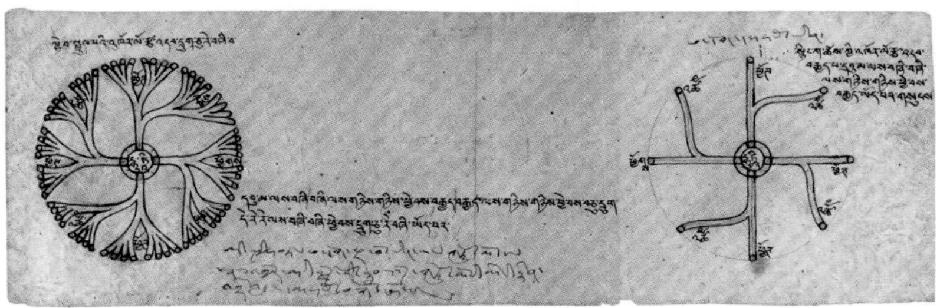

Right and below **Five primary *cakras*** within the human body correlate with Earth, Water, Fire, Air and Space as increasingly subtle, constituent elements of matter and consciousness, as shown in a Tibetan medical chart and, below, in a detail from a mural in the Lukhang temple. Although varying in number between traditions, *cakras* signify focal points of psychophysical energy along the body's central axis within a larger system of subtle energy mediating between mind and body. They are linked by the central channel, which represents a self-transcendent dimension of the human body, experienced subjectively as emptiness, clarity and sensation. Medical chart by studio of Romio Shrestha after a 17th-century original. American Museum of Natural History, New York.

Opposite **Four *cakras* at the crown, throat, navel and heart**, as illustrated from left to right on these instructional folios, represent energetic transactions within the bodymind. Although the Rigveda refers to *cakras* as 'spoked wheels' and subsequent Upaniṣads describe *nāḍis* as 'channels of breath', *cakras* as a hierarchy of energetic centres within the yogic body first appear in Buddhist Tantras in the 8th-century Hevajra Tantra, which enumerates four such centres.

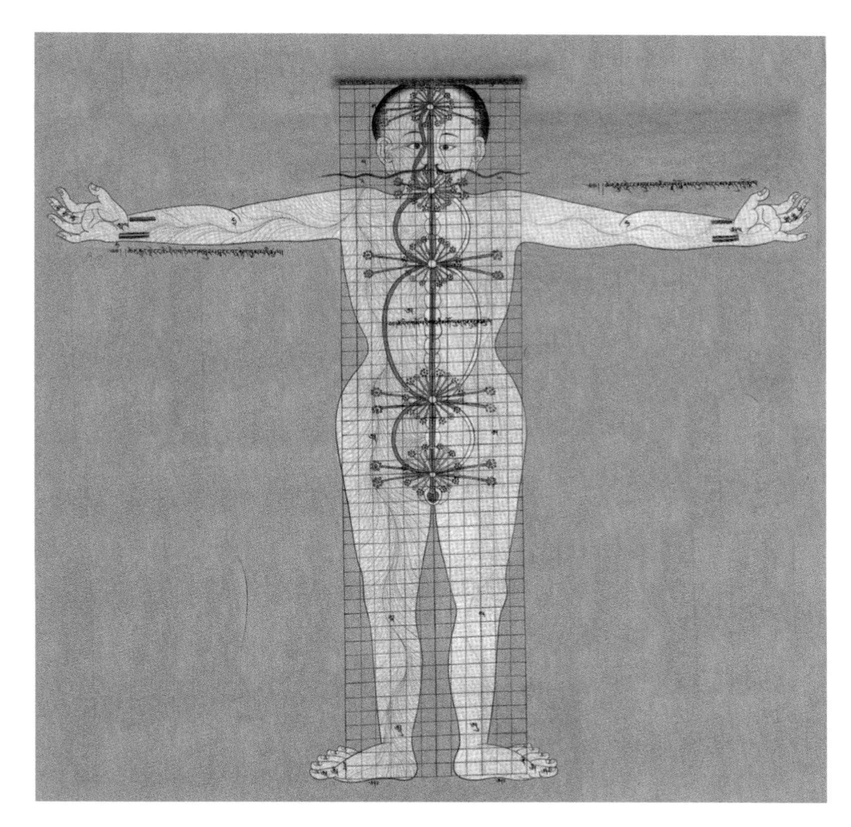

Right **Karma Lhatrul Rinpoche** sits in the meditation posture of the garuda, or celestial eagle, as transmitted within the Dzogchen lineage of Phagmo Zaptri, the 'Profound Instructions of Vajravārāhī'. Placing the soles of the feet together and stretching the knees downwards with a straight back opens subtle energy channels at the base of the central channel and awakens additional psychoenergetic centres at the navel, heart, throat and head.

Opposite **The body's inner maṇḍala** of energy plexuses, channels and subtle essences internalizes the protective circle, charnel grounds, palaces and deities that are visualized when generating a maṇḍala externally. As revealed in this Tibetan scroll painting, divine forms represent the outer appearances of internal processes within the human bodymind. As described in the 15th century by Sachen Kunga Nyingpo, 'The mind is realized and mastered through the alignment of the dependently arisen connections in the body, which is the agent of realization, and thus the explanatory continuum.' *Peaceful/Wrathful Deities* (Shitro), 18th–19th century, pigments on cloth, Rubin Museum of Art, New York, C2006.66.56 (HAR 200037).

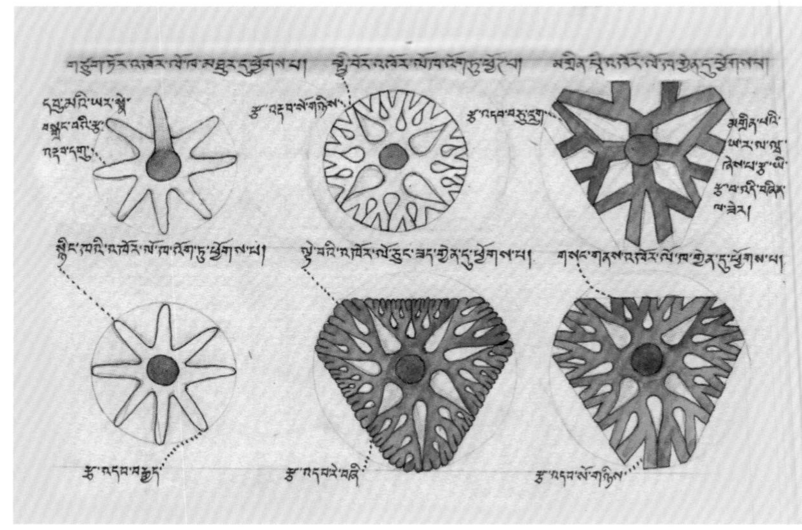

Right ***Cakras* are the basis for Tantric practice** and represent convergences of psycho-physiological processes in the genitals, lower abdomen, heart, throat, prefrontal cortex and the crown of the head. As shown in this drawing from the Shangpa Kagyu tradition, *cakras* are composed of a main channel surrounded by differing numbers of branch channels that collectively form the inner maṇḍala of the human body. Drawing by Lama Tinley.

Realization of the body's inner maṇḍala of energy channels, psychosomatic winds and subtle essences typically begins with alternate nostril breathing to balance the subtle energies of the right and left channels of the yogic body and harness their psychosomatic potential.

Empowered breathing

As the Buddha states in the *Majjhima Nikāya Sutrā,* 'If the body is not mastered, the mind cannot be mastered. If the body is mastered; mind is mastered.' Vajrayāna Buddhist practices based on a metaphysical anatomy of channels, energy currents and subtle essences are known in Tibetan as Tsa Lung Tiglé (Skt. *nāḍi*, *prāṇa*, *bindu*), representing the subjective quintessence of body, breath and mind. Tsalung practices are often combined with strenuous physical exercises called Trulkhor, the 'magical wheel of channels and winds' that reveal the body as an energetic flow of luminous awareness. Although Tantric Buddhism's Completion Phase ultimately comprises abiding in the intrinsic nature of mind without auxiliary support, Tsalung represents an internalization of Creation Phase Deity Yoga and is often upheld as the 'innermost expedient means' for realizing the innate enlightenment of body, speech and mind. As Gyalwa Yangönpa stated, 'If you do not understand the fundamental nature of the body, you will not understand the essential point of meditation.' Yangönpa further indicated the human body itself as the 'method that clarifies all the teachings.' Tsalung practices thus take the body's innermost subtle anatomy as

Tsalung breathing practices stimulate core processes within the body's myofascia, or connective tissue. Breath-controlled movements associated with Tsalung have been shown to activate the release of mesenchymal stem cells (MSC) associated with cellular regeneration and increased longevity as well as increased production of brain-derived neurotrophic factor (BDNF), a protein essential for creating and maintaining healthy neurons.

the path to realizing Buddhahood. As metaphorically described within the tradition, mind or consciousness rides the horse of *prāṇa* along the pathways of the *nāḍis*, propelled by *bindu*, the innermost vitalizing substances of the human body.

Tsalung, or Completion Phase meditation on the energetic pathways of the vajra body, typically follows Creation Phase practices of Deity Yoga. Envisioning body, breath and mind as innate expressions of enlightened awareness, practitioners of Tsalung engage in focused breathing exercises that mobilize the body's in-dwelling maṇḍala of channels, energy winds and subtle essences. This rarified expression of human physiology is held to represent the ultimate essence, nature and capacity of the bodymind, thereby leading to realization of one's innermost being as a Tantric deity. The renowned Sakyapa scholar Ngorchen Kunga Zangpo (1382–1456) clarified how the practice of Tsalung internalizes the cosmic structure of the maṇḍala, transforming a practitioner's view of his or her own body and revealing its identity with the wider cosmos. In the outer maṇḍala the central deity is visualized in union with a consort. In inner maṇḍala practice, the central deity is conceived at the heart, while the consort, in the case of a male practitioner, is placed at the 'vajra door' at the genitals. Ngorchen describes how Buddhist monks misunderstand the practice: 'What is this but an aversion towards phenomena and persons?'

As many contemporary Tibetan lamas have explained, mastering the subtle elements of the mind and body offers an accelerated path to Buddhahood, but if practised incorrectly can imbalance the nervous system and lead to physical and mental distress rather than to the intended realization of inner heat, transpersonal bliss and psychophysical illumination. Tsalung's empowered breathing techniques are thus traditionally described using the example of a snake in a hollow bamboo tube, signifying the central channel of the yogic body. Practised incorrectly, or in absence of altruistic motivation, Tsalung can lead downwards to the 'vajra hells' of ego inflation. Alternatively, rapturous identification with the bliss and emptiness of one's essential being can transport one upwards to transpersonal 'Buddha realms', while dissolving impediments to enlightened awareness.

Opposite **A Bhutanese yogini** unifies her awareness with all-encompassing space in accordance with the Dzogchen transmission of Phagmo Zaptri, the 'Profound Instructions of Vajravārāhī'.

Above **A 14th-century Tibetan manuscript** depicts the circulation of energy and awareness within the yogic body in connection with Dzogchen, the Great Perfection teachings transmitted in both Vajrayāna Buddhism and Bön, Tibet's indigenous yogic tradition. The red *rasanā* channel and the white *lalanā* channel that flank the body's central blue channel are shown shifting positions at the nostrils and unifying at the crown of the head, while the associated seed-syllable *āḥ* signifies primordial, non-dual awareness. Bönpo Meditation Manual. Private collection.

Expanding the life force

One of the earliest Vajrayāna texts to articulate yogic meditation on the body's internal maṇḍala of channels, winds and vital essences is entitled *Amṛtasiddhi*, the 'Perfection of Immortal Nectar'. Disseminated in Tibet from the 12th century, the *Amṛtasiddhi* advanced earlier Vajrayāna accounts of yogic practice by emphasizing the transformative power of 'solar fire' in the pelvic cavity. As the text states, the radiant 'sphere of the sun at the base of the central channel ... consumes the lunar secretion' at the apex of the body's medial axis, thus leading to a divinized state in which the 'yogin is made of everything, composed of all elements, always dwelling in omniscience ... Delighted, he liberates the world.' Central to this process of self-transformation involving metaphors of sun, moon and fire are psychophysical techniques that cause the body's innermost vital essences, or *bindu*, to infuse one's axial core, thereby inducing a radiant state of timeless awareness.

The word *bindu*, or *tiglé* in Tibetan, has multiple meanings depending on context. Within Tantric practice *bindu* customarily refers to the energetic potency of male and female sexual secretions. As the interface between consciousness and matter within the human body, *bindu* may also relate to information-bearing neuropeptide molecules, including endorphins, concentrated on lateral sides of the spinal cord and associated with subjective states of physiological and

Above **A Tibetan line drawing** illustrates a held exhalation (*bhaira kumbhaka*) that focuses attention at the root, navel and throat *cakras* so as to awaken *prāṇa* in the pelvic cavity and draw it upwards through the body's central channel, leading to expanded states of awareness.

Right **A former monk meditating beneath a waterfall** demonstrates *mahābandha*, a three-fold neuromuscular lock that seals energy in the body's central channel when combined with a held exhalation prior to an expanded 'vase breath' (*kumbhaka*, Tib. *bumchen*) in which respiration and discursive thought are simultaneously suspended so as to enter deeper states of meditative absorption (*samādhi*).

psychological wellbeing. As physiological correlates of emotion, peptide substrate in the human body has also been associated with the health-promoting effects of consciously controlled breathing patterns: the foundation of Tantric Completion Phase practices involving channels, winds and subtle essences.

Essentially, Tsalung practice involves consciously engaging the human respiratory system so as to optimize the flow of energy and awareness within the body's internal network of bio-energetic channels, or *nādi*, thereby removing subtle physiological, psychological and energetic blockages, called *granthi*, along the body's central axis. When practised correctly, Tsalung recalibrates consciousness by mobilizing the psychoenergetic resources of the upper and lower *cakras* and unifying consciousness at the heart centre, the nexus of the body's estimated seventy-five trillion cells. In the illuminated heart, illusions of separation vanish and, what the Buddha called *avidya*, or not knowing, transforms into radiant realization of the dynamic interconnectivity that unifies and empowers all life.

Early Tantric Buddhist texts describe the activated energies of the lower *cakras* as rising like solar flames through the body's central channel and 'melting' the luminous, lunar secretions (*bindu*) in the brain, which, in turn, stream down like nectar (*amṛta*) and give rise to increasingly subtle states of consciousness, and ultimately to the realization of the non-dual expanse of emptiness and luminosity, the Clear Light held to be the mind's innermost essence.

An accomplished yogini demonstrates breath-coordinated movements that open pathways of subtle energy within the body's innermost anatomy. In Tantric Buddhism, the inner offering of the maṇḍala is made using the flow of energies within the vajra body, while the innermost offering of the maṇḍala refers to abiding in the self-existing wakefulness of one's ultimate nature.

Harnessing the winds

In Tibetan Buddhism, breath is likened to a powerful stallion that, once tamed through the conscious control of respiration, brings one to one's desired destination. In the context of Tsalung, the ultimate essence of breath, or *prāṇa* (Tib. *lung*), is the 'indestructible energy wind' that permeates all existence. When the energy winds of the human body concentrate within the central channel, a unitary state of consciousness arises, characterized by bliss, clarity and non-conceptual awareness. Cultivation of vital breath as well as techniques for suspending respiration for extended periods constitute Tsalung's core practices that increase control over self-regulating processes within the human body, including consciousness. Tsalung's signature 'vase breath' (*kumbhaka*, Tib. *bumchen*) compresses the breath beneath the navel, where the body's three principal energy channels are said to intersect. Associated muscular contractions expand awareness of energetic processes within the physical body and further heighten sensory and extrasensory perception. Tsalung breathing practices are additionally enhanced by physically demanding yogic exercises called Trulkhor, or 'magical movements', that increase internal rapture. Breath in Tantric yoga refers not only to respiration through the mouth and nose, but also to the exchange of energy with a wider universe through the pores of the skin.

Tsalung's synchronization of awareness, breath and movement positively impacts the body's enteric, or visceral nervous system, leading to enhanced vagal tone, hormonal balance and wellbeing. Contemporary research has correlated the yogic anatomy described in Tantric Buddhism with microvascular circulation within the myofascia, the connective tissue interfacing muscles, ligaments and bones, as well as with the interstitium, the contiguous fluid-filled space between the skin and organs of the human body. The internal tingling of *prāṇa* associated with Tsalung and related practices has been further related to mechanisms of the relaxation response in which activation of the parasympathetic nervous system dilates blood vessels and markedly increases blood flow.

A horned figure on a ritual bowl from the ancient Indus Valley civilization reveals elements that later became tropes of Indo-Tibetan yoga, such as representations of a radiant energy body, a tri-striped meditation belt, and visualized wings and headdresses. Buckingham Collection.

Opposite **Tantric yogins with meditation belts** (*gomtrag*) demonstrate diverse techniques of Tsalung, beginning with clearing the body's lateral energy channels through alternate nostril breathing. The second image shows a yogin pressing the backs of his wrists into 'wind points' at the femoral arteries to draw vital essences into the central channel. The yogin at the lower right sits in a posture of regal ease (*lalita asana*) and extends his life force beyond the body, while the figure at the lower left withdraws breath and sensory awareness into the body's interior, supported by a meditation belt symbolizing the central and lateral channels of the yogic body. Ogyen Choling Manor.

Tsalung practitioners with Tantric meditation belts called *gomtrag*, signifying prowess in meditation, are depicted in this detail of a Tibetan scroll painting. Meditation belts echo the *yajñopavītam*, or sacred thread that twice-born Brahmins wear across their chests. The woven belts are typically worn around the lower back and beneath the knees to give stability and support during seated meditation, as demonstrated by the figure at the lower right.

Opposite **The mahāsiddha Virūpa** is depicted with a meditation belt that holds his body in royal ease while he points to the sun to demonstrate his control over the flow of internal energy. Solomon Family Collection.

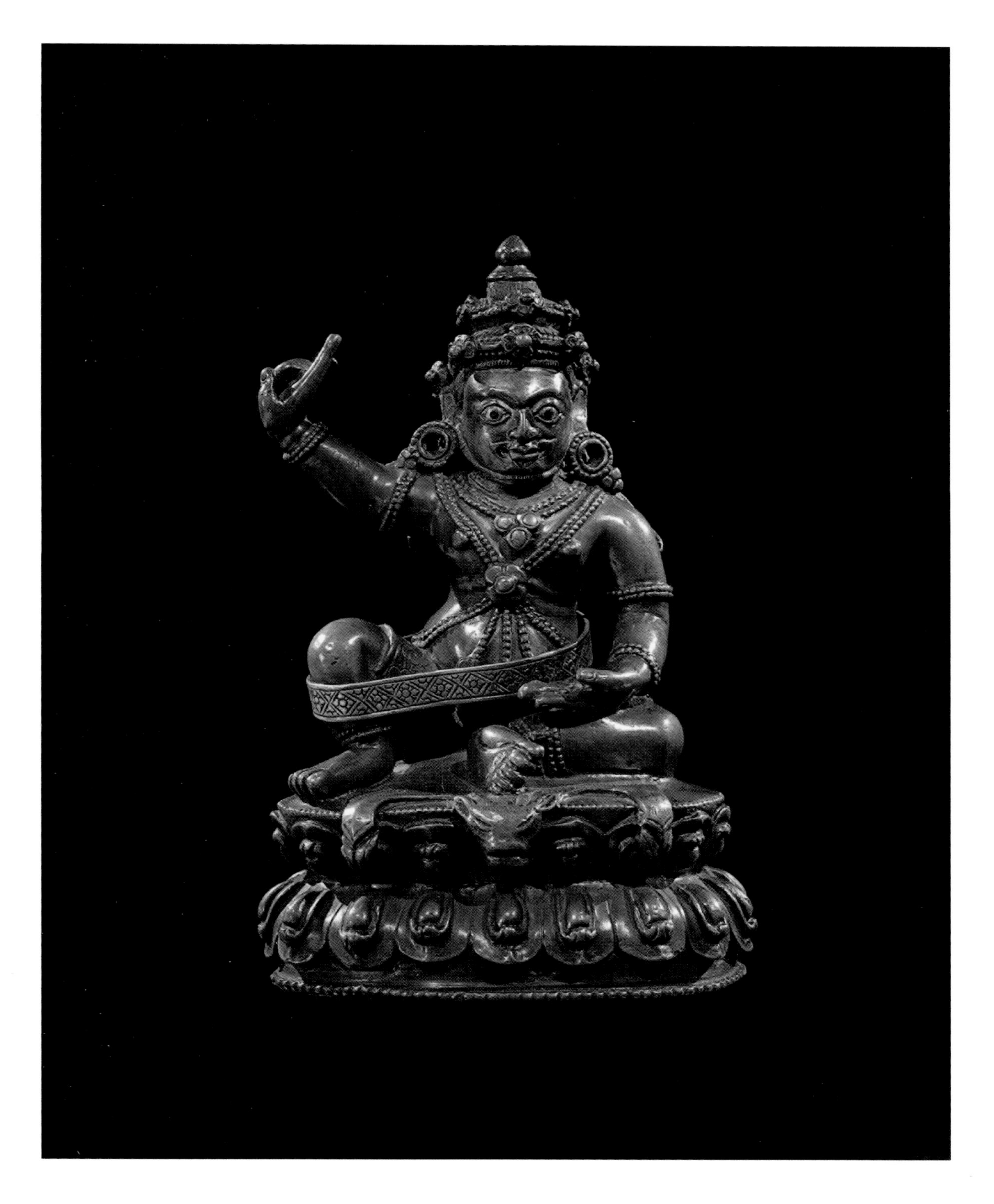

The energized flow of awareness and vital energy through the yogic body is illustrated in the painting opposite by Rolf Kluenter. Through Tantric practice, white and red essences, which are respectively held to originate at the time of conception from the father's sperm and the mother's ovum, infuse the central channel from their polarized seats at the crown *cakra* of great bliss and the junction of the three principal channels below the navel, as depicted on the body of the Tantric yogin on the right, in a detail from a mural in Tibet's Lukhang temple. The seed-syllable *āḥ* emanating from the yogin's heart *cakra* signifies the non-dual awareness that arises when the energy currents enter the body's central channel.

Illusory Body Yoga refers, at its highest level, to cultivation of an intangible divine body from the 'indestructible energy wind' of illuminated consciousness, or Clear Light. The emergent body, white in colour, typically arises in the form of one's chosen meditation deity, but may also appear in human form, as shown in this detail from a wall painting in the Potala Palace in Lhasa. An illusory body (*gyülu*) can only be perceived by those who themselves have attained an illusory body and represents a transformative dimension of being that, in Buddhist terms, neither exists nor doesn't exist.

Embracing illusion

All forms of Tantric Buddhist yoga begin with recognizing one's body as a network of energetic processes devoid of abiding material substance. The subtle channels and *cakras* represent the inner structure of the human body while the winds and vital essences refer to psychophysical propensities that are transformed through yogic practice. Vajrayāna's Creation Phase yogas conclude with recognition of the innate enlightenment of the bodymind as the ultimate deity, while subsequent Completion Phase practices begin with realization of the human body as a conduit of unimpeded, transpersonal consciousness. Within the Six Yoga system of the Completion Phase, this constitutes Illusory Body Yoga (*gyülu naljor*) in which the body is experienced as the intangible, luminescent anatomy of an ultimately illusory Tantric deity. Illusory Body Yoga thus envisions body, breath and mind – the three fundamental constituents of being – as emptiness, energy and bliss, and coextensive with space itself. Realization of the dynamic play of emptiness and appearance underlies all forms of Tantric Buddhist yoga and is further actualized through the practices of Tsalung Trulkhor, the 'magical movements of the channels and winds', that are explored in the following chapter. As the great Tibetan adept Rigdzin Jigme Lingpa pronounced, 'Unless the vitally important body is compliant and energy flowing freely, the pure light of consciousness will remain obscured. So take these physical practices to heart!'

Opposite **Magical flight**, as depicted in this image of an airborne mahāsiddha, constitutes an ultimate objective of Illusory Body Yoga. The practice ranges from recognizing the physical body as an impermanent, and thus unreal, mental construct to esoteric rites, whereby the mind can be emanated from the heart as a subtle body and used to carry out diverse activities such as remote viewing and healing. The functional separation of consciousness from the physical body is also the objective of Powa, as explored in the chapter 'Exit strategies'.

To voyage through the sky with this material body,
meditate on the subtle channels and inner winds,
and gain mastery over your energies and thoughts.
Ultimate accomplishment is nothing other than this!

Khandro Yeshe Tsogyal, 8th century

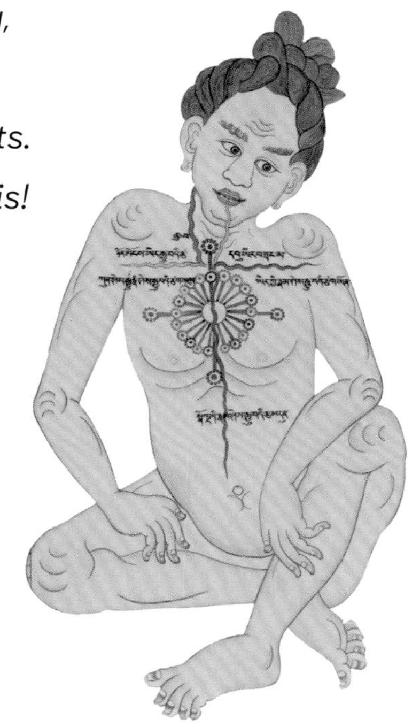

A yogin in a Bhutanese temple practises Tsalung from the Phagmo Zaptri, the 'Profound Instructions of Vajravārāhi', that focus energy and awareness in the heart centre and conceive of the body as a translucent network of subtle energy channels. Opening the subtle energy channels at the heart *cakra* through the practice of Tsalung is considered prerequisite to undertaking the more strenuous practices of Trulkhor, or 'magical movements', which concentrate energy in the pelvis and solar plexus and awaken dormant human capacities.

Flowing wholeness

The yoga of magical movement

To stabilize the mind, first tame the body with magical movements (Trulkhor) ... although you are ostensibly training the body, you are indirectly subduing and stabilizing the mind.

Karma Chagmé Rinpoche, 'Spacious Mind of Freedom', 17th century

Embodying enlightenment

Vajrayāna, the Tantric form of Buddhism practised throughout the Himalayan world, presents itself as offering the swiftest path to spiritual liberation, but the dynamic mind–body practices at the heart of the tradition are rarely revealed even to advanced initiates. As a result, Vajrayāna is better known for its publically performed monastic rituals than for the psychophysical disciplines that distinguish Vajrayāna from earlier forms of Buddhist practice. This chapter introduces the transformative exercises called Tsalung Trulkhor – literally 'magical wheel of channels and winds' – that combine visualization with vigorously held breaths, movements and yogic locks to alter the flow of psychosomatic energy through the body's myofascia and a posited metaphysical neurovascular system, leading to heightened vitality and expanded states of awareness.

Trulkhor exercises are commonly performed while imagining oneself as an aroused or semi-wrathful Tantric deity which, though appearing, is not held to be intrinsically real and can thus be considered 'magical'. The exercises thus constitute a highly embodied approach to the Deity Yoga that is foundational to Vajrayāna's Creation Phase. However, because the practices work directly on the body's interstitial network of psychic energy channels, they are normally taught as preliminaries to Vajrayāna's Completion Phase, and thus have traditionally been obscured by conventions of secrecy.

The root texts of 8th-century Yoginī Tantras such as the Hevajra and the Cakrasaṃvara Tantra describe internal yogic practices connected to the body's network of energy channels, but accounts of associated physical exercises only appear in later commentaries. However, the Hevajra Tantra makes repeated reference to the importance of ritual dance movements for purifying thirty-two specified energy channels within the yogic body and enacting the qualities of the multi-limbed and multi-faceted Hevajra deity.

Opposite **The mahāsiddha Jālandhara** reveals the body as both an instrument and agent of emancipation. His three-pronged, fire-tipped yogic staff recapitulates his activation of subtle energies within the three principal meridians of his yogic body through dynamic movement. The awakening of *śakti-kuṇḍalini* is further represented by Jālandhara's dance partner and the ambrosial waves rising from her skull cup. Gangteng Monastery, Bhutan.

This contemporary scroll painting created by Akarpa Lobsang Rinpoche codifies Tsalung Trulkhor practices within the Kagyu lineage deriving from the teachings of mahāsiddha Nāropā, the Jonangpa transmission of Trulkhor according to the Kālacakra Tantra, and the Tibetan tradition of Yungdrung Bön. As Akarpa Rinpoche explains, the erotic image of Buddha Samantabhadra, 'Awakened Universal Goodness', shown at the top centre of the painting signifies the radiant, noetic bliss that is humankind's essential nature, and which is revealed and cultivated through the practice of Tsalung Trulkhor. At the centre of the painting is the multi-armed Tantric deity Kālacakra, surrounded by six yoginis in aureales of fire, signifying the Six Vajra Yogas of the Completion Phase that reveal the intrinsic enlightenment of mind and body and transform the human condition from suffering and discontent to joy and liberation.

Until you gain control over the horse-like winds, the mount of the mind, you will not gain control over the rider-like mind.

Tsongkhapa Lobzang Drakpa, *A Lamp to Illuminate the Five Stages*, 14th century

Sacred dance

The Hevajra Tantra states that, 'When joy arises, the yogin should dance for liberation, assuming the vajra postures of the divine Heruka [Hevajra] with fullest attention … emanating them with an impassioned mind within a state of uninterrupted attention.' As the Hevajra Tantra further clarifies, the movements 'reveal the adamantine nature of the Buddhas, Yoginīs, and Mother Goddesses…. The protection of the assembly and oneself is by means of such song and dance.' Such statements suggest that the origins of Trulkhor, as a means of embodying the qualities of Vajrayāna deities and associated psychophysical processes, may lie not only in early Haṭha Yoga-related techniques, but also in traditions of Tantric dance, such as the yogic *tāndava* dance form transmitted within Kashmiri Śaivism and *caryānṛtya,* a ritual dance tradition transmitted by Newar Vajracaryās in Nepal and associated with the Cakrasaṃvara Tantra. Analogous choreographies of self-transformation are central to Tibetan ritual dances known as Cham, which prior to the 13th century were performed only within assemblies of consecrated initiates.

The 16th-century Tibetan scholar and adept Tāranātha (1575–1634) described Trulkhor as 'esoteric instructions for dissolving the energy–mind into the central channel and releasing knots in the channels, primarily using one's own body as the method', and he assigned them both medical and emancipatory effects. In his treatise entitled 'Eighteen Physical Trainings', Tāranātha consolidated yogic exercises attributed to the 11th-century Kashmiri female mahāsiddha Niguma and disseminated in Tibet by her disciple Khyungpo Naljor (c. 1050–1140). A separate transmission of six 'root' Trulkhor with thirty-nine 'branches' is said to derive from Niguma's consort, Nāropā who, in turn, reputedly received them from his Bengali teacher Tilopā, although the dating of these practices is problematic due to the absence of original Sanskrit versions of Tilopā's and Nāropā's texts and the fact that they only became part of the Kagyu transmission more than a century later.

Below left and right **A Tantric yogin** commences a series of exercises that echo the dynamic movements illustrated in a contemporary painting by Robert Powell, based on an orginal temple frieze in the former Himalayan kingdom of Mustang. The animated yoginis represent the essence of embodied experience and Tantric Buddhist yoga as an internalization of deities depicted in Tantric maṇḍalas.

Left **A Newar Caryā dancer** embodies the qualities of a Tantric deity in a ritual of sacralization and consecration, in which the human body is recognized as the locus of experience and, thus, of liberation. The Newar tradition of Tantric Buddhism in Nepal's Kathmandu Valley preserves forms of Vajrayāna that largely vanished in India after the 13th century.

Below **A yogin in a sinuous handstand**, depicted on a mural in western Tibet, illustrates the central role of the body in transforming inhibiting habits of mind, as promoted in Tantric Buddhist yoga.

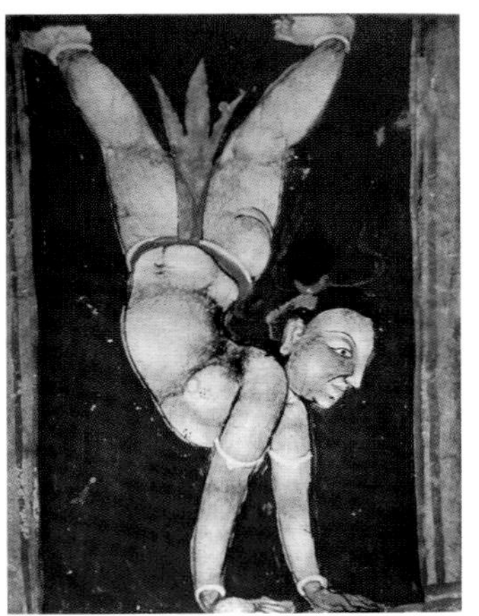

Integrating body, breath and consciousness

The earliest clearly datable descriptions of external yogic practices in Tibetan Buddhism were composed by Phagmo Drupa Dorje Gyalpo (1110–70), a 12th-century Kagyu and Sakya master whose treatise entitled 'The Path of Fruition's Thirty-two Auspicious Actions' used Sanskrit and pseudo-Sanskrit names to describe sequential yogic movements connected with the Hevajra Tantra, which had been translated from Sanskrit into Tibetan from 1041 until 1046. Phagmo Drupa also wrote 'The Path of Fruition's Five-Branch Yoga', which consists of basic instructions for loosening the neck, head, hands and legs, as well as a manual entitled 'Supplementary Verses on the Path of Method' which describes six physical exercises for removing obstacles and preparing the body for advanced internal yogas, based on drawing psychosomatic 'winds' into the body's central channel.

Trulkhor's tripartite purpose of clearing the body's subtle energy system, drawing vital essences (*bindu*) into the central channel, and distributing them throughout the psychophysical organism in preparation for Completion Phase Tantric practices, such as Fierce Heat, distinguish Trulkhor, or 'magical movements', from Lujong, a more preliminary Tibetan system of physical training. Although the movements of Lujong are analogous to those of Trulkhor, they are primarily undertaken for physical health and

Left and opposite **Tantric Buddhist art encodes internal yogic processes.** The drawing of a bow, as signified in the Trulkhor movement shown at the right, is also depicted near the base of a Tantric diagram that charts the dynamic ascent of subtle energy through the body's central meridian. Central to the practice is the compression of upward-rising and descending energy winds (*apānavâyû* and *prāṇavāyu*) in the lower abdomen so that they enter the central channel of the yogic body and pierce through all psychosomatic hindrances. The movement is also said to unblock and open the heart- centre, freeing it from stagnant 'wind' and unproductive mental states. Private collection.

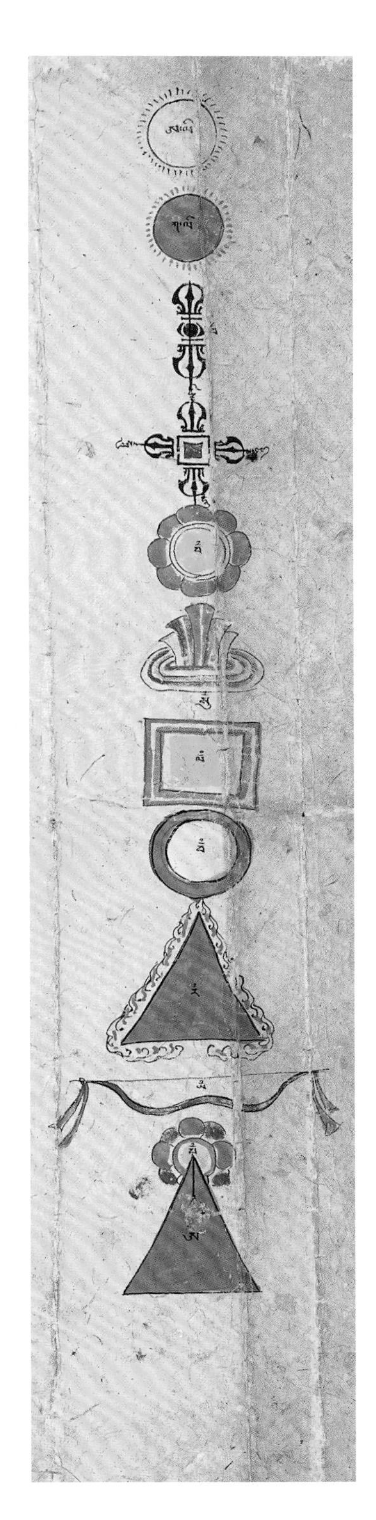

thus do not include the demanding held breaths, forceful drops and internal visualizations that characterize Trulkhor. Some of the better-known Lujong practices (also known as Nejong, or 'vital point training') transmitted in Tibet were derived from the Kālacakra Tantra – which had been introduced in Tibet in 1064 – by Butön Rinchen Drup (1290–1364), the renowned 14th-century abbot of Tibet's Shalu Monastery. Butön Rinchen Drup classified his system of Nejong as 'outer' exercises to be used both by Buddhist practitioners and physicians for balancing the body's internal energies, unblocking obstructions in the channels, and pacifying diseases of mind and body.

Butön Rinchen Drup simultaneously transmitted a system of twenty-four sequential Trulkhor exercises that he derived from the Kālacakra Tantra for concentrating the flow of psychophysical energy within the body's central channel in support of paranormal abilities such as 'swift walking' that purportedly allowed adepts at Shalu to cover vast distances on foot by modulating the effects of gravity. Based on controlling the body's internal energy flow through specialized breathing techniques and yogic locks (*bandha*), 'swift walking' was described in the early 20th century by the French explorer Alexandra David-Néel: 'The man did not run. He seemed to lift himself from the ground, proceeding by leaps. It looked as if he had been endowed with the elasticity of a ball and rebounded each time his feet touched the ground.'

Magical movements

All traditions of Trulkhor extol the exercises' remedial healing effects while emphasizing their more profound transformative influence on the body and mind, including the reputed development of supranormal powers called *siddhi*. Although attainment of the extraordinary capacities associated with yogic cultivation is rarely an openly admired or admitted goal within Vajrayāna Buddhism, provisionally useful worldly *siddhis* such as clairvoyance, invisibility and control of natural phenomena are claimed to this day to arise spontaneously as a result of dedicated practice. Vajrayāna's more transcendent goal, however, remains the *mahāsiddhi*, or 'great accomplishment' of transforming egotism, greed and aggression into empathic wisdom and unconditional compassion. Attaining this awakened disposition in the most expedient manner possible is viewed as the essential intent of Sakyamuni Buddha's Eightfold Path to Nirvāṇa and thus accounts for the inclusion of Haṭha Yoga-like 'magical movements' within Vajrayāna Buddhism's path of skilful means.

Trulkhor practices in Tibet's indigenous pre-Buddhist tradition of Bön first appear in the Bön Mother Tantra in a chapter entitled 'Elemental Essences' which outlines five foundational exercises for balancing the body's fundamental

Above **A detail of a Tibetan manuscript** illustrates a foundational Trulkhor exercise for drawing the energies of the body's lateral channels into the central meridian, an anatomical analogue of emptiness within the yogic body. The 18th-century manuscript, written in both Tibetan and Chinese, ascribes both medical and spiritual benefits to the set of thirty-two exercises based on the Hevajra and Cakrasaṃvara Tantras. Beijing Palace Museum.

Right **A clay statue of a crowned mahāsiddha**, seated on a lotus, is one of several such near life-size images that enscribe a three-dimensional model of the maṇḍala palace of the Tantric deity Cakrasaṃvara in a chapel in the Pelkhor Chöde Monastery in Gyantse, Tibet. The posture of 'drawing a bow' signifies activation of the internal energies of the yogic body so as to direct them in the service of one's own and others' enlightenment.

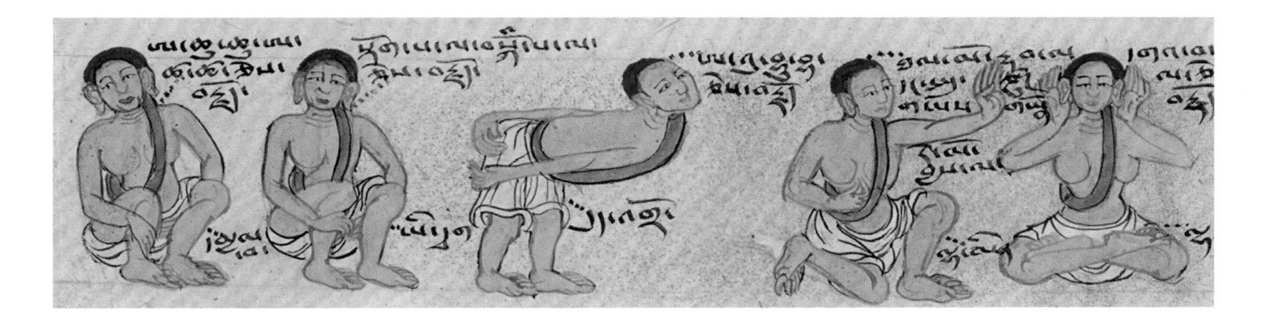

Above **A folio of a Tibetan Dzogchen manuscript** illustrates contemplative exercises preliminary to advanced forms of non-dual meditation. Royal Danish Library, Copenhagen

constituents. The practices of the Bön Mother Tantra are traditionally credited with a long line of oral transmission, but the fact that they only appeared in written form from the 11th century makes it difficult to determine to what degree they evolved independently of Buddhist influence in Tibet. Similarly, the 'Great Perfection Oral Transmission of Shang Shung: Instructions on the Magical Wheel of Yogic Movements' with its own tradition of Trulkhor practices also dates in written form to the late 11th or early 12th century, although Bön tradition maintains that the practices were transmitted orally in Tibet centuries earlier.

Below **A yogin depicted in a cave** stretches his right hand in *karana mudrā*, a compassionate gesture that wards off negativity. Ogyen Choling Manor.

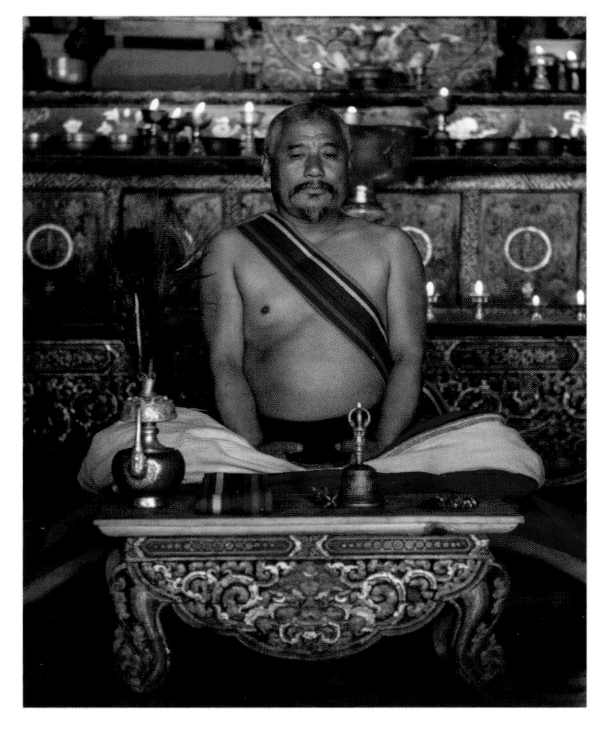

The immortal elixir

The first Vajrayāna Buddhist text to describe specific Haṭha Yoga methods is the Amṛtasiddhi, or 'Perfection of Immortal Nectar' which despite its Śaivite overtones was transmitted in Tibet from the 12th century onwards. The Amṛtasiddhi is widely held to be the source text of the Indian Haṭha Yoga tradition and makes the first known reference to the Haṭha Yoga techniques of *mahāmudrā*, *mahābandha* and *mahāvedha*. Within the context of the Amṛtasiddhi, these yogic 'locks' were used for drawing vital energies into the body's central channel and controlling their upwards and downwards flow. Described as a 'Magical Wheel of [yogic movements for realizing] Immortality', the yogic exercises of the Amṛtasiddhi were transmitted within Tibet's Shangpa Kagyu lineage from the time of Nyenton Chökyi Sherap (1175–1255), who had reputedly learned them from an Indian master. In the Amṛtasiddhi, the practitioner imaginatively transforms into the Hindu deity Śiva, who is often presented within Vajrayāna as having been converted into a Buddha by the Bodhisattva Vajrapāni. Within the Trika Śaivism of Kashmir, Śiva is synonymous with 'pure consciousness' and non-dual awareness.

Preceding pages **Tshewang Sitar Rinpoche** performs yogic exercises from the 'Magical Wheel of Wisdom Holders' (Rigdzin Trulkhor) in Gaden Lhakhang in Ura, Bhutan. (See page 132 for a description of some of the movements.)

Below **Karma Lhatrul Rinpoche** demonstrates Trulkhor movements from the Phagmo Zaptri, the 'Profound Instructions of Vajravārāhī', which channel vital energies into the central meridian of the yogic body. The practice was revealed in the 20th century by Kunzang Dechen Lingpa, based on a prior treasure tradition revealed by Rigdzin Godemchen entitled the 'Profound Transmission of Vajravārāhī'.

A 12th-century edition of the 'Perfection of Immortal Nectar' compiled by Avadhūtacandra promotes an ideal of unrestricted access to the teachings that is markedly distinct from earlier and later Tantric Buddhist lineages based on secrecy and exclusivity. A similarly open ethos in the origins of Haṭha Yoga can be discerned in another early Haṭha work, the 13th-century Dattātreyayogaśāstra, which advocates that its practices of yogic seals (*mudrās*), yogic locks (*bandhas*) and additional Haṭha Yoga disciplines of *vajrolī* (described on page 170), *amarolī* and *sahajolī* be practised freely, irrespective of ethnicity, caste or class. Due, in part, to Tantric yoga's assimilation within celibate Buddhist monastic communities, many of Haṭha Yoga's core techniques were interpreted, and practised, figuratively in Tibet within contexts of increasing secrecy. This emphasis on secrecy, which was less evident in Tibet prior to the 13th century, is gradually diminishing in light of the current globalization and secularization of Haṭha Yoga practices.

The turquoise heart essence

The earliest transmission of Trulkhor in Tibet may have been *Turquoise Heart Essence*, compiled by Sumtön Yeshe Zung in 1157, based on original writings and teachings of Yuthok Yönten Gönpo (1126–1202), the Tibetan physician and yogic adept credited with the revelation of the 'Four Medical Tantras', which consolidate Tibetan medicine's approach to the prevention, diagnosis and treatment of disease. The Yuthok Nyingthik, or *Turquoise Heart Essence*, was reputedly compiled after Yuthok's second of five trips to India where he received direct instructions from Indian Tantric masters.

Drawing in part on the Kālacakra Tantra's exposition of yogic physiology, *Turquoise Heart Essence* outlines a programme of spiritual development for non-monastic practitioners, condensing the core elements of Vajrayāna Buddhism into forty root texts, the twentieth of which describes a sequence of eighteen Trulkhor exercises for refining the body's subtle energy channels in preparation for practices of Fierce Heat and the Yoga of Sexual Union. As expounded in the Yuthok Nyingthik, these latter practices support the realization of Mahāmudra and Dzogchen and the ultimate attainment of a dematerialized body of rainbow light.

The Yuthok Nyingthik's concise treatise on Trulkhor entitled 'The Root-Text of the Magical Movements for Supreme Mastery which Clear the Darkness of Suffering' is supplemented with a longer commentary entitled 'A Concise Synopsis of the Supreme Accomplishment of the Profound Path of the Magical Wheel of Yogic Movements that Clear the Darkness of Suffering', which elucidates the therapeutic and yogic applications of *Turquoise Heart Essence*'s Trulkhor teachings. The first two of the eighteen exercises are said to clear obscuring karmic imprints from the subtle anatomy of the body, while the following five assist in generating the transformative fire of Tummo, or Fierce Heat. The subsequent eleven exercises directly prepare the body for the Yoga of Sexual Union, held by non-monastic Nyingma and Kagyu traditions to be the most efficacious means for achieving the supreme realization of Dzogchen or Mahāmudra, as prefigured in early Vajrayāna works such as the Guhyasamāja Tantra. *Turquoise Heart Essence*'s exposition of an eighteen-set Trulkhor is roughly contemporary with Phagmo Drupa Dorje Gyalpo's description of sets of six and thirty-two yogic exercises connected with the Hevajra Tantra's Path of Fruition, which he completed before his death in 1170. Both Yuthok's and Phagmo Drupa's works predate Nyenton Chökyi Sherap's codification of the 'magical movements' associated with 'The Perfection of Immortal Nectar' (Amṛtasiddhi) and thus, taken together, can provisionally be considered the earliest datable evidence of Haṭha Yoga-like practices within Tibetan Buddhism.

Opposite, above and below
The 'peacock position' (*mayûra āsana*) is described in the 15th-century Haṭha Yoga Pradīpikā as 'destroying all disease'. The upper image, from the Beijing Palace Museum, shows it as number twenty-eight in a sequence of thirty-two Trulkhor exercises from the Hevajra 'Path of Fruition' as recorded in a Qing Dynasty manuscript from China's Imperial Treasury. The lower photograph shows a contemporary practitioner placing the palms of his hands on the ground, with his navel on his elbows and, thus balanced, 'stretching the body backwards like a stick' so as to elongate the spine.

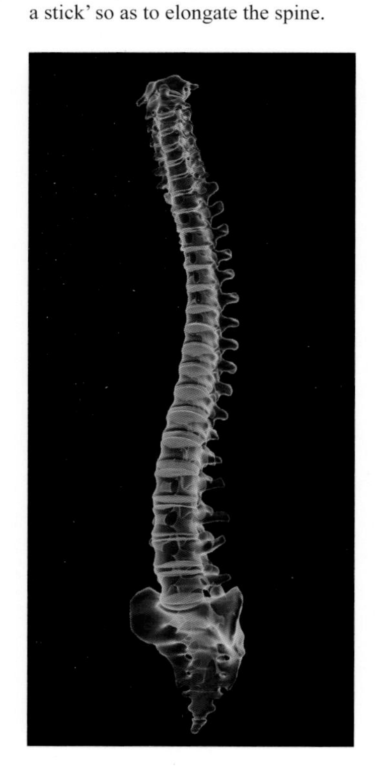

The path of fruition

Phagmo Drupa Dorje Gyalpo's 12th-century elucidations of Trulkhor practice within the Hevajra Tantra's Path of Fruition were elaborated by Drakpa Gyaltsen (1147–1216) in his 'Magical Channel Wheel of Thirty-two Auspicious Actions', which he described as removing obstacles to Tantric practice. Drakpa Gyaltsen expanded on the medical benefits of the thirty-two exercises as well as on their supporting function within the Completion Phase of the Hevajra and Cakrasaṃvara Tantras. Like Phagmo Drupa before him, he assigned Sanskrit-derived names to the various yogic movements – likening them to animals, auspicious objects and revered Indian Tantric masters – and emphasized their importance in cultivating the yogic power of Fierce Heat and other Completion Phase practices. As was also the case with the 'Perfection of Immortal Nectar', Drakpa Gyaltsen presented the yogic exercises without restrictions, indicating in his colophon that the movements remove obstacles to spiritual practice and 'are suitable for beginners as well as advanced students'. Drakpa Gyaltsen also advocated practising the set of thirty-two exercises once in a forward direction, once in reverse, and once in random order to make a prescribed set of ninety-six movements. As Drakpa Gyaltsen assures his audience: 'If one trains oneself [in the yogic exercises] as much as one can, one will achieve Buddhahood.' Drakpa Gyaltsen further claims that practising the thirty-two exercises will result in acquiring the thirty-two major body characteristics (*lakṣaṇa*) of a Buddha.

Above **The Haṭha Yoga practice of the 'great piercer'** (*mahāvedha*), in which the buttocks are gently dropped against the ground to awaken *kuṇḍalinī*, is illustrated on a mural in the Lukhang temple as the twentieth of twenty-three movements described by Tertön Pema Lingpa in his 15th-century treatise entitled 'Secret Key to the Channels and Winds'. As the accompanying wall inscription states, 'Sit in vajra posture and lift up the body [by pressing down on the hands], then drop the body against the ground. Do this three times, shaking the body into wakefulness.'

Phagmo Drupa's initial exposition of yogic exercises influenced later Tibetan masters such as Lama Dampa Sönam Gyaltsen Pelsangpo (1312–75) and Muchen Konchok Gyaltsen (1388–1471), whose *Little Red Volume* includes a chapter entitled 'Thirty-two Auspicious Yogic Movements'. Tsongkhapa Lobzang Drakpa (1357–1419), the founder of the reformed Gelug order of Tibetan Buddhism, also elaborated on Phagmo Drupa's 12th-century yogic exercises in his 'Book of Three Certainties: A Treatise on the Stages of Training in the Profound Path of Nāropā's Six Yogas' and in 'A Brief Treatise for Practising the Stages of Meditation in Nāropā's Six Yogas, compiled from the teachings of Jey Rinpoche by Sema Chenpo Kunzangpa'. Jey Sherab Gyatso (1803–75), in his commentary to the 'Book of Three Certainties', remarks that even though there are an impressive variety of exercises, 'there seems to be no great advantage in doing more than the six recommended by Phagmo Drupa [as taught by Tsongkhapa] for accomplishing the Yoga of Fierce Heat.' He further notes that 'when stability is achieved in these practices, a subtle sense of joy pervades the body'.

Unless energy flows freely through the body,
the pure light of consciousness will remain obscured.
So take these physical practices to heart!

Rigdzin Jigme Lingpa, 18th century

Evolving traditions

Tsalung Trulkhor and versions of the associated Six Yogas developed within all schools of Tibetan Buddhism in both monastic communities and among non-celibate male and female yogins. Phagmo Drupa's principal disciple Jikten Gonpo Rinchen Pel (1143–1217) founded the Drigung Kagyu school of Tibetan Buddhism, which transmitted elaborated Trulkhor practices based on 'Cakrasaṃvara's Oral Transmission of the Magical Wheel of Channels and Winds' and 'The All-Illuminating Mirror: Oral Instructions on the Magical Wheel of Yogic Movements for Training the Body to Progress in the Practice of Fierce Heat from the Six Yogas of Nāropā'. The Drigung Kagyu also continues to transmit a cycle of thirty-seven Trulkhor movements revealed by the Second Karmapa, Karma Pakshi (1204/6–83). The Drigung Kagyu's elaborate and complex systems of Trulkhor were periodically condensed, emphasizing five core movements combined with retained 'vase breaths', visualization and internal neuro-muscular 'seals' for activating and harmonizing the body's five elemental winds.

Within Tibet's Nyingma tradition, the transmission of Trulkhor and the Six Yogas of the Completion Phase closely paralleled emergent practices in the new translation schools, but they were expediently presented in the form of revealed 'treasure texts' attributed to Nyingma's iconic 8th-century patron saint Padmasambhava. Although no descriptions of Trulkhor can be found in original texts associated with Tibet's earliest Vajrayāna lineage, early Nyingma masters such as Rongzom Chökyi Zangpo (1012–88) and Nyang Ral Nyima Özer (1124–92) were closely associated with early 'New School' proponents such as Smṛtijñānakīrti and Padampa Sangye and are likely to have received

Previous page (above) **Tolāsana is an arm-balancing variation of lotus pose**, or *padmasana*, and is practised together with *mahābandha* (a combination of root lock, upwards abdominal lock and throat lock) and *mahāvedha mudrā* in both Ashtanga Vinyasa Yoga and Tibetan yoga to draw energies into the body's central channel. The practice involves retaining (or alternatively exhaling) the breath, pressing down with the palms, contracting the abdominal and perineal muscles, lifting the legs and buttocks, and then, after holding the position without strain and with the chin pressed into the notch of the larynx, gently and repeatedly dropping the buttocks onto the ground. According to Haṭha Yoga texts, this causes the 'winds' in the body's side channels to enter the central channel and confers longevity and spiritual powers.

Previous page (below) **Kukkutāsana, or 'rooster pose'**, is a variant of *tolāsana* and is performed by slipping the arms into the creases between the thighs and calves and, as in *tolāsana*, lifting the torso and legs above the ground without pressing the shoulders upwards. With the breath held out, the coccyx is tucked under, the pubic bone dropped back to meet it, and the sitting bones drawn together in an intensified root lock (*mula bandha*). The abdomen is drawn upwards in *uddiyana bandha* and the chin tucked inwards in *jalandhara bandha*. The same sequences are applied in Tibetan yoga.

Right **Karma Lhatrul Rinpoche** performs Tsalung Trulkhor movements from the 'Profound Instructions of Vajravārāhī' (Phagmo Zaptri), which is attributed to the

15th-century Bhutanese treasure-revealer Tertön Pema Lingpa. The thirteen sequences are divided into three sections. The first five movements open the energy channels of the yogic body. The second set of five cultivates vital essence (*tiglé*), while the last three movements distribute the vital essence throughout the body.

Above **Padmasambhava encircled by Eight Wisdom Holders**, as shown on a mural in Gaden Lhakhang in Ura, Bhutan. The eight tiger-pelted, dancing *vidyādharas* are associated with a twenty-one movement Trulkhor cycle called the 'Magical Wheel of Wisdom Holders' (Rigdzin Trulkhor) revealed by Rigdzin Jigme Lingpa.

Tsalung Trulkhor transmissions from them, thus gradually introducing codified practices of breath and movement into the Nyingma corpus. The new material entered the Nyingma tradition as revealed 'treasure texts', 'mind treasures' and 'pure visions' that allowed Trulkhor to be recontextualized within Dzogchen's view of self-existing enlightenment.

After the cycle of eighteen yogic exercises described in the 12th-century *The Turquoise Heart Essence*, Trulkhor further entered the Nyingma tradition through the literary works of the 14th-century Dzogchen master Longchen Rabjampa Drimé Özer (1308–64). Longchenpa synthesized earlier Nyingma treasure texts in his multi-volume *Nyingthik Yabshi* that quotes widely from the foundational Seventeen Dzogchen Tantras. But the first instance of Trulkhor practice in Longchenpa's writings occurs within his subsequent *Wishfulfilling Treasury*, later catalogued as one of his 'Seven Treasuries'. The book elucidates Buddhist cosmology and philosophical systems, but the concluding section of its final chapter, 'The Fruition that is the Culmination of Meditation', describes twenty yogic movements for clearing obstacles according to the 'profound

Bhutanese Lama Tshewang Sitar Rinpoche performs an 'adamantine drop' (*dorje kyiltrung beb*) from the Rigdzin Trulkhor cycle of the 'Heart Essence of the Vast Expanse' (Longchen Nyingthik) in Gaden Lhakhang in Ura, Bhutan. The forceful movements are a Tibetan elaboration of the earlier and more subtle Haṭha Yoga practice of *mahāvedha*, 'the great piercer', as shown on pages 128 and 129.

meaning of the vajra essence, the ultimate instruction of the *Wishfulfilling Treasury*'. These exercises include sequenced stretching movements in support of the Dzogchen contemplative technique of Kadak Trekchö, or 'cutting through [discursive mental activity] to primordial purity'. Unlike preceding forms of Trulkhor presented within Tibetan Buddhism, Longchenpa's rendition is not based on visualizing oneself as a Tantric deity, but on vibrant awareness of one's innate Buddha Nature, on the basis that, from the perspective of Dzogchen, all divine forms arise from the luminous expanse of the heart that is the ultimate deity.

The Trulkhor exercises described in the twenty-second chapter of Longchenpa's *Wishfulfilling Treasury* formed a template for later and more elaborate Heart Essence presentations of Trulkhor. The twenty movements include interlocking the fingers against the chest and stretching them outwards (no. 3), twisting the shoulders down to the hands and knees (no. 4), pushing outwards from the chest with the hands held as fists (no. 5), twisting the body with the arms crossed and the hands on the shoulders (no. 6), drawing the hands along the arms as if shooting a bow (no. 8), pushing the fists outwards as if against a mountain (no. 9), bending forwards and backwards (no. 10), and joining the little fingers of the hands and forming a *mudrā* on the top of the head (no. 11).

Below **A radiant boar-headed yogini** standing on a moon disk represents the transformed vision and experience resulting from Tantric Buddhist practice. Trulkhor involves mastery of the body's internal energy system and is typically undertaken while envisioning oneself as a Tantric deity.

Subsequent revealed treasure texts connected to the Dzogchen Nyingthik, or 'Heart Essence of Great Perfection' transmission, largely all include Trulkhor practices. For example, in 1366, two years after Longchenpa's death, Rigdzin Godemchen (1337–1408) revealed his highly influential 'Northern Treasure' with a Trulkhor cycle based on the meditational deity Vajravārāhī. These teachings were expanded upon by the treasure revealer Tenyi Lingpa (1480–1535), whose writings elaborated on the movement of energy through the channels during sexual union and the discipline of *vajrolī*, in which sexual fluids are circulated through the body's yogic anatomy. Tenyi Lingpa's elaboration of Rigdzin Godemchen's Trulkhor, as first revealed in the Gongpa Zangthal – the highest Dzogchen teachings of the Northern Treasure lineage – consists of twelve preparatory exercises, thirteen principal movements and twelve concluding movements.

All systems of Tsalung Trulkhor typically include sequences of forceful 'drops' (*beb*), as described in greater detail later in this chapter. As illustrated above, the practice purportedly drives subtle energies into the body's central channel to promote expanded states of awareness.

Tertön Pema Lingpa's 15th-century 'Secret Key to the Channels and Winds' describes a sequence of twenty-three yogic movements that were illustrated around 1700 on the walls of the private meditation chamber of Tibet's Sixth Dalai Lama, Tertön Pema Lingpa's direct blood descendent. The movements are performed with held 'vase breaths' with self-visualization as the Tantric deity Hayagrīva in union with Vajravārāhī. The sequential movements begin in the upper right corner, continue from left to right in the second register, and from right to left in the third register. They culminate with an illustration of a yogi sitting in the seven-point meditation posture of Vairocana, as described on page 53. The series of movements is said to clear hindrances to contemplative practice while also ensuring physical and mental health.

A Tantric mahāsiddha, twirling a double-headed skull drum and ringing a vajra-topped hand bell, embodies the existential orientation of the 'magical wheel of channels and winds' that are based on the unity of emptiness and appearance. Although Tantras such as the Hevajra do not mention Trulkhor, 'breath yoga' in the Hevajra Tantra is associated with the Tantric activities of 'overthrowing' (exhaling), 'controlling' (inhaling), 'attracting' (filling) and 'paralyzing' (holding). These breathing practices are, in turn, related with associated gazing techniques. Ogyen Choling Manor.

Opening the heart mind

Opposite above **Lama Tashi Tenzin** of Thimphu, Bhutan, demonstrates Trulkhor movements from the 'Sky Teachings' (Nam Chöd) which conclude with an 'auspicious circle of drops' in which the adept performs a clockwise series of yogic falls.

Opposite below **Trulkhor's 'magical movements'**, when practised from a Dzogchen perspective, are often presented as direct expressions of enlightenment rather than a means of attainment. Practitioners of Tsalung Trulkhor typically wear short, pleated kilts called *angrak*, the colours of which symbolize the elemental energies of space, air, fire and water.

The twenty-two yogic movements described by Longchenpa in his *Wishfulfilling Treasury* do not include either forceful 'drops' (*beb*) nor the 'adamantine wave' practice of pressing on the carotid arteries at the sides of the neck to induce altered states of awareness (see page 184). These were added by Longchenpa's ostensible 15th-century Bhutanese reincarnation, Tertön Pema Lingpa (1450–1521), who revealed a text entitled 'Secret Key to the Channels and Winds', which outlines twenty-three sequential movements preparatory to the Dzogchen's visionary practice of 'Leaping over the Skull' (Tögal). The practices are performed with the breath retained in a 'vase' in the lower abdomen, in combination with *mūladhara bandha*, and are described as 'clearing hindrances' to contemplative practice while also ensuring optimal health. Tertön Pema Lingpa revealed a longer system of Trulkhor in his 'Lama Jewel Ocean' and an abridged version of only seven exercises in his revealed treasure 'Adamantine Necklace of Introductions on Longevity'.

Following Tertön Pema Lingpa's 'Secret Key to the Channels and Winds', further cycles of Trulkhor emerged within the Nyingma Heart Essence tradition through 'The Universal Embodiment of the Precious Ones', a 17th-century treasure text revealed by Rigdzin Jatson Nyingpo (1585–1656), and the approximately contemporaneous 'Accomplishing the Life Force of the Wisdom Holders' revealed by Lhatsun Namkha Jigme (1597–1650/53). The Dzogchen adept Namchö Mingyur Dorje (1645–67) subsequently revealed a 'Sky Teaching' with a Trulkhor cycle of more than sixty movements based on the Buddhist deity Vajrakīlaya, 'Wielder of the Adamantine Dagger', which concludes with an 'auspicious circle of drops' in which the adept performs a clockwise series of yogic falls and also jumps with his or her legs in lotus posture from one padded yogic seat (*beb den*) to another.

Trulkhor's place within the Nyingma Heart Essence tradition was further established with the visionary treasure revelation of Rigdzin Jigme Lingpa whose 'Heart Essence of the Vast Expanse' includes the 'Magical Wheel of Wisdom Holders', a Trulkhor cycle of twenty-one movements elaborating on Longchenpa's *Wishfulfilling Treasure*. The Rigdzin Trulkhor practice begins with five initial exercises for clearing the body's elemental winds followed by eight movements that embody the qualities of eight Indian 'wisdom holders', acclaimed as enlightened contemporaries of Padmasambhava. These and subsequent exercises in the series include vestiges of ritual dance as well as forceful movements reminiscent of Chinese systems of Wei Gong and Yang-style Taijiquan.

Some later Heart Essence treasure works such as the Chetsün Nyingthik revealed by Jamyang Khentse Wangpo (1820–92) make no mention of Trulkhor, whereas the 'All-Perfect Heart Essence' revealed by Chokgyur Dechen Lingpa (1829–70) contains a Trulkhor series based on the Tantric Buddha Ācala Caṇḍamahāroṣaṇa. The later 'Heart Essence of the Sky Dancers', revealed by Dudjom Jikdral Yeshe Dorje (1904–87) in 1928, contains a widely practised Trulkhor cycle of sixteen movements which draws from the 'Profound Transmission of Vajravārāhī' revealed by Rigdzin Godemchen. Similarly, the 'Profound Instructions of Vajravārāhī' revealed by Kunzang Dechen Lingpa (1928–2006) contains an extensive Trulkhor cycle with elaborate 'drops', although Dechen Lingpa modified the practice in recognition that 'drops' could be harmful if not commenced at a sufficiently early age.

Falling free

Opposite above **A practitioner in Bhutan** demonstrates a 'yogic drop' (*beb*) central to the practice of Tsalung Trulkhor. As a method of self-consecration combining the Creation Phase and Completion Phase of Vajrayāna Buddhist practice, the 'magical wheel of channels and winds' concentrates vital essence and awareness in the body's central channel and is traditionally practised in preparation for Tummo, the Yoga of Inner Fire. Like Cham and Caryā dance – which were originally practised in secret and are now performed openly – Trulkhor is also increasingly being revealed as an iconic practice of the Vajrayāna Buddhist tradition. The maṇḍala-like mats that cushion the falls are traditionally filled with either compressed yak wool or the hollow hairs of musk deer.

Opposite below **A 3D scan of the pelvis and the lumbar spine**, the physical foundations of the body's innermost energy channel, the *vajranāḍi*. Science Photo Library, London.

Below **A Tibetan manuscript folio** depicts 'magical movements' as practised within the Kagyu lineage of Vajrayāna Buddhism. The yogic exercises open subtle energy channels and enhance the flow of vitality and awareness.

Trulkhor customarily includes intermittent forceful 'drops' (*beb*) of increasing complexity that purportedly direct the body's subtle energies into the central channel to induce expanded states of awareness. The most demanding, and potentially injurious, 'drops' involve leaping into the air from a standing position and landing cross-legged on the ground in the lotus posture with the breath held in a 'vase' in the lower abdomen. Forceful 'drops' are categorized as 'small' (*beb chung*), 'medium' (*bar beb*), 'big' (*beb chen*) and 'adamantine' (*dorje beb*), during which the legs are crossed in the vajra posture in mid air. There are also *kyang beb* in which the adept extends their body and drops on to their side (see pages 140–41 and 144), *chu beb* that are performed after first spinning in a circle, and 'ornamental' *gyen beb* performed at the end of a Trulkhor series. It is likely that *beb* evolved from originally gentler Haṭha Yoga practices such as *mahāvedha mudrā*, which is central to Trulkhor practice in the Amṛtasiddhi and Yuthok Nyingthik. Mahāvedha, the 'great piercer', is normally performed with the legs crossed in *padmāsana*, or lotus posture, the palms pressed against the ground, and the throat pulled inwards in *jālandhara mudrā* while retaining the breath below the navel and successively dropping the backs of the thighs and buttocks on to the ground to cause *prāṇavāyu* to leave the two side channels (*iḍā* and *piṅgalā*) and enter the *suṣumnā*, or central channel. However, *mahāvedha mudrā* as practised in the Amṛtasiddhi differs from the medieval Haṭha Yoga exposition and does not involve dropping onto the thighs and buttocks but sitting on the heels of the feet, which are joined and pointed downwards. An analogous exercise to *mahāvedha* called *tāḍana kriyā*, or 'beating action', is performed in Kriyā Yoga with the eyes concentrated at the point between the eyebrows in *śāmbhavī mudrā*, and is also said to cause vital energy to ascend the central channel.

Beyond the forceful 'drops' that punctuate the movements of Trulkhor, an even more invasive exercise for opening the central channel often concludes a Trulkhor session. The 'vajra wave' (*dorje balap*) involves pressing on the carotid arteries at the sides of the neck to reciprocally increase blood flow through the cranial arteries in the brain stem, engendering a non-conceptual experience of the indivisibility of Saṃsāra and Nirvāṇa. This technique, which is also used in non-dual Śaivism to 'astonish' the mind, is given as the sixth of Phagmo Drupa's foundational thirty-two Trulkhor exercises, with the idiosyncratic appellation '*tsarang gagana'*, implying an intentional blocking (*gag*) of the vital channels (*tsa*).

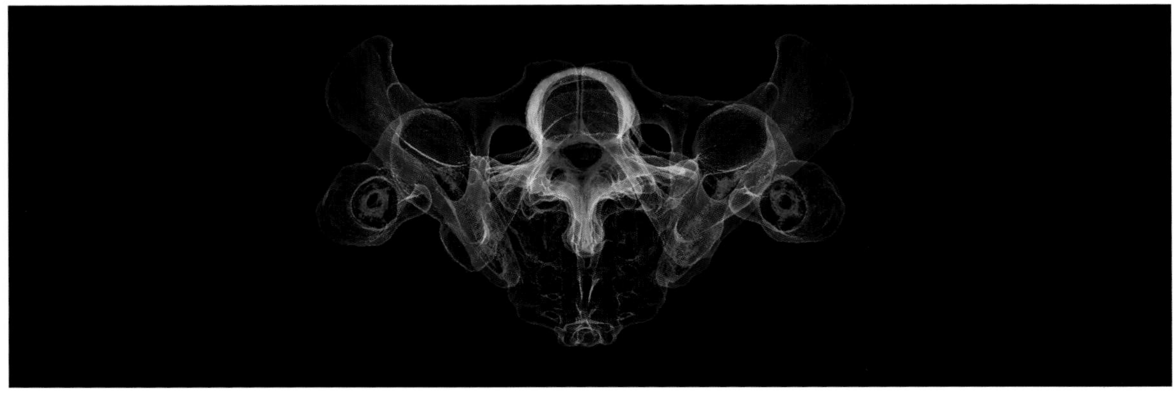

A Bhutanese yogi, concealed behind a mask of Milarepa, demonstrates sequential 'yogic falls' (*beb*) that are integral to Trulkhor practice in the tradition of the Six Yogas of Nāropā. The 'Vajra Verses of Oral Transmission' ascribed to Nāropā refer to six 'root' Trulkhor with thirty-nine 'branches'. Sequential yogic exercises have been practised in the Himalayan world from at least the 12th century, as evidenced by texts such as Phagmo Drupa Dorje Gyalpo's 'The Path of Fruition's Thirty-two Auspicious Actions'.

Yantra yoga

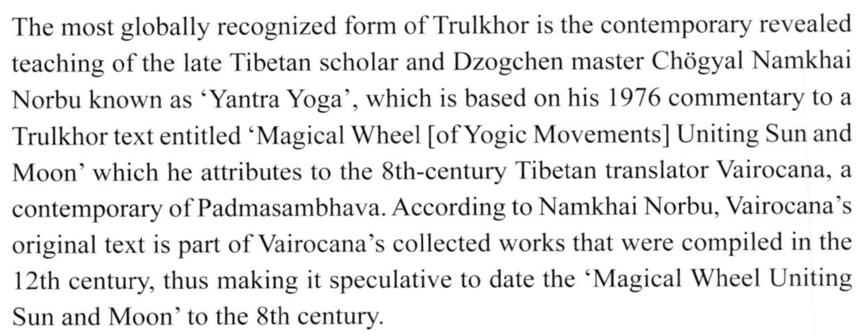

The most globally recognized form of Trulkhor is the contemporary revealed teaching of the late Tibetan scholar and Dzogchen master Chögyal Namkhai Norbu known as 'Yantra Yoga', which is based on his 1976 commentary to a Trulkhor text entitled 'Magical Wheel [of Yogic Movements] Uniting Sun and Moon' which he attributes to the 8th-century Tibetan translator Vairocana, a contemporary of Padmasambhava. According to Namkhai Norbu, Vairocana's original text is part of Vairocana's collected works that were compiled in the 12th century, thus making it speculative to date the 'Magical Wheel Uniting Sun and Moon' to the 8th century.

Namkhai Norbu's commentary, 'A Stainless Mirror of Jewels', extends Vairocana's system of poses and breathing practices into one hundred and eight interconnected movements. Many of the positions are well known within modern postural yoga, giving further evidence of the heuristic nature of Tsalung Trulkhor which, like Haṭha Yoga, continues to evolve through its interactions and exchanges with analogous traditions. According to Namkhai Norbu, Vairocana is said to have received the transmission of Yantra Yoga directly from Padmasambhava who, in turn, is said to have learned the practices from a Nepalese mahāsiddha named Hūṃkāra who himself reputedly learned them from Śrī Siṃha, an early Dzogchen master who lived for a considerable period at the sacred mountain Wutai Shan in western China where similar Taoist-Chan Buddhist methods of what is now called *qigong* were transmitted from before the 8th century. The close parallels of the 'Magical Wheel Uniting Sun and Moon' with Indian Haṭha Yoga and its potential links with Chinese systems of *dao yin* and *qigong* invite further comparative research and may eventually indicate greater transcultural origins for Tibet's Trulkhor practices than has so far been supposed.

A Tibetan yogini stands in vajra posture, a fundamental pose in Yantra Yoga as well as a dynamic isometric exercise in the transmission of Dzogchen. Yantra Yoga translates the Sanskrit term *nāḍivāyuyantra*, or 'instrument of channels and winds', which refers to a transformative technology, in the case of Tantric yoga, for reconfiguring human experience. Yantra Yoga, as taught by Chögyal Namkhai Norbu, largely omits forceful 'drops' (*beb*) as well as self-visualization as a Tantric deity. It does, however, envision the body as a luminously transparent network of energy channels.

Opposite **A Chöd practitioner** performs a ritual dance. In all its forms, Tantric Buddhist yoga directs neurobiological energies into the body's central channel, quelling obscuring mental activity and arousing the blissful 'fierce heat' of Tummo.

Trulkhor awakens in-dwelling capacities through a synergy of body, breath, and movement. Forceful drops on the sides of the body drive energies from the two lateral channels into the body's central meridian, an anatomical analogue of self-transcendent emptiness. From the perspective of Dzogchen, the dynamic actions of Tsalung Trulkhor are useful only in so far as they enhance effortless awareness of 'pure and perfect presence'.

Natural wisdom

In a text entitled 'Realization of Reality through its Bodily Expressions', the 8th-century female mahāsiddha Sahajayoginī Cinta expresses an enlightened view concerning the nature of movement-based practices in Vajrayāna Buddhism: 'Spontaneous movements of the body are sacred gestures. Whether graceful, heroic, terrifying, compassionate, fierce, or peaceful, they are all without exception naturally perfected expressions of enlightened mind.' Sahajayoginī's verses maintain that authentic transformational movement arises spontaneously in an infinite variety of forms. In Trulkhor, prescribed physical actions are undertaken in ritualised emulation of Tantric deities, but Tantric root-texts often place more emphasis on dance and ecstatic play for awakening divine qualities in oneself and the world. This latter approach accords with the spirit of the early mahāsiddhas who advocated naturalness and spontaneity in place of contrived practices.

As described in the chapter 'Primal radiance', Trulkhor practice in Dzogchen often consists of spontaneous, integrated expressions of the body, voice and mind, so as to distinguish conditioned states of Saṃsāra from the existential freedom of Nirvāṇa. The 14th-century Dzogchen master Longchen Rabjampa, an uncompromising advocate of naturalness, counselled that structured yogic practices often inadvertantly estrange us from our innate perfection. As he wrote his *Precious Treasury of Natural Perfection*: 'Exhausting exercises involving struggle and strain are of short-lived benefit … we strive in meditation because we desire excellence, but any striving precludes attainment … remaining constantly at ease in uncontrived spontaneity … non-action is revealed as supreme activity.'

Thus from the perspective of Dzogchen, the forceful Haṭha Yoga-like practices of Trulkhor ultimately matter less in the process of psychophysical integration than the expanded and ungrasping consciousness to which they ideally lead. As Longchenpa's proclaimed 15th-century Bhutanese reincarnation Tertön Pema Lingpa stated in his 'Secret Key to the Channels and Winds': 'By seeing reality as it is, the conceptual mind naturally comes to rest … and the body itself naturally manifests enlightenment.' When undertaken with such an illuminated attitude, the practices of Tsalung Trulkhor can rapidly transform subjective experience and open awareness to self-transcendent dimensions. In this sense, the 'magical wheel of channels and winds' that is varyingly described within different traditions of Vajrayāna and Dzogchen ultimately transcends its geocultural origins and points towards the awakening of collective, if unrealized, capacities of a consciously illuminated bodymind in spontaneous cycles of waking, dreaming and sleeping and the beguiling spaces beyond.

The ultimate purpose of Trulkhor is to loosen the knots of conceptual mind and reveal the incandescent joy of Buddha Nature. As Rumi wrote in the 13th century: 'The Heart is the essence … How many more phrases, ideas, metaphors can I stand? It's burning that I want, true burning!'

A flying mahāsiddha exemplifies the natural spontaneity of enlightenment. From the perspective of Dzogchen, choreographed Trulkhor exercises are often considered unnecessary. The 14th-century Dzogchen master Longchen Rabjampa likened the results of forceful Trulkhor exercises to 'a sand castle built by a child'. As Śrī Siṃha proclaimed, 'When we have understood the yoga that takes us to the end and from which there is neither joining or parting, we dwell in brilliant and blissful presence. Everything desirable arises spontaneously, like a wish-fulfilling jewel.'

༄།གྲུབ་ཐོབ་ལ་

Incandescence

The yoga of unbound fire

Meditation on the essence of mind is good.
But for immediate results nothing compares with the yoga of inner fire.
Milarepa, 11th century

Primal heat

In the *Dhammapada*, one of Buddhism's earliest scriptures, the Buddha speaks of fire as a principle of transformation: 'The spiritual seeker is like fire. Fire consumes everything great or small … all life's vanities, passions and terrors.' Fire was also the basis for the Haṭha Yoga practice of *caṇḍālī,* the 'blazing goddess' invoked by Tantric Buddhist adepts to immolate psychosomatic impediments to a transpersonal state of bliss and incandescent awareness. Analogous to the Kuṇḍalinī yoga of Tantric Śaivism, the practice of *caṇḍālī*, or Tummo in Tibetan, gives rise to four enstatic states associated with specific focal points in the yogic body. As the first of Six Yogas that confer *siddhi*, or supranormal powers including enlightenment, Tummo is traditionally practised only after achieving unwavering insight into the emptiness, or boundless potentiality that underlies all phenomena, and only under the guidance of an accomplished mentor. Otherwise, it is said that the arousing qualities of inner fire can inflame the ego and imbalance the nervous system. Practised correctly, however, the sequenced application of visualization, breath control and yogic seals are held to direct the body's 'winds and essences' into the central channel and to thus reveal the immortal mind of Clear Light (*ösel*) that the Buddhist Tantras correlate with Nirvāṇa. Although Nirvāṇa is often held to refer to the extinguishing of the afflictive fires that fuel Saṃsāra, or conditioned existence, Nirvāṇa refers more accurately to a fire that has been liberated and unbound from its source (un, *nir* + binding, *vāṇa*) and is thus self-blazing. This ardent and undying flame within the pelvic cavity is the basis of the Tantric Buddhist practice of blissful heat that gives rise to a 'mind like unbound fire', rapturously awakened to the infinity of human potential. As the great 8th-century yogini Yeshe Tsogyal summarized the practice, 'Recognize the intrinsic unity of bliss and emptiness … Raise and suffuse your vital energy and seal it with the iron nails of your imagination.'

Opposite **A Tantric mahāsiddha**, or realized adept, demonstrates a sitting posture for awakening Tummo, literally the 'Fierce Feminine', in a mural detail from the Lukhang temple in Tibet. The yogin's posture is stabilized with a meditation belt while the figure above his head supports his self-visualization as a Tantric deity. Combining breath retention with subtle contractions of the pubococcygeus muscle in the pelvis, the Yoga of Inner Fire illuminates subconscious processes of the mind and body and facilitates control over the autonomic nervous system.

Thermogenesis

Above **A Tantric yogin** depicted on the wall of a private temple in Bhutan holds his thumbs against the base of his ring fingers in the position of 'vajra fists' to retain and intensify internal heat during the practice of Tummo. The great yogini Yeshe Tsogyal likened Tummo to 'sealing one's body like a lighted butter lamp.'

Above right **The mountain Gyala Pelri**, in Tibet's Pemakö region, is held to represent the head of the incandescent Tantric meditational deity Vajravārāhī with whom practitioners of Inner Fire identify in support of rapturous self-transcendence. 'Taking blissful heat as the path' is traditionally practised in high mountain settings where cold temperatures work in synchrony with internally generated heat to induce altered physiological and psychological states.

Yogic practices based on the cultivation of thaumaturgic heat originate in the Indian ascetic tradition of *tapas*, a Sanskrit word that derives from the verb *tap*, meaning 'to burn', and which denotes an ardent discipline that burns away the physical, mental and emotional obstacles to the unitive state of yoga. The fiery enthusiasm inherent in the practice of *caṇḍālī*, or Tummo, parallels the rising of *kuṇḍalinī*, the coiled energy at the base of the spine, and in the heart, which is first referred to in 8th-century Indian Śaivite texts. In its earliest sources, *kuṇḍalinī* is described as a female manifestation of the life force that rises serpent-like through the body's central channel to unite with Śiva, as effulgent consciousness. The 10th-century Pādmasamhitā similarly describes *kuṇḍalinī* as ascending from below the navel through breath and fire and 'bursting forth into the cavity of the heart in the form of a brightly blazing snake'. The Khecarīvidya describes *kuṇḍalinī* as rising through a luminous channel to the abode of Śiva at the crown of the head, and 'sprinkling the body of the yogin with dewy, unctuous, cool nectar.' The practice is later elaborated with instructions for generating intense heat through breath retention and yogic seals that cause the 'goddess of the [central] channel' to pierce through psychophysical blockages that obstruct awareness of the integral freedom and spontaneity of supreme 'sky-like' consciousness.

The illuminating fire of *caṇḍālī* is described in the 8th-century Hevajra Tantra as a primal energy that blazes upwards through the adept's core and incinerates in-dwelling Buddhas that signify conventional, and thus inhibiting, Buddhist beliefs. The practice epitomizes the more radically illuminating and antinomian approach to liberation propounded in the Buddhist Tantras. *Caṇḍālī*, the Buddhist version of *kuṇḍalinī*, was thus the foundation of the Six Yogas that the Bengali mahāsiddha Tilopā transmitted to Nāropā on the banks of the

Above **A dancing tiger-headed deity** evokes the electromagnetic current and amplified bioelectrical field that are subjectively experienced at advanced stages of Tummo practice. Private collection.

Ganges River in the first half of the 11th century as the key teaching from the otherwise highly complex Hevajra Tantra. *Caṇḍālī* subsequently became the basis of Completion Stage practices in other lineages of Vajrayāna Buddhism. The core methodology in which sequenced Haṭha Yoga exercises (Trulkhor), combined with visualization and breath retention, ignite the 'solar fire' in the pelvic cavity and induce a flow of nectar from the 'moon' in the head is first elaborated in the Vajrayāna Buddhist Amṛtasiddhi Tantra, the 'Perfection of Immortal Nectar'. Composed in the 11th century, the Amṛtasiddhi shares a common methodology with Nāth Śaivism and presents a template for unifying experiential polarities within the human nervous system, corresponding, in contemporary medical terms, with the hypothalamic – pituitary – gonadal axis. The Seventh Dalai Lama described the practice in a fervent invocatory prayer: 'Vital essences generated by inner and outer means are drawn into the central channel, igniting the fire of inner heat. Inspire us in this yoga, that we may realize the innately arising bliss aroused by the drop of the immortal nectar.'

Right **A Tantric Buddhist master** from Derge, in eastern Tibet, demonstrates a primary posture for cultivating the inner fire of Tummo. After subtly contracting his diaphragm and perineal floor, he places his thumbs against the base of his ring fingers and presses the back of his hands against specific points in the groin to concentrate sensation below the navel, while his arms press against the sides of his torso to draw energies into the body's central channel. The heat generated in the pelvic cavity is visualized as flames that rise through the core of the body to 'melt' subtle essences in the brain that, in turn, flow downwards and blaze from the heart and lower abdomen.

Opposite **Tummo's 'inner alchemy'** is illustrated in this painting by Rolf Kluenter as conversions of red and white seed-essences within the body's central channel. After generating heat in the pelvic cavity through visualization and forcefully held 'vase breaths', the aroused energy ascends to the limbic region of the brain, causing the dispersal of mood elevating substances symbolized by the bija mantra *hāṃ*.

Below **The primary posture for Tummo** involves pressing the backs of the wrists into the inguinal crease between the thighs and the lower abdomen so as to redirect the circulation of blood through the femoral arteries and stimulate the flow of vital energy in the body's central channel. In medical terms, Tummo engages the 'second brain' of the enteric nervous system and its intricate web of more than one hundred million neurons which, in addition to regulating metabolism, convey information to the brain through the vagus nerve that influences immune response, mood and emotion, including intuitive 'gut feelings'.

Fire and ice

Opposite **The 'snow-curtained' hiddenland** of Beyul Yolmo Kangri in northern Nepal was one of Milarepa's favoured locations for Tummo practice.

Below **A 19th-century Tibetan scroll painting** of Padmasambhava. The detail shows two yogins being instructed in the Yoga of Inner Fire. The lower figure stretches the side channels of his body so as to open the juncture where three principal energy currents meet beneath the navel. The figure behind him uses a meditation belt to stabilize an alternate posture. Rubin Museum of Art, New York, C2006.66.440 (HAR 897).

Tibet's celebrated yogi Milarepa proclaimed in the 11th century that, 'For attaining liberation in this lifetime, nothing surpasses the secret yoga of inner fire, the life blood of the sky-dancing ḍākinīs.' It was at Mount Kailash that Milarepa asked his beguiling female disciple Rechungma, 'Though you cast off your fine, soft woollens, can you kindle the bliss and heat of Tummo?' Traditionally undertaken in high-altitude environments, Tummo's beneficial effects on the autonomic nervous system are further enhanced by exposure to cold temperatures that induce positive metabolic changes, including replacement of white adipose tissue with more metabolically active brown adipose tissue. These metabolic transformations are triggered by the increased action of a protein called brain-derived neurotropic factor (BDNF), a neuron-producing stress response hormone in the hippocampus region of the brain. BDNF is linked with cognitive enhancement and mood elevation and, besides cold exposure, is also elevated by exercise, intermittent fasting and caloric restriction. Tummo is initially practised forcefully, to generate heat, and then more gently, to maintain the heat. Studies of Tummo practitioners in eastern Tibet show correlations between the length of breath holdings and increase in core body temperature and energetic states. But as the explorer and Tummo adept Alexandra David-Néel wrote in 1929, 'To spend the winter in a cave amidst the snows, at an altitude that varies between 11,000 and 18,000 ft (3,350 to 5,500 m), clad in a thin garment or even naked, and escape freezing, is a somewhat difficult achievement.'

Ecstatic asceticism

The early 20th-century French explorer Alexandra David-Néel was one of the first scholars to write about the Yoga of Inner Fire for a Western audience. In *Magic and Mystery in Tibet*, she describes a midwinter scene by a mountain stream in which Tummo practitioners 'sit on the ground, cross-legged and naked. Sheets are dipped in the icy water, each man wraps himself in one of them and must dry it on his body. As soon as the sheet has become dry, it is again dipped in the water and placed on the novice's body to be dried as before. The operation continues in that fashion until daybreak. Then he who has dried the largest number of sheets is acknowledged the winner of the competition.' She further comments that, 'Besides drying wet sheets on one's body, there exist various other tests to ascertain the degree of heat which the neophyte is able to radiate. One of these tests consists in sitting in the snow. The quantity of snow melted under the man and the distance at which it melts around him are taken as measures of his ability.' However, as all traditions of Tummo maintain, elevated body temperature is simply a sensational side effect of the mind and body surpassing conventional limits in the shimmering radiance of 'unbound fire'.

Akarpa Lobsang Rinpoche, a highly accomplished practitioner of diverse traditions of Tsalung Trulkhor, the 'magical movements of channels and winds', demonstrates an outwardly held vase breath for activating Inner Fire. A comparable breath hold (*bhaira kumbhaka*) is also used in Haṭha Yoga to still the movements of the mind and arouse liberating heat.

Science's ongoing dialogue with Tibetan Buddhism did not begin with clinical investigations of relaxation-inducing mindfulness practices, but with Dr Herbert Benson's groundbreaking Harvard Medical School study of Tibetan practitioners of Inner Fire, as urged by H.H. the Dalai Lama in the late 1970s. Dr Benson's analysis of metabolic and electroencephalographic (EEG) alterations during the practice of Tummo has been advanced by more recent research by neuroscientist Dr Maria Kozhevnikov among female Tummo practitioners in eastern Tibet. Dr Kozhevnikov's study has demonstrated that Tummo's dynamic combination of meditative visualization and forceful vase breathing stimulates the sympathetic nervous system, rather than relaxing the parasympathetic nervous system, thus leading to heightened states of wakefulness, mental resilience and enhanced cognitive performance correlated with increased alpha, beta and gamma wave activity in the brain. Contemporary medical studies of a secular form of 'inner fire' meditation developed by 'Iceman' Wim Hof have also demonstrated highly beneficial effects of Tummo-related practices on the human endocrine and immune systems.

Right **Togden Amtin, Togden Achos and Togden Semdor** were highly revered yogis in the Drukpa Kagyu lineage of Himalayan Buddhism. Their uncut hair, coiled on top of their heads, and their Tantric shawls – symbolizing the merging of the red and white elements within the yogic body – distinguish them as advanced practitioners of Tummo. In their tradition, when one yogi passes away they are replaced by another. Tashi Jong, a Tibetan settlement in the Himalayan foothills of northern India, remains a vital centre of Tantric Buddhist yogic practice.

Below **The 16th Karmapa Rangjung Rigpe Dorje** (1924–81) demonstrates the Yoga of Inner Fire. Tummo involves four phases of respiration: slow inhalation (*jugpa*), open holding of the breath (*dangba*), pressing down (*zhilba*) and exhalation (*phenpa*). An 'empty' breath is held after exhalation (*tsa tong khilba*) with stretched arms and the back supported by a meditation belt.

The reincarnate Tibetan lama, Lopon Ugyen Rinpoche, who studied western biomedicine in China, has speculated that the 'blazing and dripping' of vital essences (*tiglé*) within the yogic body, central to Tummo practice, correlates with increased production and secretion of mood-elevating hormones and neurotransmitters such as dopamine, oxytocin, serotonin and anandamides that similarly interface with human consciousness. Current research initiatives in Bhutan are leading to changes in traditional attitudes regarding the 'secrecy' of advanced Vajrayāna Buddhist practices, which increasingly have been shown to actualize latent capacities of the mind and body and to advance insight, compassion and wellbeing.

Four phases of joy

The practice of *caṇḍālī*, or Inner Fire, is described in the Hevajra Tantra as leading to four increasingly powerful states of inner rapture known as the 'four joys' (*caturananda*) that parallel the four *dhyānas*, or states of meditative absorption, central to early Buddhist practice, which result in perfect equanimity and awareness. In their Tantric iteration, these four meditative stages are highly eroticized and likened in the Hevajra Tantra to experiences of blissful absorption associated with stages of sexual consummation, while ultimately transcending conventional notions of sensual pleasure. On an inner level, the Four Joys are experienced as the white *bodhicitta*, or male seminal essence, and corresponding female 'red element' ascending and descending through the four principal *cakras* of the yogic body, leading to joy (*ananda*) at the crown *cakra*, supreme joy (*paramanada*) at the throat *cakra*, culminating joy (*viramananda*) in the heart *cakra* and innate joy (*sahajananda*) at the navel centre. The Four Joys are then re-experienced in ascending order in an intimate continuum of emptiness and delight. In the 13th century, the Tibetan adept and medical practitioner Gyalwa Yangönpa (1213–87) described the Four Joys naturalistically as innate to human embodiment, clarifying that the body is born and dies with innate joy and that the essence of the body and mind while living is great bliss. Further overturning early Buddhist views of life as intrinsically faulted, Yangönpa concluded that, 'Therefore the body is bliss throughout the three times.' The Yoga of Inner Fire differs from forms of meditation that intentionally calm the parasympathetic nervous system. By stimulating the sympathetic nervous system, Tummo has been shown to heighten arousal, cognition and psychological resilience.

A Bhutanese adept draws energy into the midline of the body and channels it to the brain by pressing his wrists against energy points on the upper thighs. Thermoregulation is governed by the preoptic region of the hypothalamus which, by extrapolation, can be identified as the primary area of the brain that the Yoga of Inner Fire engages.

Right above **An accomplished yogini** demonstrates the opening of the body's central energy channel, which brings awareness of the mind's natural state of unconditioned rapture. Research in the neurobiology of forceful vase breathing combined with meditative visualization correlates significantly with amplified alpha wave activity in the brain. As signified by the red and white Tantric shawl, trainees in Tummo were often required to sit through the night in sub-zero temperatures, successively drying cotton sheets soaked in ice water with their elevated body temperature.

Right below **A yoga practitioner** sits in the Tummo posture known as the 'six-cornered stove', a position favoured by the 11th-century Tibetan yogin Milarepa. As Milarepa's contemporary, the 11th-century mahāsiddha Niguma instructed: 'Imagine that fire as fine as a thread reaches through the central channel from top to bottom and, focusing the mind there, meditate clearly.'

A detail from an 18th-century manuscript at the Beijing Palace Museum shows a yogin practising Tummo within the context of a sequence of thirty-two yogic exercises (Trulkhor) elaborated in the 12th-century by Drakpa Gyaltsen and associated with the 'Path of Fruition' (Lamdré) of the Hevajra and Cakrasaṃvara Tantra. The sequence of thirty-two Trulkhor exercises is significant in its reference to the thirty-two subtle energy pathways listed in the Hevajra Tantra as well as to the thirty-two *nādi* that reputedly radiate from the eight petals of the heart *cakra*. The seed-syllable *āḥ* at the yogin's navel signifies the ascending fire that melts, and inverts, the seed-syllable *haṃ* at the crown of the yogin's head. The seed-syllable *oṃ* is depicted at the yogin's throat, and an inverted *hung* at his heart centre. The syllables represent vibrational currents within the yogic body, while the *āḥ* and *haṃ* reversed become *mahā*, signifying the 'Great Bliss' that overturns ignorance and suffering.

A contemporary painting, created in Nepal by artist Rolf Kluenter, represents the merging of the red and white female and male essences within the yogic body that are central to the practice of Tummo and related methods for drawing energy and awareness into the central channel, signified here by a blue sphere and midnight-blue border representing the all-encompassing element of Space.

The noetic bliss that results from merging upward-rising energy winds (*apānavāyu*) and descending energy winds (*prāṇavāyu*) at the navel *cakra* is the basis for awakening to the ultimate state of consciousness.

Transcendent rapture

Above **The Yoga of Inner Fire** catalyzes all bodily processes, as illustrated in this line drawing, which shows an upturned skull cup brimming with ambrosia on top of a yogin's head while his lower body blazes in transformative flames.

Above right **The Tantric deity Vajravārāhī** represents the initial, outer stage of Tummo practice when a practitioner visualizes themself as the flaming, incandescent goddess, as depicted in this Tibetan scroll painting. Inner Tummo involves meditating on the channels and *cakras* of the yogic body, while secret Tummo consists of 'blazing and melting'

In Book Six of his *Treasury of Knowledge*, Jamgön Kongtrül Lodrö Thayé (1813–99) characterized Tummo as the 'burning away of impure psychophysical constituents and utterly vanquishing emotional afflictions.' He further explains that, 'the ultimate inner fire is the attainment of utter luminous clarity, the flame of pristine awareness ... which cuts through all conceptual elaboration.' In a work entitled *Hidden Description of the Vajra Body*, Gyalwa Yangönpa likens Tummo to internal alchemy: 'The union of the *āḥ* at the navel and the *haṃ* at the crown of the head symbolizes the action of inner heat, in which the junction of the three channels below the navel is the fire pit; the short *āḥ*, the fire god; the side channels *rasanā* and *lalanā* the implements used in the fire rite; winds and vital essences, the fire offering substances.' Yangönpa concludes that, in the Yoga of Inner Fire, 'a natural fire-offering rite is performed within the body in which channels and bodily constituents are the circle of deities of the maṇḍala.'

In his analysis of Tantric yogic practice, Yangönpa writes of pleasure as the natural state of existence, and thus an essential component of true meditation. The author Henry Miller wrote in his memoirs of a 'joyous illumination in ardent, non-dual communion. Vajravārāhī's numinous iconography includes a severed skull held at her heart, signifying the reorientation of consciousness brought about by fervent burning and the associated co-emergent blissful awareness.

Below **Tummo is often performed outdoors** with a minimum of clothes, as shown in this photograph from the Nangchen region of eastern Tibet. The Tibetan yogin Shabkar Tsokdruk Rangdrol travelled extensively in Nangchen. In his writings on Inner Fire, he described the almost 'unbearable bliss' that pervades the body 'like milk filling a leather pouch' and which reveals the mind's 'natural state as the realization of bliss and emptiness'.

... a metaphysical bliss which makes everything clear without being known.' His assessment recalls mahāsiddha Saraha who described the effortless bliss of Sahajananda as the lived intuition of a totality that can only be realized in a perfectly non-dual state of mind. As Saraha proclaimed, everything originates and merges back into this primordial unity which 'is free of existing or not existing.' The philosopher Pierre Teilhard de Chardin referred to joy as 'the infallible sign' of the presence of divinity. He also wrote of conducting one's life 'as if limits to our ability did not exist.' Tummo, the yoga of blazing fire, expresses this same ardour for infinity and, in its original sense, signifies the incineration of limits. Ray Bradbury began his dystopian novel *Fahrenheit 451* with the memorable words, 'It was pleasure to burn', but that fervent passion only becomes meaningful when it serves a greater good. Yeshe Tsogyal, the 8th-century Tibetan princess-turned-yogini who attained enlightenment through the Yoga of Inner Fire, clarified the matter succinctly: 'Unless bliss is mingled with boundless compassion, one strays from the path of the Inner Tantras ... Taste rather the coalescence of bliss and emptiness as they arise in union! ... So-called Buddhahood is nothing other than this!'

A Tummo practitioner pictured on the wall of a private temple in Bhutan meditates on Inner Fire while a tiger curls beneath him, signifying the taming of the mind. The cultivation of pelvic fire opens the central channel of the yogic body and is thus the foundation for all subsequent yogic practices of the Inner Tantras. As Milarepa's closest disciple Rechungpa summarized: 'Blending inner heat with meditation on the illusory body is the practice of the daytime. Blending dream and luminous clarity is the practice of the night. Blending the intermediate state of Bardo with the transference of consciousness is the practice at the time of death.'

Numinous passion

The alchemy of desire

If thoughts of desire arise, conduct yourself like a joyful elephant!

Mahāsiddha Maitrīpa, 'Vajra Song of Twelve Instructions', 11th century

Dialectics of desire

The Buddha's early life as a privileged prince was devoted to the pursuit of pleasure, but he found it wanting as a source of lasting fulfillment. The Buddha's later teachings were thus a critique of desire, which he came to view as the source of life's perennial dissatisfactions. According to Buddhist Sutrās composed centuries after his death, the Buddha advocated a life of abstinence from emotional, psychological and sensual entanglements. The Buddhist Tantras, however, which appeared from the 6th century with the 'Assembly of Secrets' (Guhyasamāja Tantra), reversed the logic of early Buddhist thought and promoted sexual union as a path leading to a state of numinous communion in which dualistic passions could resolve in an all-encompassing unity of bliss and emptiness, compassion and wisdom. Early commentaries on the Caṇḍamahāroṣaṇa Tantra went so far as to rewrite the Buddha's life story, presenting his encounter with Sujata, his first female disciple, as an erotic union, and his offering bowl flowing upstream afterwards, brimming with rice milk, as a coded metaphor for the ascent of *bodhicitta*, or reproductive essences, through his awakened anatomy. By altering established narratives of desire and consummation within a context of transgressive sexuality, the Buddhist Tantras offered skilful means for de-pathologizing desire as perennial distress and recasting it as a vehicle of enlightenment. As mahāsiddha Saraha sang: 'Can that be called perfect knowledge if one is not released while enjoying the pleasures of the senses? If it is already manifest, what is the use of meditation?' As Saraha further proclaimed, 'That which I have heard by the word of my master why should I speak of it secretly? That blissful delight that arises in the union of lotus and vajra [female and male sexual organs], who does not rejoice there? In this triple world, whose hopes does it fail to fulfil?'

Opposite **Indian princess Mandarava and Padmasambhava** generate the non-dual bliss that directly perceives the ultimate nature of mind and reality, as shown in this detail of a Tibetan scroll painting. As Yeshe Tsogyal declared in the 8th century: 'Let male aid female, female aid male; let each penetrate each other as in weaving … Merge emptiness with bliss … and allow the vital essences to pervade your being … Realize the fruit of passion, the Great Bliss (*mahāsukha*) … and let doubts and confusion disappear!' Orgyen Dorje Chang, 19th century, ground mineral pigment on cotton, Rubin Museum of Art, New York (Item No. 656).

Eros and emptiness

Passion within Tantric Buddhism was not without its perils, and a traditional sequence of four Tantric consecrations (*abhiṣeka*) sought to purify desire of any proprietary grasping. In the 8th century, the Hevajra Tantra famously proclaimed that its revisioning of human experience was not for everyone. But, according to the Tantras, what can lead to confusion and distress for the ill-prepared, brings liberation for the Tantric initiate. Yet in the absence of compassion and an all-encompassing view of Śūnyatā – the unbounded openness within which all experience occurs – Tantra can manifest as a maze of self-delusion. Tantric practice is thus on its innermost levels an elite endeavour, subject to rigorous guidance by qualified preceptors. For those who enter Tantric maṇḍalas with discernment and altruistic intent, the path of desire offers skilful means for resolving delusory oppositions of spiritual and worldly life. But as Chögyam Trungpa maintained, Tantra is a delicate matter, like 'licking honey from a razor blade.' The 15th-century Bengali poet Chandidas set the bar even higher and described perfected passion as the capacity to make a frog dance in the mouth of a snake or to bind an elephant with a spider's web.

Tantric deities in erotic embrace signify the union of wisdom and compassion, as exemplified in the scroll painting of Cakrasaṃvara and Vajravārāhī to the left and Yogambara and Jñāna Ḍākinī to the right, from the Chaturpita, or 'Four Thrones' Tantra. Whether actual or imagined, Tantric eroticism supports the transformation of desire into the ecstasy of enlightenment. It differs from ordinary sexuality in that its object is not the satisfaction of desire, but an omniscient and compassionate arousal that blurs distinctions between the human and the divine. Private collections.

The Buddhist Tantras repeatedly proclaim the inherent unity of the ego-bound state of Saṃsāra and the self-liberation of Nirvāṇa, maintaining that only deluded, dualistic attitudes divide them. Tantra was thus the loom on which the tapestry of non-duality was woven, expanding the range of the Buddhist Sutrās for those both inclined and ready. The non-duality of emptiness and material form intrinsic to the Tantric worldview resonates in the words of the British novelist E. M. Forster who wrote: 'Our life on earth is and ought to be, material and carnal. But we have not yet learned to manage our materialism and carnality properly; they are still entangled with the desire for ownership.' The Buddhist Tantras sought to resolve the human habit of appropriation through radical formulations of the Buddhist view of selflessness, to which desire, refined into offertory and unwanting joy, can paradoxically give access. As French author André Gide wrote, 'It is in pleasure that we become wholly conscious of ourselves … The secret workings of carnal desire drove me out of myself towards an enchanting confusion … When I stopped looking for myself it was in love that I found myself again … my desires alone were capable of instructing me: I yield to them.'

Tantric consorts, both male and female, are categorized in Tantric Buddhist texts. According to the Womb of Secrets Tantra, the optimal partner for a man is a jasmine and sandalwood-scented 'lotus woman', whose diverse endowments include seventy-two more energy channels than a male. The visionary female Tibetan treasure revealer Sera Khandro (1892–1940) furthered her own and her male consorts' spiritual evolution through the practice of sexual yoga. The illumination that arises through compassionate and equanimous arousal transcends ordinary conceptions of pleasure and can give rise to penetrating insight, as indicated by the three-eyed mask of a wisdom ḍākinī held by this contemporary female practitioner.

Rapturous means

Above left **The Tantric Deity Yogambara, united with Jñāna Ḍākinī, evokes the exalted, transpersonal nature of** Tantric eroticism. The accoutrements of vajra and bell, crossed at the heart, symbolize the mingling of the male and female attributes of compassionate means and innate wisdom. Theopathic consort practice is undertaken in Vajrayāna Buddhism in order to realize Mahāmudra, the 'total coalescence' in which all apparent, yet illusory, oppositions, including life and death, are resolutely transcended. 17th-century scroll painting, Rubin Museum of Art, New York, C2001.1.2 (HAR 65002).

The mahāsiddha Tilopā, who formulated the Six Yoga system that he transmitted to Nāropā, summarized the practice of *karmamudrā*, or consort practice, in the following words: 'Pure awareness of bliss and emptiness arises through ecstatic service to the consort. United as penetrating insight and skilful means, slowly let fall, retain, and draw back the inner essences and, conducting them to their source, suffuse them throughout the body. But only in the absence of infatuation and attachment will supreme awareness arise. Then, with vitality and eternal youthfulness, waxing like the moon, radiant and clear, with the strength of a lion, you will quickly realize worldly powers and ultimate enlightenment.' Marpa Chökyi Lodrö, who received the transmission of the Six Yogas from Nāropā, put them into practice and stated: 'By means of Inner Fire, I actualized the four joys; and by means of consort practice, I developed them to completion.' Although publicly hidden, the oral tradition of Tibetan Buddhism generally upholds the yoga of sexual union in the context of absolute and mutual compassion, to be the most expedient method for manifesting enlightenment in mind and body. Yet as Lama Thubten Yeshe cautioned, 'In Tantra it's not the man who enters the woman, but the woman who enters the man.'

Right **Tibet's renowned yogin Milarepa** is depicted in sexual communion with the mountain goddess Tseringma, in this detail from a Tibetan scroll painting. Although the 'yoga of union' (*jorlam*) in which dualistic passion transforms into ego-dissolving non-dual bliss is central to most Buddhist Tantras, the practice was interpreted metaphorically within monastic communities. A visualized 'wisdom consort, or Jñānamudrā, is thus substituted for an external 'action consort', or Karmamudrā, while the ultimate consort is upheld as Mahāmudrā, the experiential unity of empty knowing and imperishable joy. (See full image on page 282.)

Right **The mahāsiddha Dombi Heruka**, a master of the Hevajra Tantra, was originally Cakravarman, a Kashmiri king who renounced his throne in 936 AD to dwell in the forest with the daughter of a mendicant entertainer. The ecstatic couple is depicted here ornamented with human bones, riding a pregnant tigress, and holding skull cups overflowing with ambrosia. The venomous cobra that Dombi Heruka brandishes above his head signifies his mastery of his internal energy system. As the Saṃpuṭra Tantra states: 'At dawn, in the afternoon, and at sunset; at midday, and at midnight ... realize ultimate wisdom through union with the consort.' (See full image on page 287.)

Opposite right **A ḍākinī initiatress** into the Tantric mysteries wields a flaying knife that severs objectifying thoughts and a skull cup brimming with blood and ambrosia. Ḍākinīs are traditionally depicted in charnel grounds where, ornamented with human bones, they triumph over life and death. Ḍākinīs are characteristically shown in 'dancing pose' (*ardhaparyankāsana*), with one foot held up beneath the opposite thigh. (See full image on page 13.)

Refining the essence

In its earliest instance, Haṭha Yoga was a means for preserving reproductive essences within the physical body, with the goal of engendering both vitality and union with the divine. As promoted in the oral tradition of the Caṇḍamahāroṣaṇa Tantra, 'One can use one's vital essence to give birth to children outside one's body, or to gods inside one's body.' Although there were practical considerations for semen retention during Tantric rites – such as avoiding pregnancy – the principal purpose was sustaining arousal and thus transforming desire into undiminishing rapture and empathic bliss. The technique of *vajrolī mudrā* – preliminary exercises for which are illustrated on this

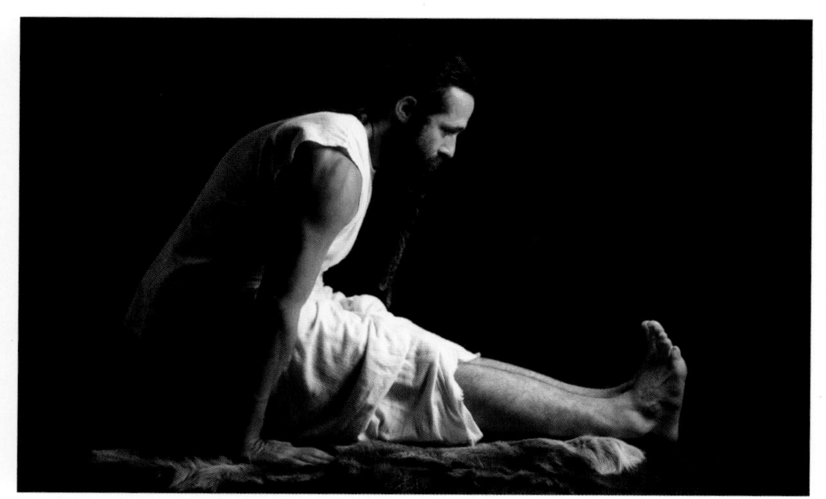

Above and right **Yogic movements connected with *vajrolī mudrā*** assist in reabsorbing reproductive essences to promote longevity and self-transcendent awareness, signified by the yogini's human bone ornaments. The related practice of *amarolī*, common to both Hindu and Buddhist Tantra, involves the absorption through the urethra of the combined 'solar' and 'lunar' fluids produced through ritual union. *Sahajolī* is performed when the male *bindu*, or procreative essence, has been aroused but not expended. The diverse techniques for circulating vital substances within the human body are described as the 'secret of all secrets', evoking the etymological root meaning of the word 'secret' as bodily secretion.

page – developed between the 9th and 14th centuries as a method for redirecting the flow of vital essences – one's own and one's consort's – through the body's central channel in connection with the awakening of *kuṇḍalinī* and the cultivation of expanded states of consciousness. While suspending emission – and thus dopamine suppressing surges of prolactin – can lead to vertiginous pleasure, Tantric Buddhist empowerment originally involved the ritual ingestion of conjoined male and female essences as a transformative, alchemical substance contributing to mutual consecration and divinization.

Below right **Tantric paramours depicted on a temple** exemplify the athletic self-transcendence, as opposed to sexual bypassing, that can arise through sexual yoga. According to the Buddhist Tantras, cultivating and reversing instinctual currents of mind and body engenders transpersonal dimensions of love and awareness. As Padmasambhava stated: 'Without a consort, a partner in skilful means, there is no way to experience the mysteries of Tantra … without wood a fire cannot burn.'

Below **A *mudrā*, or ritual hand gesture**, signifying the creative potentiality of a woman's womb. As anatomical analogues of primordial emptiness, female genitalia are referred to in the Buddhist Tantras as 'palaces of wisdom'. Although women are naturally endowed, male practitioners must engender the fecundity of space that wombs represent through yogic practices connected with *cakras* and internal energy channels.

Synergetic pleasure

Sigmund Freud defined the pleasure principle as the instinctual avoidance of pain or production of pleasure in order to resolve tensions and satisfy biological and psychological needs. In the context of Tantric Buddhism, the yoga of sexual union fulfils an entirely different function in subverting autonomic biological instincts and engendering a continuum of ecstatic arousal. As mahāsiddha Āryadeva stated in the 7th century, 'Erotic love, enjoyed by the ignorant, becomes bondage. That very same love, tasted with understanding, brings liberation.' But achieving personal pleasure and avoiding pain was never the crucial point. The Kālacakra Tantra clarifies that the purpose of cultivating heightened states of bliss through consort practice is to bring transpersonal love and wisdom into all human activities. As the Kālacakra claims: 'There does not exist a greater transgression than lack of passion, and there does not exist a greater merit than bliss. Therefore, O King, apply your mind continuously to immutable bliss.' Central to the agenda of emancipating rapture is overcoming what the Kālacakra Tantra refers to as the 'passion for emission': 'From emission is born dispassion, and from dispassion comes suffering … dissipation and death.' In the 1730s, the visionary Tibetan Lama Lelung Shepai Dorje challenged monastic attitudes by teaching 'magical techniques of sexual yoga' to celibate monks, proclaiming it as a skillful means for merging one's being with the unchanging bliss of ultimate reality. His controversial transmission included recipes for medicinal ointments designed to stimulate and fortify the erogenous zones of one's chosen consort. As he memorably stated: 'May those who desire to practise this rite of sexual union look upon it with … a desire to achieve enlightenment for the sake of all sentient beings … and may they be spontaneously liberated into the body of light.'

Below **The primordial Buddha Samantabhadra**, 'Immutable Goodness', represents the innermost, pristine nature of human consciousness, as presented in Dzogchen, the resultant Great Perfection stage of Tantric Buddhism. The entwined figures also address the earliest reference to Dzogchen in the Guhyagarbha Tantra, chapter thirteen of which associates 'great perfection' with the state beyond thought in the climactic moment of sexual yoga. In an invocation of non-dual joy, the French intellectual Georges Bataille characterized sacred eroticism as two lovers contemplating in speechless wonder the continuity that unites them'.

Right **The meditational deity Kurukullā**, also known as 'Lotus Dākinī', embodies the magnetizing power of transmuted desire. Two of her four arms hold a bow and arrow entwined with flowers, while her other two hold a hook and noose. As a beguiling emanation of the Tantric deity Hevajra, Kurukullā is is garlanded with skulls and freshly severed heads. She dances on the body of Kamadev, the Hindu god of love, signifying her transubstantiation of compulsive, ephemeral passion into altruistic, non-dual rapture and transpersonal bliss. Potala Palace, Lhasa.

Opposite right **Vajrayoginī ornamented with severed human skulls** and holding a skull cup of ambrosia above her upraised leg exemplifies the intertwining of desire and death central to Tantric Buddhist iconography. Tantra's explicit eroticism evokes both Eros and Thanatos, the dual drives of creation and dissolution that are equally fundamental to modern psychoanalytic theory. Georges Bataille observed that, 'There are staggering similarities and even corresponding and interchangeable characteristics in the two spheres, erotic and mystical … to live to the limits of the possible and impossible, with ever increasing intensity.' Private collection.

'This is myself and this is another'. Be free from this binding thought, and your true nature is thereby released. Do not err in the matter of self and other. Everything is Buddha without exception … Immaculate perfection in which mental forms are pure in their very essence.

Mahāsiddha Saraha, 'Treasury of Songs', 8th century

Numinous communion

Tantra is often viewed one-dimensionally in the Western world as a sacral form of sexuality. But in the Guhyasamāja Tantra, Tantra is explicitly defined as the continuum of compassionate awareness within all spheres of human experience. Nonetheless, eroticism has been central to Tantric Buddhist iconography and practice from its earliest inception. Saraha, the most celebrated of the mahāsiddhas, proclaimed that true spirituality lies in attuning to 'that by which one is born, lives, and dies', an orientation that came to be known as Sahajayāna, the 'way of effortless perfection', in recognition that the ritual procedures of Vajrayāna's creation and completion stages are spontaneously realized in embodied erotic experience. As Saraha proclaimed, 'In this state of highest bliss, there is neither self nor other.' Self-transcendent rapture through sexual yoga was identified within Sahajayāna as actualization of the practitioner's Buddha Nature. The tradition controversially upheld that without *karmamudrā* – or sexual union with a consort – there is no Mahāmudra, or ultimate spiritual attainment. The 8th-century mahāsiddha Śabara, reputedly phrased it more anatomically: 'Without genitals there is no Mahāmudra.' A chapter in the Hevajra Tantra entitled 'The Means to Attain the Innate' states the matter directly: 'Making the consort for Mahāmudra naked, the wise yogi always serves her. The adamantine yogi makes love repeatedly, thus attaining numerous powers and becoming equal to all the Buddhas.'

The mutual merging of energy and awareness in Tantric consort practice transcends ordinary pleasure and desire and reveals the innate bliss of one's innermost being as a numinous communion with all existence. It thus exemplifies Vajrayāna Buddhism's transcendence of inhibiting doctrines and its essential message of bringing wisdom, joy and compassion into all human activities. Saint Augustine of Hippo wrote of the 'peculiar intensity of arousal, compulsive urgency, pleasure and pain that characterizes the human fulfilment of desire.' The practice of *karmamudrā*, or sexual union with a consort, transcends such dichotomies and seeks fulfilment in all-encompassing loving awareness. As pervasively represented in Tantric Buddhist art, ecstatic rapture can intensify into expansive states of being that transcend the confines of conventional desire. As Lama Thubten Yeshe stated, 'This is the central point of the tantric approach. The same desirous energy that ordinarily propels us from one unsatisfactory situation to another is transmuted, through the alchemy of tantra, into a transcendental experience of bliss and wisdom.'

Below **Padmasambhava and Yeshe Tsogyal in synergetic union** exemplify the integral role of sexuality in Tantric Buddhist practice. Although Buddhist monastics such as Candrakīrti likened desire to a 'mirage' that 'makes the flames flare up', Tantras such as the Buddhakapāla present passion as a skilful means for transcending subject-object duality: 'Compassion is ignited with a mutual glance, benevolence with an embrace, joy through contact, and immutable bliss by equanimous merging. How can anyone exalted through such yogic practice be said to be bound by attachment?'

Opposite below left **Dancing male and female mahāsiddhas** on the walls of Pelkhor Chöde Monastery in Gyantse, Tibet, express the joyous intent of Tantric eroticism. As Marcel Proust wrote, 'The limits we set to love are too restrictive and derive solely from our great ignorance of life.'

Right **The Tantric deities Hayangriva and Vajravārāhī,** encircled by flames and trampling on outmoded thoughts and conceptions, transform passion into exalted compassion. Participating in such ecstatic iconography assists *karmamudrā* practitioners to transcend conventional notions of selfhood and to realize numinous, non-dual awareness. By enhancing the dissolution of the body's subtle constituent elements (*bindu*) into the central channel, consort practice intensifies the inner fire of Tummo and parallels the natural process of dissolution that occurs in the post-mortem dimension of the Bardo. In each existential circumstance the practitioner seeks the exalted illumination of Nirvāṇa.

Below right **Tantric deities on the walls of a temple** in western Tibet signify blissful realization of the creative entanglement of emptiness and form. The Tantric Buddhist master Drukpa Kunley (1455–1529) put conventional sensuality into perspective in his song of the 'Three Pleasures': 'A virgin finds pleasure in her rising desire; a youthful tiger finds pleasure in consummation; an old man finds pleasure in his fertile memory.'

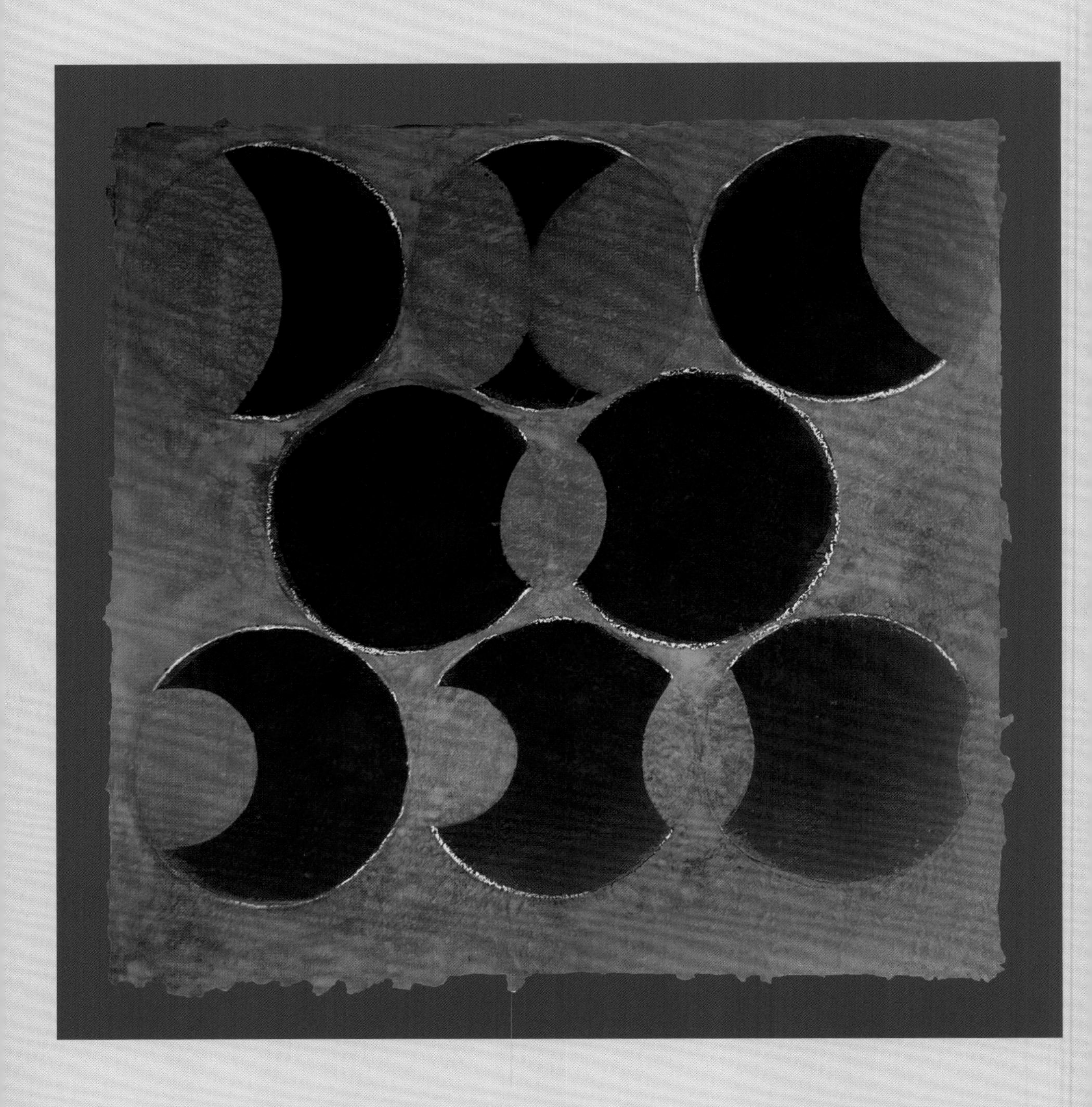

Noetic light

The infinite brightness of being

This self-originated Clear Light … Although it exists in everyone everywhere, it has gone unrecognized – how amazing!

Padmasambhava, 'Self-Liberation through Seeing with Naked Awareness', 8th century

Yogas of fire and light

Opposite **A contemporary painting** by Rolf Kluenter evokes the meditative arising of the subtle mind of Clear Light. The intersecting spheres illustrate the merging of solar and lunar energies in the central channel of the yogic body and the corollary 'eclipse' of dualistic consciousness. In the Buddhist Tantras, Clear Light represents the mind's innermost nature of radiant luminescent knowing, as experienced in meditative states of waking, sleeping and dying.

The 'blazing and melting' of the Yoga of Inner Fire directly reveals the bliss, clarity and non-conceptual awareness that is the basis for the Yoga of Clear Light (*ösel naljor*) or, as known in Sanskrit, *prabhāsvara*. The Yoga of Clear Light encompasses practices during the waking state as well as during deep, dreamless sleep. The waking state practice of Clear Light is undertaken in conjunction with the self-transcendent rapture that arises through the Yoga of Inner Fire and Karmamudrā. As mahāsiddha Tilopā taught, 'After meditation with a consort and the spontaneous arising of blissful wisdom, the yogin meditates on the Illusory Body and the Yoga of Clear Light.'

The Yoga of Clear Light describes the recognition of the mind's innermost photonic nature in similes progressing from ephemeral mirages, to flickering fireflies, to all-pervading luminosity 'like a moonlit sky in autumn'. The 13th-century Tibetan adept and physician Chen Ngawa described the innate mind of clear light as 'totally pure, self-perfected, imperturbable luminescence … the all-pervasive, uncreated essence of consciousness'. The mind's innate luminosity is said to appear spontaneously at the time of death as well as during deep, dreamless sleep. The Yoga of Clear Light brings this self-transcendent luminescence into ever-greater awareness through the blissful heat aroused by Inner Fire as well as by illuminating the subconscious during meditative sleep. The boundless luminosity revealed through the Yoga of Clear Light thus comprises the base, path and fruition of the Six Yogas during recurrent cycles of intensified awareness, wakeful sexuality, conscious dreaming and death. At the most advanced stages of Dzogchen, the body itself is said to dissolve into a noetic luminescence that is referred to as a 'rainbow body' (*jalu*).

All-pervading brightness

In his oral instructions to Nāropā, mahāsiddha Tilopā stated that the Yoga of Clear Light is the 'most wondrous of yogic paths'. He described how, at the moment of sleep and in deep meditation, consciousness enters the central channel at the heart *cakra*, giving rise to various visions such as 'lights, light-rays, rainbows … apparitions of deities and divine forms'. Even for the untrained, the transitional period between wakefulness and sleep encompasses dream-like visions in which artists such as Salvador Dalí discovered creative inspiration and which neuropsychologists identify as hypnogogia, a hyperassociative state in which vivid, fragmentary imagery offers potential insight into subconscious mental processes. But the Yoga of Clear Light lies beyond the hypnogogic mental state that Dalí referred to as 'sleeping without sleeping', and it is also distinct from the trainable capacity for lucid dreaming during rapid eye movement phases of wakeful slumber. Rather than attending to an unconstrained continuum of inner imagery and associations, the Yoga of Clear Light involves concentrating vital energies at the heart *cakra* while maintaining a lucid state of awareness that ultimately transcends waking, dreaming, sleep and death. This continuum of illuminated awareness, or clear light consciousness, derives from the Sanskrit word *prabhāsvara,* 'brilliantly shining.' In the context of Tantric Buddhism, the word relates to Buddha Sakyamuni's spontaneous visionary experience of enlightenment, the 'clear seeing' of reality beyond conventional constraints of time, space, knowledge and matter, which all subsequent forms of Buddhist yoga seek to reproduce. Practices based on radiant luminescent knowing, although inherent to Buddhism's earliest doctrines, developed further as Buddhism co-evolved with light oriented mysticism, including Zoroastrianism, Neoplatonism and Syriac Christianity, in the Indo-Iranian frontiers of Bactria, Gandhara and Uḍḍīyana.

The clear light of consciousness arises at the heart *cakra* after the body's internal energies have entered into the central channel at a point, the width of four fingers below the navel, as illustrated in this 18th-century manuscript. Although the subtlest manifestations of human consciousness can arise during deep states of meditation, the Clear Light appears spontaneously in the hypnagogic state between waking and sleeping as well in the dying process, although these recurring opportunities tend not to be recognized. Beijing Palace Museum.

Right **A yogini in meditative retreat** in a cave near the north face of Mount Everest in Tibet abides in natural luminescence. *The Turquoise Heart Essence* describes Clear Light as 'the mind shining forth without bias or limit … the vast expanse of primordial awareness free from either meditation or meditator'.

Above **The mind's ultimate nature** is likened to a crystal that, though empty and transparent, spontaneously produces visionary forms reflective of the innate creativity of human consciousness. Crystals, such as this one with a gilded lotus base, are used in Dzogchen to point out the mind's empty yet radiant luminescence.

Right **A mural detail** from the Lukhang temple in Tibet depicts the refractive qualities of light as it passes through a crystal to illustrate the illusory nature of sensory appearances. Dzogchen draws from diverse sources to point out the ultimate co-substantiality of matter, light and consciousness. As Shabkar Tsokdruk Rangdrol stated, 'The nature of the mind is as vivid as a flawless piece of crystal; intrinsically empty, naturally radiant and ceaselessly responsive.'

Timeless presence

While the subtlest levels of human consciousness remain unsusceptible to physical measurement, neuroscientists have associated hypnogogia, the transitional state into deep sleep, with the otherwise rare convergence of alpha brain waves – the dominant wave pattern associated with relaxed wakefulness – and theta brain waves, which arise when dreaming. The hypnogogic state also reveals reduced activity in the prefrontal cortex, an area of the brain involved in decision-making and evaluative thought. Attuning to the non-conceptual luminosity of the heart centre during the transition into deep sleep thus opens perceptual channels between the conscious and subconscious mind, and intimates the ultimate clear light awareness that the Tibetan yogi and poet Shabkar Tsokdruk Rangdrol (1781–1851) characterized as an intangible and ineffable emptiness. If you chase after the mind, Shabkar argued, 'it vanishes and dissolves … yet it experiences untold suffering and joy'. The ultimate mind nature, however, lies beyond all such fluctuations. Accessing and abiding at that subtlest level of consciousness is the principal objective of the Yoga of Clear Light. As the 15th-century Bhutanese treasure-revealer Tertön Pema Lingpa instructed, 'Meditate on clarity and emptiness free of grasping so that sleep naturally arises as unimpeded Clear Light. Meditate in this way repeatedly and the movements of outer and inner thoughts will dissolve into all-pervasive luminosity.'

Tantric Buddhism describes four fundamental conditions of consciousness: reflecting on the past, speculating about the future, preoccupation with

Inverted images of sky and mountains reflected in Gokyo Lake in Nepal illustrate the illusory nature of perceived reality. The Buddhist Tantras refer to appearances as habits of perception that bear only a tangential relationship with reality itself. The Yoga of Clear Light cultivates experiential awareness of the subtlest levels of consciousness and is often described as 'taking appearances as the path'.

Chatral Sangye Dorje Rinpoche, the 'Adamantine Buddha', was considered one of the greatest 20th-century exemplars of Dzogchen, or natural Great Perfection. In regard to temporal mental states that obscure pristine, heart-centred awareness, he advocated practising according to one's individual capacity, 'whether by avoiding [afflictive states], transforming them, taking them as the path, or seeing into their very essence.' His core teachings centred on the luminous continuum of compassion and pristine awareness within all experience.

the present, and a transcendent 'fourth state' of consciousness characterized as luminescent awareness, beyond conventional limits of time and space. Although the potentiality of clear light consciousness is most fully developed in the Great Perfection teachings of Dzogchen, early Buddhist luminaries such as the Indian scholar Candrakīrti (570–650) wrote in his commentary to the Guhyasamāja Tantra that, 'Luminosity is ultimate truth' and the essence of spiritual practice. As the immanent, all-pervasive brightness of pure consciousness is 'beyond the three times' of past, present and future, it is further characterized as selfless, timeless, effortless and radiant. As Candrakīrti wrote of this imperishable brightness, 'There is no view and nothing to meditate on. There is no specified conduct and no result. The mind is the meditation; free of concepts and naturally at ease. There is nothing that recognizes [this innate clear light consciousness] and nothing that does not.' Several centuries later, mahāsiddha Tilopā, who systematized the Six Yogas as essential extracts of the Buddhist Tantras, further distilled them into 'six words of advice' for abiding in the non-dual continuum of Clear Light. As he instructed Nāropā: 'Let go of what has passed; Let go of what may come; Let go of what is happening now; Do not try to figure anything out; Do not try to control anything; Relax, right now, and rest', in the radiant, luminescent coalescence of emptiness and appearance.

Above **An Indian master**, identified by the inscription as Vajrahāsya, ‘Smiling Vajra’, sits on a lotus and moon disc on a wall mural in the Piyang caves in western Tibet. A contemporary of Padmasambhava, Vajrahāsya composed a commentary to the Guhyasamāja Tantra, the ‘Assembly of Secrets’, which invokes the transformative power of laughter in realizing the luminous mind of Clear Light.

Opposite **Buddha Nature,** the innate perfection of human consciousness, is illustrated in this detail of a late 17th-century mural in the private meditation chamber of Tibet’s Sixth Dalai Lama. A stream of five-coloured rainbow light links the central figure with a radiant Buddha, signifying the process of self-illumination central to Ati Yoga, the resultant Great Perfection stage of Tantric Buddhism. As stated in the ‘Perfection of Wisdom Sutrā’, ‘The nature of mind is luminous clear light, yet it is habitually obscured by adventitious defilements.’

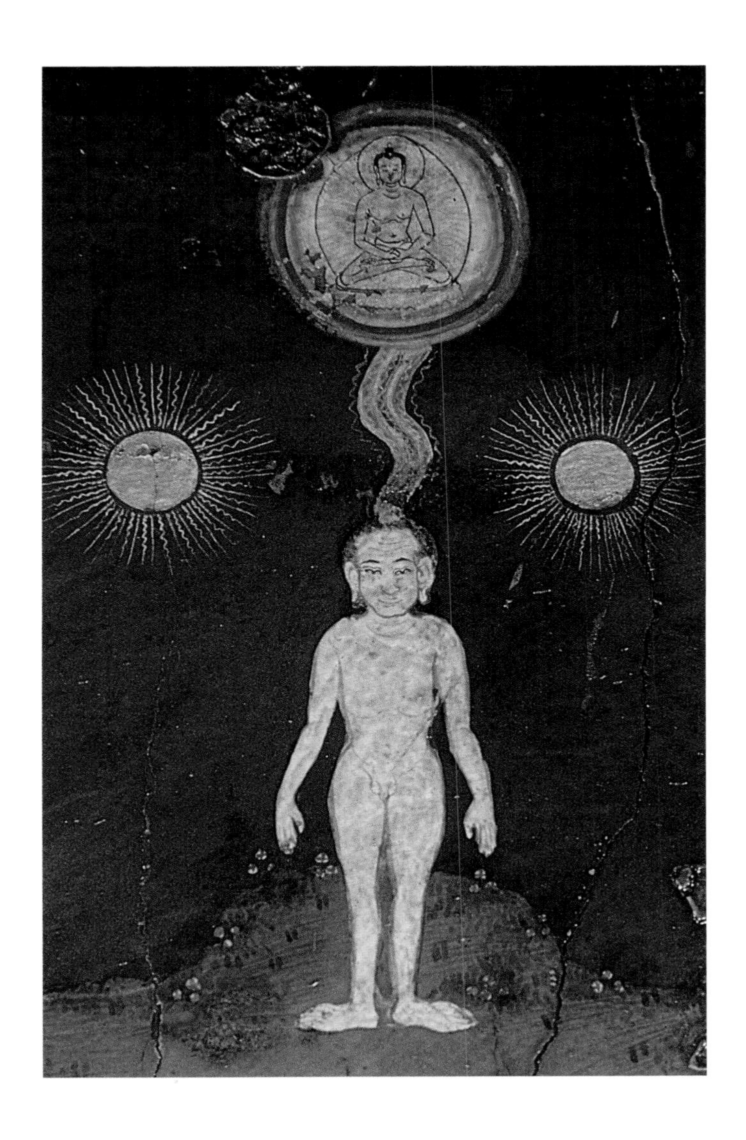

Having established that all perceived phenomena arise within consciousness, recognize that emptiness itself appears as radiant displays of light ... Beyond all thought and expression, inconceivable and ineffable, naked primordial awareness is clear and bright ... uncontrived, spontaneously manifesting and radiant.

Turquoise Heart Essence (Yuthok Nyingthik), 12th century

A Tantric master presses on a disciple's carotid arteries to induce an illuminated state of awareness identified as the 'clear light' of emptiness and bliss. The image appears on a mural in the private meditation chamber of Tibet's Sixth Dalai Lama and illustrates a 15th-century text by Tertön Pema Lingpa entitled 'Pearl Garland of Introductions [to the Nature of Mind]'. As stated in the accompanying inscription: 'In a dark room, the master should suddenly press the pulsating channels in the disciple's neck, inducing visions … When consciousness is restored, the nature of the visions is clarified.'

The wave of light

Although the intrinsic clear light of consciousness manifests spontaneously under specific conditions, Tantric Buddhism also includes techniques for forcibly inducing it. One of the most expedient means is referred to in Tibetan as the 'vajra wave' (*dorje balap*), in which pressure is exerted on the carotid arteries at the neck to arouse a direct experience of Clear Light. The method is presented in Tibet's Kagyu lineage as a substitute for dark retreats to enhance recognition of the mind's innate luminosity. To stimulate such awareness, the preceptor presses precise points on the sides of the student's neck and recites the words that Tilopā reputedly said when he slapped Nāropā on his head with his sandal to arouse non-conceptual awareness: 'This is self-arising primordial wisdom, beyond words and imagination. I have nothing more to show you. Now you should know yourself from this direct introduction to the Clear Light of Awareness.' By lucidly expanding beyond the reactive patterning of the fight or flight response produced in the brainstem through the redirection of blood to the basilar artery, the yogin's bodymind flows with non-conceptual wakefulness. An analogous technique of noetic near-asphyxiation is practised

A Tibetan yogini, supported by a meditation belt (*gomtrag*), demonstrates the practice of the 'vajra wave'. According to the oral teachings of the 12th-century *Turquoise Heart Essence*, the technique can be used to clarify the non-conceptual nature of primordial awareness through direct introduction to the Clear Light which also arises spontaneously in the process of dying. By remaining lucidly present within the acute stress response brought about by reducing oxygen flow to the brain, awareness intensifies of the mind's innermost nature of self-transcendent luminescence.

within non-dual Kashmiri Śaivism in conjunction with a 'floating vase breath' (*plavini kumbhaka*), during which the teacher or an assistant presses on the sides of the disciple's neck to 'surprise' or 'astonish' the mind. The wave-like pulsations that spread throughout the body are identified as manifestations of *spanda*, the primal vibration through which consciousness recognizes its divine nature as effulgent light.

An 18th-century Tibetan manuscript illustrates a self-administered form of the 'vajra wave' in which a yogin seated on a tiger skin crosses his arms in front of his chest to press subtle energy channels at the sides of his neck. The technique is shown here as the sixth in a series of thirty-two 'magical movements' (Trulkhor) devised by Phagmo Drupa (1110–70) to arouse the mind of the Tantric deity 'Joyous Vajra' (Hevajra). The points at the neck also intersect with the vagus nerve, thus stimulating the parasympathetic nervous system. Beijing Palace Museum.

The illuminated heart

In Dzogchen, the Great Perfection, the ontology of light refers to the postulated photonic substratum from which all appearances arise, characterized as an inseparable unity of primordial purity (*kadak*) and natural perfectedness (*lhun-drup*), the Dzogchen iterations of emptiness and luminescence. The Dzogchen Tantra entitled 'Necklace of Pearls' describes this source of being as 'beyond any locality, directionality, and partiality. It is neither being nor nothingness, and … is beyond all words and measurement.' This manifestation of reality as 'ground luminosity' is the basis of the Dzogchen practice of Lhündrup Tögal, 'leaping over the skull into natural perfection', in which multi-coloured displays of light signify stages of the path leading to the body's ultimate dissolution into light at the time of death, leaving behind only nails and hair. The photonic phenomena that arise in the practice of Dzogchen recall the *nimitta*, or visual signs of meditative progress described in the 5th century by the Theravada Buddhist monk Buddhaghosa in the *Visuddhimagga*, or 'Path of Purification', which include stars, clusters of gems, chariot wheels and moon disks. Similar 'empty forms' appearing in darkness as well as in the sky are described in the 10th-century 'Treatise on Stainless Light', a commentary on the Kālacakra Tantra, the 'Wheel of Time', which may also have influenced the later development of Dzogchen in Tibet.

The culminating manifestation of clear light awareness is likened in the Buddhist Tantras to the full moon illuminating a cloudless sky. As stated in the 'Tantra of Unimpeded Sound', visionary experiences arising out of the ground luminosity of consciousness continue to expand and develop 'like the moon in autumn', as seen in this moonrise over the Annapurna range in Nepal.

Common to these diverse traditions are the spontaneous manifestations of Clear Light that reveal every moment of perception as a creative act, and that all is altered when seen from the heart – just as photons, the energy units of light, are simultaneously waves and particles or, in Buddhist terms, emptiness and form, changing in response to how they are viewed. Although light is the fundamental nature of all reality, its subtle dimensions can be experienced most vividly during states of lucid, dreamless sleep. Various methods are used for awakening to the clear light of sleep, but all focus on the heart-centre as the locus of awareness. The Tibetan adept and physician Gyalwa Yangönpa (1213–87) identified the heart as the 'essential birthplace of realization' and described the Yoga of Clear Light as drawing the winds of consciousness into the lotus of the heart and visualizing the seed-syllables *āḥ*, *nu*, *ta*, *ra* on each of its four petals, with either *oṃ* or *hūṃ* at the centre, so as to light up the interior of the body and 'capture the Clear Light during deepest sleep'. Tibet's Fourth Panchen Lama Lobsang Chökyi Gyaltsen (1570–1662) described the process evocatively in 'The Golden Key: A Profound Guide to the Six Yogas of Nāropā', which invokes the following instructions by mahāsiddha Nāropā to the Tibetan translator (*lotsawa*) Marpa Chökyi Lodrö: 'In the space between sleep and dreams lies the essence of reality, a vast unknowing. Draw this into your experience as unimaginable and inexpressible emptiness. Whatever arises thereafter is bliss. This is the uncontrived primordial nature of being; the essential instruction regarding Clear Light. Have you fathomed this unborn mind, O Lotsawa?'

Ani Rigsang, a highly accomplished Tibetan yogini, meditates beneath prayer flags at the edge of Draksum Lhatso lake in Tibet's Kongpo region. Mindfulness in Dzogchen is often characterized as emptiness experiencing bliss.

By perceiving reality just as it is, the conceptual mind naturally comes to rest ... Free of conflicting perspectives, everything arises in its intrinsic luminescence ... Conditioned aggregates dissolve, and the body itself naturally manifests enlightenment.

Tertön Pema Lingpa, *Dzogchen Kunsang Gongdu*, 15th century

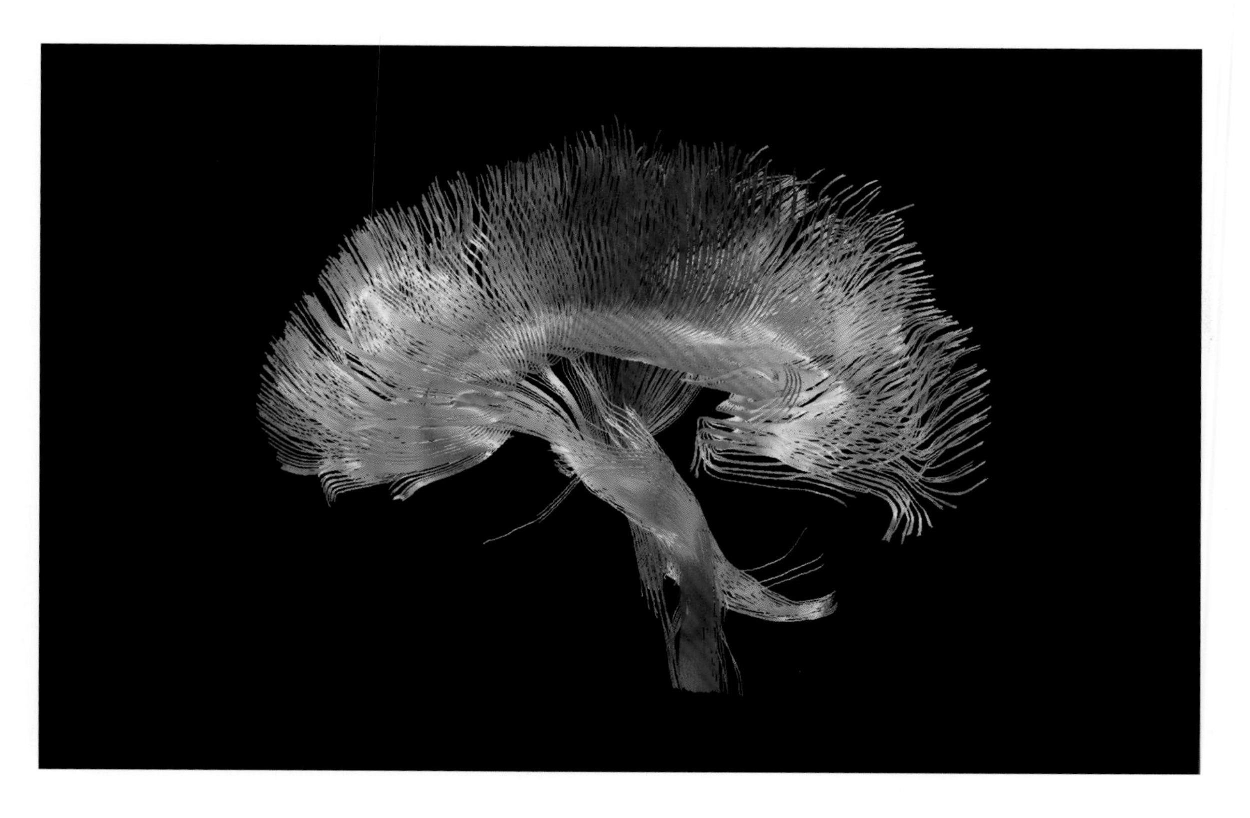

Luminous rapture

One of the earliest scriptures of Mahāyāna Buddhism, the 'The Perfection of Wisdom in Eight Thousand Lines' (*Aṣṭasāhasrikā Prajñāpāramitā Sūtra*), provisionally dated to the 1st century BC, provocatively states that, 'Mind is not mind. The nature of mind is clear light.' Although the statement supports later Tibetan accounts of a luminous substratum underlying consciousness, it refers more precisely to the 'clear light awareness' held to be the subtlest level of the mind that, free of conceptual cognition, continues even beyond death as the basis for enlightenment. The Dzogchen adept Patrul Rinpoche (1808–87) described this subtle ground of being as 'the nature of the mind of all beings, pure from the beginning and innately luminous', although 'ordinary beings perceive it only as a flash when dying.' Patrul Rinpoche further clarified this natural luminosity as the ever-present 'potentiality of Buddhahood' that can be realized through the profound meditative practices of the Great Perfection.

Opposite above **A Dzogchen manuscript** illustrates methods for illuminating consciousness by inducing experiences of luminosity and non-dual presence. The figure to the left cultivates clear light awareness by gazing at rays of the sun. Other figures on the folio brighten the mind by alternately interiorizing and expanding sensorial awareness. Royal Danish Library, Copenhagen.

Opposite below **Neural pathways in the brain** can be mapped by magnetic resonance imaging (MRI), as seen in this image revealing microscopic myelin-coated nerve fibres carrying information between nerve cells in the cerebellum and the brain stem. Neurobiological changes in the brain associated with meditation manifest in brain scans as increased functional connectivity and correlate with enhanced cognition, emotional wellbeing and subjective experiences of internal brightness. Science Photo Library, London.

Right **The Bhutanese adept Amchi Sherab Tenzin** meditates by the Yangsang River in Tibet's hiddenland of Pemakö. Supported by a meditation belt, he opens subtle energy channels in the neck that interface with the eyes and heart and enhance experience of radiant luminescence.

Dreamtime

The yoga of lucid sleep

Like a drop of dew, a bubble in a stream,
a flash of lightning in a summer cloud,
a flickering lamp, an illusion, a phantom, or a dream.
So is all conditioned existence to be seen.

The Buddha, Vajracchedikā Prajñāpāramitā Sūtra, 2nd century

Visionary sleep

Opposite **Tibetan Dream Yoga,** as expressed in this contemporary painting by Rolf Kluenter, is often initiated by visualizing a stream of vibrating seed-syllables *āḥ* – symbolizing the awakened state of consciousness – transiting through the body's central channel between the heart and the glabella region between the eyebrows while in a hypnogogic state between waking and sleep.

Right **The recommended body posture** for Tibetan yogas of sleep and dream is illustrated in a detail from a Bhutanese meditation treatise. Lying on his right side, the practitioner visualizes a glowing moon disc at the heart where, as stated in the accompanying Tibetan inscription, he merges his consciousness with the mind of his spiritual teacher (lama).

Waking experience often has a dreamlike quality because of the disparity between the way things appear and their actual reality. Tibetan Dream Yoga (*milam naljor*) capitalizes on this discrepancy and cultivates an illuminated state of consciousness both during rapid eye movement (REM) sleep and waking experience. Dream sleep follows successive nightly phases of slow-wave delta sleep when the brain is less active and normally unaware. While deep, dreamless sleep is physically and mentally restorative, REM sleep, when the mind is dreaming, plays a vital role in learning and memory consolidation. Dream Yoga advances these effects by consciously altering one's dreams, as well as one's mental projections during the waking state, by aligning oneself with the all-pervasive 'ground luminosity' within which all experience occurs. The 16th-century Spanish mystic and Carmelite nun Saint Teresa of Ávila described this state of consciousness as 'infused brightness … a light which knows no night.' In the Tibetan Buddhist tradition, this clear light of consciousness is the basis for gaining mastery of the apparitional nature of mind both while dreaming and while awake. To instill detachment, Tibetan Buddhism often likens apparent phenomena to dreams. As Chöying Thobden Dorjé, a 19th-century Buddhist master, wrote: 'Like appearances in a dream, all phenomena of Saṃsāra and Nirvāṇa have never come into being … What the senses experience externally as mountains, valleys, towns, and sentient beings and, internally, as one's physiology, sensory awareness, and thought process, are all appearances in a dream … at no point do they objectively exist … Meditate on this until even while you are dreaming all phenomena arise as dreams.'

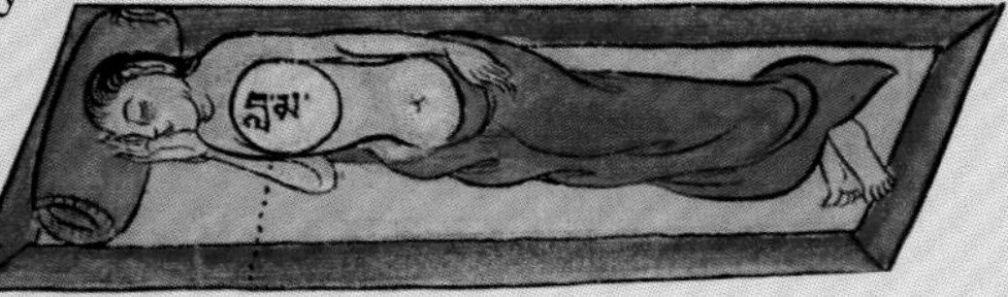

Transforming experience

Awakening during the dream state to the fact that one is dreaming is the entry point for both lucid dreaming and Tibetan Dream Yoga. Lucid dreaming implies becoming fully conscious during rapid eye movement (REM) sleep in order to restructure subconscious scripts of the sleeping mind, whether for problem solving or sheer entertainment. Dream Yoga focuses on recognizing that what arises in dreams is illusory and therefore alterable. Illusion does not mean that what is experienced is unreal, but only that it is not what it appears to be. In Dream Yoga, the luminous ground from which dreams appear is the clear light consciousness that recognizes dreams as ephemeral displays without intrinsic reality. As with lucid dreaming, Dream Yoga begins by waking up within the dream state by attending to specific signs that distinguish dreams from ordinary reality, such as the presence of a deceased relative or phenomena that defy the laws of physics, such as flying or walking through walls. When the dream state is recognized for what it is, it becomes a negotiable if paradoxically insubstantial reality. If anxiety or panic emerges in a lucid nightmare, it offers a powerful opportunity to confront the seeming source of fear and alter the dream's outcome, while simultaneously realizing that fear often arises in falsely assuming illusory events and unconscious projections to be real. By bringing an inquiring and meditative mind into the dream state, Dream Yoga offers the opportunity to cut through subconscious mental patterning and to discover at the heart of experience an unexpected dimension of openness and possibility that is often obscured in everyday waking life.

In Dzogchen, the culmination of the completion phase practices of Tantric Buddhism, the phenomenal world is perceived as inseparable from primordial

Dream Narratives, as shown in this detail from a Tibetan painting, often involve unfortunate, yet never fatal events, such as being swallowed by a giant fish or drowning in a swamp. In Dream Yoga, a practitioner lies on their right side so that the heart remains unrestricted and, and as a locus of consciousness, luminously aware even during dreamless sleep, and thus able to alter the outcome of both dreams and reality.

A monk flying through banks of clouds, as illustrated in this detail from a Tibetan wall painting, evokes the most advanced stage of Dream Yoga in which a practitioner may attain an 'illusory dream body' which, unrestricted by the laws of physics, allows them to undertake compassionate activities during sleep, including remote viewing, divination and healing.

Below **Walking through walls** can be a profitable undertaking during lucid dreams. As shown in this detail of a Tibetan mural, dreaming allows for actions that are normally impossible while awake, thus cultivating increased mental flexibility.

consciousness, the nature of which is described as radiant, all-pervasive luminosity. As stated in the Guhyagarbha Tantra, the 'Womb of Secrets': 'When all actions are realized to be like dreams without substantial existence, one's perception becomes divine and faultless', beyond conceptual attachment to an externally existent reality. Just as photons of light can be perceived as either ephemeral elementary particles or wave signatures in space, 'reality' can be alternately viewed as either truth or illusion, or their intrinsic inseparability. The advanced practitioner of Dream Yoga actualizes this perspective during nocturnal dreams so as to manifest enlightened non-dual vision in daytime waking reality. The Buddha is held to have stated in the Sūtra on Perfection of Wisdom (*Prajñāpāramitā*) that, 'All phenomena are like dreams and magical illusions. Nirvāṇa is also like a dream or magical illusion. If anything exists beyond Nirvāṇa, it too is like a dream or a magical illusion.' From the perspective of liberation as transcendence of illusion, Dream Yoga offers a direct path to enlightened vision and the re-engineering of experience both while dreaming and in the waking state. Traditional Dream Yoga meditations for transmuting fear include invoking a dream tiger that one can either ride or befriend, leaping off cliffs with impunity, or entering harmlessly into raging fires. Such illusory acts performed in the dreamtime can carry over into creative and courageous action when confronting threatening circumstances and unconscious projections in the waking state.

Mastering darkness

Opposite **A Dream Yoga visualization technique**, depicted in a painting by Rolf Kluenter, illustrates a flow of vibrating blue and white seed-syllables rising from the heart to the forehead through the body's central channel during subtle inhalations and descending back into the heart during exhalations. The luminous circles at the lower left signify the associated transformation of the five elemental qualities of the bodymind.

Below **A lion-headed dākinī**, depicted on a mural in Gangteng Monastery in Bhutan, signifies the unsettling imagery that can arise both in dreams and in deep meditation.

Below right **A ravenous dream tiger** consumes a grinning corpse. Charnel ground imagery is ubiquitous in Tantric Buddhism and habituates the mind to the non-duality of life and death as well as waking states and dreams. Gangteng Monastery, Bhutan.

Clear Light Yoga is the direct experience of the dissolution of mental concepts during meditation or slow-wave delta sleep and the concurrent arising of luminescent awareness. Dream Yoga is applied when visionary phenomena appear during cycles of rapid eye movement sleep, and involves consciously re-engineering fragmentary 'picture puzzle' narratives of dreams so as to gain mastery of the mind. To do so involves navigating the indivisible terrain of emptiness and appearance, the 'ground luminosity' that underlies all experience. Dream Yoga thus refers to emptiness and luminosity manifesting as awareness, and consequently seeing and acting with ever-greater clarity and precision until consciousness awakens from inhibiting dualistic constructs such as self and other, attachment and aversion, birth and death. Dream Yoga is often preceded by specific breathing practices, along with establishing a clear intention to stay aware during the dream state. In a Dream Yoga method presented in Dzogchen, the practitioner visualizes a glowing moon at her or his heart, from which a phonemic stream of seed-syllables *āḥ*, representing infinite space and potentiality, rises upwards through the throat to a point between the eyebrows, associated in Haṭha Yoga with the *ājñā cakra* and transcendent insight. According to Dzogchen teachings, the visualization of flowing syllables enables one to maintain awareness of the groundless luminosity of being both while dreaming and while deeply asleep. A more concise method involves meditating on a pulsating red lotus at the throat. Once lucidity is established within a dream, a dreamer can begin to reshape the dream's contents and choreograph its outcome. With practice, consciously altering events within a dream carries over to being able to shift emotional states and transcend conceptual limits while awake.

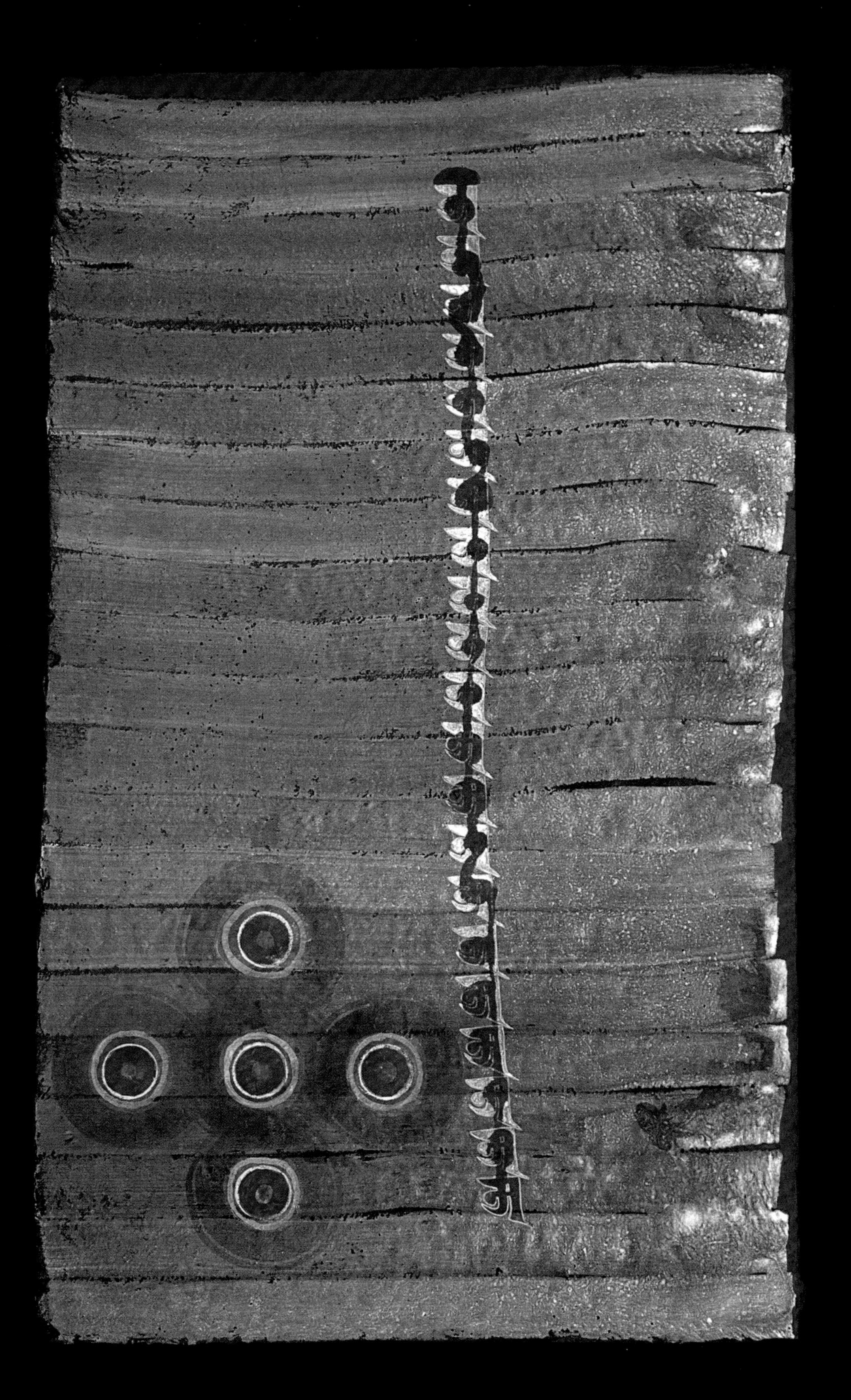

Living beyond illusions

An illustrated meditation manual from Bhutan depicts vignettes of the human condition, from the impermanence of riches to suffering, death and rebirth. All such experiences can also arise in the dream state and thus be transformed through Dream Yoga. As stated in the accompanying inscriptions, neither monks nor cave-dwelling hermits can escape death, and nor is 'pretending to be a Buddha entering Nirvāṇa' effective for escaping mortality, as illustrated by the figure lying on his right side with his hand beneath his head – the standard posture for Dream Yoga. The figure at the bottom, visualizing his annihilation in a charnel ground, signifies the terrifying experiences that can arise in dreams, even though the events and states of consciousness associated with them have no objective existence.

The 'awakening' that is referred to in Buddhist teachings is not awakening from sleep but from a state of inattention and automation. The root verb *budh,* 'to awaken', refers in the Upaniṣads and the Rigveda to an alert and vigilant consciousness. In Buddhism, the word infers an expansive abiding attention that self-oriented mindfulness can unintentionally occlude. Presenting life as a dream, as commonly stated in Tibetan Buddhist teachings, implies that the dreamer too is only an illusion, without any inherent identity. Yet it is often in dreams and illusions that we paradoxically awaken to what is most true within ourselves: the imaginal realities that shape and determine our waking actions. Dream work, from a psychoanalytic perspective, is thus to restore to consciousness repressed elements of the unconscious mind. Whether undertaken during REM sleep or in waking life, Dream Yoga is a deeper disposition that can be carried into all experience. By viewing disquieting events as 'dream like', the stress of existence can be significantly abated, without regressing into states of denial. Within this illuminating frame of mind, dream and waking states are no longer opposed, but complementary and interactive polarities. As life takes on renewed vividness and wonder, one's response, in turn, can become one of engaged creativity rather than passive detachment and reaction.

As neuroscience has revealed, perception and reason do not faithfully reflect reality, and we live more accurately in a kind of dream world of

Above **A yogi on a tiger skin**, pictured on a folio from an 18th-century manuscript, demonstrates a dream yoga posture for 'capturing luminosity at the heart'. The relativity of form and emptiness central to Buddhist thought is based on the experiential insight that the pure potentiality within which all phenomena arise and dissolve can be experienced subjectively as a luminous continuum of consciousness, within which both dreams and waking experience are neither real nor unreal. Beijing Palace Museum.

ever-altering, interdependent appearances. Tibetan Dream Yoga, in its largest sense, is to recognize that when everything is viewed as dream-like, everything becomes potentially possible. To view life as a lucid dream is not to see it as a deceptive illusion but as a creative process in which one's actions continuously redefine life's unfolding, both for oneself and others. Experiencing life as a negotiable dream is central to all aspects of Tibetan yoga, from the Creation Phase of viewing all appearances as empty, the Completion Phase of experiencing all sensations as emptiness and bliss, and the resultant Great Perfection of non-dual realization of the luminous continuum of all existence. The practice of Dream Yoga thus ultimately cultivates a vision of human possibility that recalls the words of Henry David Thoreau who observed, in another context, that, 'Our truest life is when we are in dream awake.'

Even though, with training, life can appear to be dream like and illusory, viewing life's shape-shifting occurrences as if they were actually real offers a potentially deeper level of engagement. Detachment might be lost, but intimacy

and vivid presence gained. The 14th-century Tibetan meditation master Longchen Rabjampa Drimé Özer advocated going 'to places that make the mind waver', where emotional and mental discomfort enliven our sensibilities. Before him, the 11th-century Indian mahāsiddha Padampa Sangye said, 'Go to places that scare you and discover the Buddha within yourself.' Through such perspectives, distinctions between desirable and undesirable experiences begin to dissolve. They address Tibetan Dream Yoga's ultimate application as a preparation for end of life experiences in which the mind takes on an increasingly independent existence from the physical body, leading to both disorienting visions and potential awakening within the noetic light beyond the range of the discursive, dreaming mind.

A Skull Mask, as used in Tantric dance ceremonies connected to the 'Lords of the Cremation Grounds', protector deities who guard the peripheries of the Buddhist universe, as well as the mind, from negative forces. The mask's grinning countenance and 'wisdom eye' at the forehead signify the transformation of being that occurs with transcendence of fear. The rainbow wings that extend beyond the cranium represent the body's ultimate dissolution into light.

Glorious Lords of the Charnel Ground (*Shmashana Adhipati*). These male and female dancing skeletons are characterized in Tantric Buddhism as 'wisdom protectors'. They invoke the impermanence of all phenomena, including the human body. Encircled by flames of 'pristine awareness', the vibrantly entwined cadavers are not a morbid *memento mori* but rather a paradoxical celebration of the transcience of existence, signifying freedom from fear and attachment and inviting more inclusive forms of awareness. Painted terracotta, Tibet, 18th century, Rubin Museum of Art, New York.

Exit strategies

The yoga of transcendent death

When you arrive at the extinction of reality, all that remains is the spontaneity of your pure, innate potential. Only then can you dance in the sky.

Khandroma Yeshe Tsogyal, 8th century

Transcending death

Opposite **Great Transference, or Powa**, refers to ejecting one's consciousness beyond the physical body to a celestial Buddha Realm, thereby bypassing the after-death state of the Bardo, a vignette of which is shown at the upper right of this mural detail from the northern wall of the Lukhang temple in Tibet. As indicated by the flame emanating from the top of the yogin's head, this image also illustrates the Yoga of Inner Fire.

Below **A practitioner of Chöd**, or 'severance', ritually simulates his own death and liberation at a charnel ground at the base of Mount Kailash in Tibet.

The Buddha's life story informs the narrative of Vajrayāna Buddhism and the pedagogy of its yogic practices. Fundamental to this narrative is the Buddha's own series of encounters with old age, sickness, and death – the generative source of the existential discontent that ultimately drove him from his palace to a life of mendicancy, meditation and, ultimately, enlightenment. The traditional narrative presupposes that the cloistered prince who was to become the Awakened One was already in the third decade of his life before becoming aware of the existence of mortality, having hitherto been sheltered from the pain and uncertainty of the outside world by a well-meaning, if overly protective, father. In the prince's third revelatory sojourn beyond the palace walls, the sight of a corpse being borne towards a funeral pyre led him to question what he was seeing, to which his charioteer replied that death, a state in which neither life nor consciousness animates one's body, awaits every living being. His driver also told him that what happens to consciousness after the dissolution of the body is a mystery that no religion or philosophy has ever convincingly resolved, despite the visionary accounts of those who have neared that extinction and returned with alternately consoling and disturbing interpretations. The predicament of unknowing remains unchanged through time, although comparative research has revealed much about what occurs at the threshold. Accounts of near death experiences tell us much about the subjective phenomenology of the initial stages of dying, but they tell us virtually nothing about what happens when all sense organs have ceased to function, when the heart and respiration have stopped, and when all brain activity – assumed by science to be the physiological support for consciousness – has come to an end. The Tibetan Yoga of Transference (Powa), often described as 'liberation without meditation', seeks a comprehensive solution to the problem of death by forgoing it altogether.

The art of dying

In the moment that consciousness is freed from physiological constraints, does it begin a disembodied journey to a transcendental end? This is the premise of the teachings constituting much of *The Tibetan Book of the Dead* or, more properly, 'Liberation through Hearing in the Bardo', wherein Bardo refers to a posited postmortem reality in which personal consciousness, stripped increasingly of memory, transits through a hallucinatory intermediary realm of alluring and terrifying sounds, lights and spectral forms before taking rebirth. Powa, the yoga of consciousness transference at the moment of death, refers to the fifth of the Six Yogas of the Completion Phase, and represents a skilful means whereby the perils of the Bardo and rebirth can be summarily bypassed. Powa originates in the yogic technique of *utkrānti*, or 'ascent from the body', as practised within the Atimārga and Mantramārga traditions of Tantric Śaivism. Recognizing the signs of approaching death, the practitioner either ends their life by ejecting their vital energy out of the body to a paradisiacal realm, or takes possession of another body. In the Powa tradition taught by the Kashmiri mahasiddhā Sukhasiddhi, one visualizes oneself as a Tantric deity and, compressing one's breath, uses the sound of the chosen deity's mantric seed-syllable (such as *hūṃ*, *hik* or *phat*) to forcefully open the 'aperture of Brahma' between the frontal and parietal bones at the crown of one's head. Doing so allows consciousness to be ejected from the body at the time of death and to enter the transcendental Land of Bliss associated with Amitābha, the Buddha of Infinite Light.

A Tibetan monastery typically includes a 'protector chapel' in which rituals are performed to remind Tibet's pre-Buddhist gods of their vows to assist Tantric Buddhist practitioners on their path to enlightenment. Surrounded by walls depicting decomposing and dismembered bodies, a pilgrim makes an offering of light, symbolizing the illumination of the subconscious contents of the mind. As the analytical psychologist Carl Gustav Jung once wrote in regard to such practices, 'enlightenment does not consist in imagining figures of light, but in making the darkness conscious'.

A Rainbow Buddha, as pictured on a Tibetan scroll painting, illustrates the transformation of the elements of the human body into effulgent light. In contrast to this photonic dissolution of the body at the time of death, as promoted in Dzogchen, the practice of Powa involves forcibly ejecting consciousness through the crown of the head and directing it towards a desired 'pure land.' Both practices involve transcendence of ordinary conceptions of death. As mahāsiddha Padampa Sangye famously sang, 'Birth, sickness, aging, and death flow ever onwards, a river with ford or bridge … Have you prepared yourself a boat?' Private collection.

The yogic practice of transferring one's consciousness to a Buddhist 'pure land' at the time of death is referred to within Tibetan tradition as 'Buddhahood without Meditation', in that the practice can reputedly be applied in the final moment of one's life and achieve the same result as a lifetime of meditation. In an invocation attributed to Padmasambhava entitled 'Root Verse on the Bardo of Dying', the yogin reflects as follows at the moment of death:

'Now as the Bardo of dying dawns upon me,
I abandon all grasping, yearning, and attachment,
Enter without distraction into the clear meaning of the teaching,
And eject my consciousness into the space of primordial unborn awareness.
As I leave this compound body of flesh and blood
I know it to be a transitory illusion.'

Separating mind and body

Unlike other Completion Phase practices such as Inner Fire, Consort Practice and Clear Light, Powa was eventually taught openly in what are often today large-scale public initiations. Those who receive the Powa teachings typically practice intensively for a week to ten days, following which many manifest physical signs, such as the emergence of fluid from a small hole in the area of the fontanel into which the retreat master traditionally inserts a stalk of grass as a mark of success. The technique recalls trepanning, or boring of holes into the skull, that archeological evidence suggests is one of the world's oldest surgical procedures and associated by its contemporary advocates with enhanced cerebral blood flow and mental abilities.

The 'opening of the sky door', as some texts refer to Powa, ensures that, at the time of death, one's consciousness will exit the body by the most auspicious route – the aperture of Brahma at the top of the head – and avoid the body's less favourable outlets. Learning Powa also allows one to perform it on behalf of others and to transfer the consciousness of the deceased to one or another desirable Buddha Realm, from where final enlightenment can be attained. As a means for realizing Buddhahood without spending a lifetime in meditation, Powa is the ultimate life insurance policy. But the practice is not without its hazards. Unless one enacts the ejection of consciousness – one's own or someone else's – at the correct moment in the process of bodily dissolution (when outer respiration has ceased and inner breathing continues), Powa can bring about premature death. Other forms of Powa are performed as daily meditations, however, in which the mind is projected from the body as an expanded, unobstructed field of awareness. Mastery of death can also be achieved while sleeping. Sakya Paṇḍita (1182–1251), for example, advised that one go to sleep while visualizing Amitābha, the Buddha of Infinite Light, dissolving into one's heart. 'By practising this, in the future, sloughing off this body like a serpent's skin, you will be miraculously reborn from a lotus in Sukhāvatī', Amitābha's effulgent Land of Bliss.

Pure lands such as Sukhāvatī represent idealized intermediary worlds from where enlightenment can be more readily achieved, while their celestial geographies signify transcendence of the dichotomy of life and death. At the time of his own final passing into Nirvāna, Buddha Sakyamuni re-enacted his enlightenment by ascending and descending through visionary states of meditative absorption, echoing the words that he is said to have spoken at the time of his spiritual awakening: 'Opened for those who hear are the doors to the Deathless.'

Buddhist 'pure lands' represent the general view of Indic religions that the power of an individual's final thought at the time of death conditions their future rebirth. The practitioner of Powa thus typically focuses their mind on an image of one or another transcendental Buddha in order to be reborn in their celestial realms.

The practice of Powa involves three fundamental components of recognition: the central channel of the yogic body as the path; consciousness as the traveller and the salvational environment of a Buddha Realm as one's destination. As in the Greek term *ekstasis*, Powa ultimately implies a 'stepping out' or transcendence of one's ordinary condition, as illustrated in this detail of a 17th-century Tibetan scroll painting. (See full painting on page 152.) Rubin Museum of Art, New York.

Abandoning distress

'The dead do not speak', Buddha's charioteer is said to have told him. 'They can tell us nothing about what happens after death. We know that we will eventually die, but we know nothing beyond that. Death ends all understanding.' The charioteer's words prompted Prince Gautama to leave his palace for good. After recognizing rather late that all things come to an end, he no longer found solace in habitual comforts and what once were pleasures became perfunctory distractions. Neither did he find consolation in children's laughter or abundant feasts or among the concubines in his harem, for all experience was tinged with inevitable decay. And although death is the prerequisite for ongoing life, he found all things wanting and dedicated his existence to discovering a way out of the conundrum of seemingly purposeless pursuits and attendant disappointments. Life itself appeared to the Prince as a senseless struggle for survival and ephemeral pleasures that, in all instances, were infused with sorrow and futility. Even death could bring no relief for the unenlightened for, based on the prevailing belief system of his time, it brought only further births, and perennial discontent. When his own life came to an end, he approached it with ease, letting go into the great mystery that awaits us all while inviting those he left behind to discover the self-luminous source of their being – to be lamps unto themselves.

Tibet's Great Perfection teachings present two distinct methods for entering the natural luminosity of death. The superior approach is described as abiding in the nature of mind 'like a newly born child' as the clear light of death arises as one's field of awareness. The second method involves visualizing one's primordial nature as the syllable *āḥ*, and ejecting it from the heart through the crown of the head into the Buddha Realm of one's choice.

Opposite and above left **The practice of Chöd**, or 'severance', prepares both mind and body for the death process by ritually visualizing one's corporeal dismemberment and afterwards offering one's body parts to famished spirits. Both Chöd and Powa remind us that we assume death to be terminal simply because we can not imagine what happens next, not because nothing does. In the Tibetan arts of dying, death, like life, is perceived as an alterable dream, changing its manifestation in response to how we choose to engage it.

Above right **Charnel grounds** inspire active contemplation of life's fundamental pain and impermanence, while encouraging transcendence of identification with the physical body. Success in the practice of Powa and Chöd confers fearlessness in facing death and other potential adversities, such as having one's heart eaten by a lammergeier, as depicted in this detail of a Tibetan scroll painting.

Embracing possibility

Three distinct forms of Powa are described in accordance with the three 'bodies' of reality – Nirmāṇakāya, Sambhogakāya and Dharmakāya – which refer reductively to matter, energy and space. Nirmāṇakāya Powa, in which an adept could project his or her consciousness into an undecomposed corpse and bring it back to life, is generally held to be a lost art. Sambhogakāya Powa, in which the mind is energetically transferred to a visualized Buddha Realm, is the most common form of Powa. Dharmakāya Powa is analogous to the Dzogchen practice of Kadak Trekchö, or 'cutting through to primordial purity', in which the mind is spontaneously freed from attachment and delusion. In its ultimate expression, at the time of death, the constituent elements of the body dissolve into their fundamental nature of radiant, all-illuminating light. Although rarely achieved and imperfectly documented, the so-called rainbow body (*jalu*) is the ultimate exit strategy from the limited views that constrain the full expression of human potential. Rather than dissolving into oblivion at the moment of death, realization of the rainbow body posits nothing less than resurrection as cognizant luminosity, beyond distinctions of emptiness and form, spirit and matter. As the Italian physicist Carlo Rovelli wrote, 'We are born and die as the stars are born and die, both individually and collectively. This is our reality. Life is precious to us because it is ephemeral.'

A yogini meditating on the flow of a waterfall embodies the Dzogchen view of 'naked awareness', the moment-to-moment, concept-free realization of impermanence and perpetual becoming. The flow of life that unceasingly arises and dissolves within consciousness is less about entropy than unending rebirth. In its ultimate sense, Powa offers not only transcendence of the confusion and distress of end of life experience, but liberation of consciousness while fully alive. As the Indian mahāsiddha and Dzogchen master Padampa Sangye proclaimed, 'Pure awareness is without fixation, like a rainbow in the sky.'

Above **The Bodhisattva Vajrasattva** embraces his consort Vajra Garvi amidst billowing blue clouds. Jñāna Ḍākinī is pictured on the left and the heavenly paradise of Abhirati on the right. Mahāyāna 'pure lands' represent idealized destinations for transferring consciousness at the time of death. Varying techniques and traditions of Powa are associated with different visionary dimensions, all of which testify to the fact that, while it can never be known, death can be richly imagined. (See full image on page 168.) Rubin Museum of Art, New York.

Below **A rainbow on the Tibetan plateau** recalls the luminous *mu*-cords by which Tibet's earliest kings travelled freely between earth and heaven. Dzogchen characterizes enlightenment as the realization of a photonic 'rainbow body' that manifests when the coarse elements of the physical body are reabsorbed into their pure light essences. In early Dzogchen, the dissolution of a practitioner's body into light is referred to as 'Buddhahood without physical remainder'. Both instances represent transcendence of the physical body at the time of death.

Liminality

Navigating transitional states

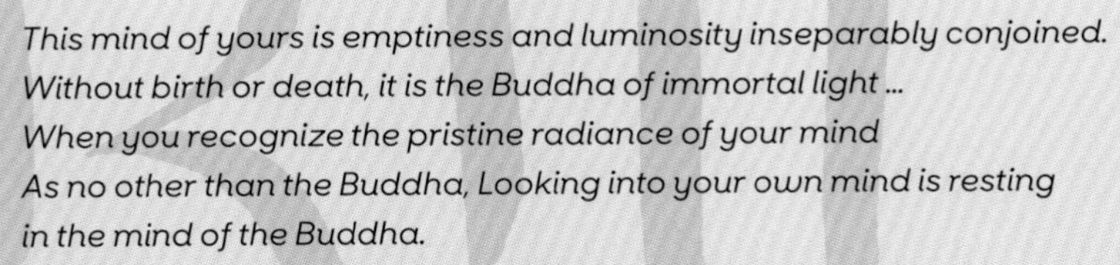

This mind of yours is emptiness and luminosity inseparably conjoined.
Without birth or death, it is the Buddha of immortal light ...
When you recognize the pristine radiance of your mind
As no other than the Buddha, Looking into your own mind is resting
in the mind of the Buddha.

Padmasambhava, 'Great Liberation through Hearing in the Bardo', 14th century

Opposite **Bardo Yoga is the culmination of the Six Yogas** and encompasses the practices of Illusory Body, Dream Yoga and Clear Light. Harrowing imagery, such as seen on this temple mural in Bhutan, is said to familiarize one with 'peaceful and wrathful' deities that manifest in an intermediary dimension between death and rebirth as projections of unresolved thoughts and emotions. The six transitional states of the Bardo are equated in some Tibetan traditions with the Six Yogas that likewise provide opportunities for transforming inner experience during all stages of waking, dreaming, sleeping and dying. Ogyen Choling Manor.

Perpetual becoming

The Six Yogas represent essential extracts from the prevailing Buddhist Tantras of 11th-century India. When Tilopā transmitted them to Nāropā he explained that the Yoga of Inner Fire derives from the Hevajra Tantra, the practice of Clear Light from the Cakrasaṃvara Tantra, Dream Yoga from the Mahāmāya Tantra and Illusory Body and Bardo Yoga from the Guhyasamāja Tantra. Bardo Yoga, in which an adept negotiates a transitional state between death and rebirth, or its psychological equivalent, was not a prominent teaching within Indian Vajrayāna. The practice developed in Tibet in connection with instructional advice on transforming the experience of death and dying. According to his 'Instructions on the Six Yogas', Tilopā received teachings on the intermediate state (*antarabhāva*) from the female mahāsiddha Sukhasiddhī, a contemporary of Nāropā's Kashmiri consort Niguma. In his 11th-century transmission of Bardo Yoga, Tilopā advises the practitioner to 'gather the winds of the sun and moon at the heart', and further describes how 'the visions of death appear for seven or seven-times-seven days', followed by rebirth. Tilopā counselled that, while transiting through the Bardo, one could either remain in a state of non-conceptual lucidity or emanate as a Tantric deity so as to bring the dream-like displays of the Bardo to an end, and thus prevent an undesired rebirth. Nāropā elaborated the Bardo teachings in his subsequent *Vajra Verses* and distinguished three distinct intermediary states: the Bardo from Birth to Death, the Bardo of Dreaming and the postmortem Bardo of Becoming, in which 'without seeing there is supreme seeing ... natural awareness, radiant, empty, non-conceptual, free from all obscurations ... utterly pure pristine wisdom'.

Transforming death

The interior experience of the dissolution of mind and body at the time of death led to further elaborations of the early Bardo teachings brought from India to Tibet. The 13th-century adept Gyalwa Yangönpa articulated a six-fold system of intermediary states during recurring cycles of waking, dreaming and dying, as well as during deep meditation. In regard to the transitional period between death and rebirth, Yangönpa's *Deliverance from the Perilous Straits of the Bardo* emphasizes the initial arising of the clear light of consciousness followed by the emergence of an illusory mental body and subsequent hallucinatory dream-like visions. As with Tilopā's instructions two centuries earlier, Yangönpa's exposition focuses on 'interrupting' the spontaneous visions of the disembodied state so as to block the 'womb door' leading to rebirth.

Descriptions of the Bardo between death and rebirth culminated a century later with the revelation of the 'Great Liberation through Hearing in the Intermediate State' (Bardo Thödol) by Tertön Karma Lingpa (1326–86). Fusing Tantric contemplative practices with indigenous Tibetan funerary rites, the text became known in the West centuries later as *The Tibetan Book of the Dead*. Outwardly, the Bardo Thödol is a guide for directing consciousness through phantasmagoric experiences associated with the dissolution of the mind and body at the time of death, towards an optimal rebirth. On an inner level, the Bardo Thödol articulates the ever-occurring transitional states within which we are born, live and die. As with the Six Yogas, the Six Bardos present opportunities for actualizing awareness within dimensions of existence that otherwise remain largely unconscious. Bardo Yoga thus extends beyond preparation for navigating transitional states after death and, by dissolving rigid mental constructs while fully alive, brings heightened awareness and attention to all human activities, while cultivating creative appreciation for uncertainty, ambiguity and the unknown. As novelist E.M. Forster wrote, 'Our final experience, like our first, is conjectural. We move between two darknesses.'

Left **A sojourner in the Bardo** reveals that only those who can sustain clear light awareness can transcend the dubious prospects of a non-volitional rebirth.

Opposite **A yogi seated on a leopard skin** gazes past a nimbus of weapon-wielding, animal-headed dākinīs that herald the ambiguous appearances that occur in the postmortem dimension of the Bardo until one awakens to one's innate Buddha Nature, as depicted in the paradisiacal realms beyond.

Right **A gleeful lion-headed dākinī**, trampling on a corpse, characterizes the kinds of equivocal encounters that are said to arise in the liminal dimension after death. The Bardo Thödol presents the postmortem journey as a hazardous passage that determines one's future rebirth or, more optimally, allows one to transcend the ever-recurring cycle of birth, death and rebirth in the realization of Nirvāṇa. Through Bardo Yoga, the practitioner learns to recognize the visions of the intermediate state as projections of his or her mind. Whether such visions appear demonic or benign, the adept regards them with equanimity so as to merge with the Clear Light from which the visions arise. As the Bardo Thödol states: 'O son or daughter, whatever you see, however terrifying it is, recognize it as … the natural, undefiled radiance of your mind.' Ogyen Choling Manor.

Moving between worlds

A 14th-century treasure text entitled 'Introducing the Moment of Death' attributed to Padmasambhava and revealed by Tertön Dorjé Lingpa (1346–1405) describes the process by which, at the time of death, the body's earth element dissolves into water, water into fire (as the mouth and nose dehydrate), fire into air (when the body's heat is lost) and air into consciousness with one's final exhalation. 'At the that time', Dorjé Lingpa's treasure text clarifies, 'you may feel that you are being pressed down by a great mountain, or forced into darkness, or cast into empty space, while all appearances are accompanied by sounds of whirring and hissing. The entire atmosphere becomes glaringly bright, as if a silken canopy had been thrown open. Within a canopy of rainbow light, one's extended awareness fills with peaceful, wrathful and ecstatic spirits, with varieties of heads and limbs and brandishing weapons, and roaring in all sorts of ferocious tones … and light shining like a hundred thousand suns rising at once. At that time, know that the thought that a mountain is crushing you is the dissolution of your own physical constituents … The thought that you are being forced into darkness … is the dissolution of your five sensory organs. The thought that you are falling through space is not falling, for when mind and body part, and the breath ceases, the mind is without support. All manifestations of rainbow light are the radiance of your own awareness. All peaceful and wrathful forms are your own awareness. All sounds are its natural expression. All lights are its natural luminosity. Have no doubt about it! For if you doubt, you will be thrown into cyclic existence.'

A mask of Mahākāla signifies the state beyond time and death, as invoked in Tantric dance rituals that enlist the powers of Tibet's wrathful protector deities. Mahākāla's upturned third eye, framed by flaming eyebrows, represents the enlightened vision that sees between dimensions, while his crown of skulls signifies the full embrace of life's impermanence. Mahākāla's blackness is said to absorb all forms and colours, thus symbolizing his all-embracing, comprehensive nature. Wood, Tibet, 19th century, private collection.

As Dorjé Lingpa's text makes clear, the process of dying and the subsequent stages of the Bardo, during which consciousness assumes an unobstructed illusory body, present a spectrum of opportunities for recognizing the nonduality of emptiness and appearance and actualizing enlightened awareness. By traditional accounts, the initial phase of the Bardo between death and rebirth is characterized by the natural dawning of Clear Light, inseparable from one's intrinsic being. But unless one merges with that light, habitual mental tendencies reappear in peaceful and abhorrent visionary displays. This Bardo of Becoming (*sipé bardo*), when the mind is no longer conditioned by the physical body, refers to the infinite possibilities of being reborn, whether literally or figuratively, into one or another realm of existence, as well as to emerging from cyclic existence through recognizing one's innate nature as radiant light, infused with self-transcendent wisdom and compassion.

Right **The Tibetan shaman Pawo Wangchuk** guides the life force of the dead through immanent worlds of darkness and light while possessed by pre-Buddhist tutelary deities. Tibetan Buddhism integrates a rich tradition of indigenous shamanism in which spirit mediums known as lhapa enter altered states of consciousness in order to perceive and interact with a spirit world, and channel those transcendental energies to diagnose and heal disease. The lhapas' visionary journeys through parallel dimensions of supernal lights, sounds and phantasmal forms reflect in many respects the passage of the deceased through the Bardo.

Right **The leopard-skin skirted Chagdor Rinpoche**, born in 1869 in the Golok region of Tibet, manifests like an apparition from the Bardo. Visionary accounts of the interim dimension between life and death were propagated by such Tantric yogins. The so-called *Tibetan Book of the Dead* reflects indigenous Tibetan religious concerns for the safe passage of the deceased within a Buddhist context of death and rebirth.

A denizen of the Bardo contemplates a potential meal. As consciousness migrates unencumbered by a physical body through the interim dimensions of the Bardo, innumerable 'peaceful and wrathful' forms manifest as mental projections, determined in part by one's past actions and dispositions. According to the Bardo Thödol, distinguishing awareness from its contents during the visionary displays leads to liberation from conditioned existence and the uncertain prospects of rebirth in one or another dimension of sentient life. Ogyen Choling Manor.

Opposite above **A female shaman**, or lhapa, in Lhasa, Tibet, moves readily between dimensions, as signified by her crown of skulls and a doorway embellished with a painting of a flayed human skin.

Opposite below **Scenes of dismemberment** in the protector chamber at Pelkhor Chöde Monastery in Gyantse, Tibet, free the mind from inhibiting comforts and promote openness to the unknown.

O son or daughter, whatever you see, however terrifying it is,
recognize it as your own projection ...
the natural, undefiled radiance of your mind.

Padmasambhava, 'Great Liberation on Hearing in the Bardo', 14th century

Opposite **Charnel ground scenes** from the White Temple at Toling Monastery in western Tibet invoke the scenery of the liminal states of the Bardo. *The Tibetan Book of the Dead*, or Bardo Thödel, is part of a larger corpus of teachings entitled the 'Profound Dharma of Self-Liberation through the Intention of the Peaceful and Wrathful Ones', revealed by Karma Lingpa. The text is intended as a guide through experiences that arise during the intermediate state between death and rebirth, but it can be applied to all circumstances in which consciousness confronts the unknown. According to the Bardo Thödel, all appearances, however alluring or abhorrent, are projections of the mind and thus to be integrated on the path of liberation.

Right **A sword-wielding skeleton** from the Donkhar Caves in western Tibet evokes the fearlessness stance associated with Bardo Yoga and contemplation of a dimension of experience beyond human mortality. The dancing 'Lord of the Charnel Ground', where divisions between life and death are porous, specifically represents transcendence of the fear of death and is thus a catalyst for psychological growth and spiritual insight.

Myriad hallucinations occur in the Bardo,
surpassing in horror all description,
and causing your very heart to quiver with fear.

Shabkar Tsokdruk Rangdrol, 19th century

Near-death experiences

The fate of consciousness after death remains a mystery, although investigation of near death experiences has become an increasingly accepted field of scientific inquiry. Western biomedicine defines death as the irreversible cessation of circulatory and respiratory functions as well as all activity of the brain. But observations that delta brain wave patterns that occur during deep sleep continue after cardiac rhythms and arterial blood pressure have ceased complicate the matter of exactly when death occurs, as does the fact that genes continue to function even more energetically in the days after people 'die'. Tibetan medicine maintains that despite the outward signs of clinical death, 'inner respiration' and subtle states of consciousness continue within the body until either blood or pus exudes from the nose or sexual organs, at which point the body can be discarded.

It has long been observed that near death experiences parallel many aspects of Tibetan accounts of the Bardo. One central difference, however, is that near death experiences tend, with notable exceptions, to be presented as overwhelmingly positive, with the disembodied state of near death experiences typically characterized by those who experience them as infused with love and meaning. As no one can, by definition, fully die and return to life, it is obviously impossible to account empirically for the traditionally harrowing descriptions of the Bardo following the initial experience of Clear Light. Near death experiences thus tell us only what can happen at the threshold of death, not what happens after.

Opposite **Rotating seed-syllables** depicted in this painting invoke a vibratory field that opens the seal of primordial awareness within the body's central channel, which terminates by some accounts at the pineal gland at the base of the brain.

Right **Disembodied consciousness** experienced in the Bardo is analogous to the illusory body that manifests in lucid dreams. Unconstrained by laws of physics, the mind acts with increasing freedom, flying unobstructedly through rock and sky, as illustrated in this detail from a mural in the Lukhang temple, Tibet. Neuroscience has shown that out of the body experiences can be reliably induced by stimulating the juncture between the temporal and parietal lobes of the human brain.

Unbound awareness

The survival of consciousness after death is foundational to most religions, including Buddhism, and is the basis for Bardo Yoga. Descriptions of the initial phases of the Bardo of Dying share common features with near death experiences, including a deeply transformative phenomenology of light and, often, a consequent fearlessness of death. Near death experiences can be induced by oxygen deprivation, acute trauma, high fever or exposure to hallucinogenic substances, and are often associated with out-of-body experiences characterized by light tunnels, celestial topographies and divine apparitions. The stream of memories, images and ideas that typically occur in near death experiences are often associated with positive life changes and subjective states of compassion and insight, despite the fact that they arise through temporary impairment to blood circulation in the brain. Neurologically, near death experiences are partly explained as an intermediary state between dream sleep and waking consciousness, associated with REM paralysis in response to acute stress. It is generally held that near death experiences occur in the interval between normal brain function and the onset of, or recovery from, unconsciousness. Analogously to the Bardo, they are also known to result in the phenomena of 'panoramic memory', involving detailed recall of autobiographical events. Near death experiences are also typically associated with spiritual or religious emotions of unity, tranquility, absence of pain, and they are associated neurochemically with increased production of dopamine and endogenous opiates. Customary visions of tunnels of light are caused by reduced blood circulation to the eyeball, beginning at the periphery of the field of vision. The bright, alluring colours that typically appear at the end of the tunnel in near death experiences are caused by stimulation of the visual cortex, as in the state of dreaming. Although deeper stages of the Bardo experience remain immeasurable, initial phases suggest a similar phenomenology with near death experiences, understood as dream sleep surfacing during conscious awareness in response to the dissolution of bodily functions. In regard to the decomposition of the pineal gland at the time of death, psychopharmacologist Dr Rick Strassman has speculated that a consequent flood of endogenous N-Dimethyltryptamine may partly account for the disembodied visionary states integral to the Bardo experience. As Strassman writes, 'DMT opens our inner senses to these betwixt states with their myriad visions, thoughts, sounds, and feelings. As the body becomes totally inert, consciousness has completely left the body and now exists as a field among many fields of manifest things.'

A Bönpo meditation manual from 1350 entitled *Instructions on the Four Wheels and Sounds* depicts spontaneous visionary experiences associated with meditation on the Bardo as an intermediary dimension between physical and immaterial reality. According to the manuscript, the Bardo commences with visions of spinning water particles and progresses to apparitions of wind, sun and moon, followed by manifestations of five light-emanating, transcendental Buddhas. Private collection.

Paraliminal visions

In traditional accounts, the Bardo of Dying (*chikhai bardo*) continues until 'inner respiration' ceases and the Clear Light of consciousness dawns as one's field of awareness. The manifestation of Clear Light at the time of death is associated with the dissolution of ordinary thoughts and emotions and the emergence of increasingly subtle states of consciousness. According to the teachings of Dzogchen, the pristine awareness that arises at this stage of the Bardo is characterized by spontaneously manifesting sounds and multi-coloured lights that parallel the successive visionary experiences of Lhündrup Tögal, the advanced Dzogchen contemplative practice of 'leaping over the skull into spontaneous presence.' These four phases of visionary experience are designated as Appearance, Increase, Full Attainment and Intrinsic Luminosity and represent pre-eminent opportunities for realizing the non-duality of emptiness and appearance, and thus enlightenment. During the process, the male 'white essence' at the crown of the head descends through the body's unbounded central channel to merge at the heart with the red female essence ascending from below the navel, leading to a state of innate bliss as forty designated thought forms associated with desire naturally dissolve into non-dual awareness. As the lunar and solar essences eclipse at the heart a phase of utter 'blackness' ensues, free of all concepts. This is referred to as 'Full Attainment'.

A Dzogchen practitioner, depicted on the walls of the Lukhang temple in Tibet, unifies his awareness with the light essences of the five elements, signified as male and female Buddhas in photonic union. By attuning to such visionary phenomena associated with the five psychophysical aggregates, practitioners of Tögal are said to be able to bypass the Bardo after death.

From the dimension of pure potentiality, the Ground Luminosity of consciousness arises as the innermost essence of the mind, the basis for enlightenment. Unless one has prior experience in deep meditation, however, this pristine Clear Light generally passes unnoticed and, after a period of unconsciousness, the mind departs from the body and enters the subsequent Bardo of Intrinsic Reality (*chönyi bardo*), characterized by spontaneous, shimmering visions that also support awakening. In this phase of the Bardo, the disembodied mind takes the form of a luminous body and becomes aware of a dazzling, flowing world of sound, light and colour, unlimited by dimension, direction or identity. But as with the initial dawning of Clear Light, this manifestation of the innermost nature of the mind also passes unrecognized in absence of advanced meditative experience, in which case the rays of coloured lights transform into luminous spheres that coalesce into a brilliant all-encompassing maṇḍala of 'forty-two peaceful and fifty-eight wrathful deities' that eventually dissolves within one's heart centre. If again one fails to recognize intrinsic non-dual

Right **Couples in sexual union** in a charnel ground illustrate the interconnected nature of love, death and reincarnation. A disembodied being from the Bardo – the intermediate state between death and rebirth – enters through the lower woman's nostrils at the moment of conception to reincarnate in her womb. Another figure remains suspended in the clouds, 'closing the womb door' and forgoing the call of further birth. The simultaneity of dismembered body parts and images of foetal development emphasize that life and death, self and other, wisdom and compassion are ultimately a single continuum.

Above **A row of Buddhas** depicted in a Tibetan meditation manual are linked with the elemental geometry of the body's internal energy system. In accounts of the Bardo, wrathful deities emanate from the head whereas peaceful deities, such as those shown here, issue from the heart. In all instances, the dazzling appearances of the Bardo are held to be spontaneous expressions of the nature of mind. Bardo Yoga can be viewed as a process of constructive defamiliarization in which the familiar is made to appear strange in order to expand the range of perception and sympathetic imagination. Private collection.

reality, a shaft of light emanates from one's heart as resplendent displays of luminous spheres, likened to unfurled carpets crowned by an outspread canopy of peacock feathers. This manifestation of the mind's intrinsic potential for enlightenment culminates in a limitless apparition of unutterable wisdom and clairvoyance, the spontaneous radiance of the mind's innermost nature. The entire vision of one's intrinsic nature then dissolves back into its original essence, like a tent collapsing once its ropes are cut. If the brilliant, unfolding visions are mistaken as objectively real, consciousness does not self-liberate from the cycle of birth and death and one moves into the dimmer realms of the Bardo of Becoming (*sidpa bardo*), and ultimately incarnates in the womb of one's future mother. As the 18th-century adept Shabkar Tsokdruk Rangdrol summarized the perils and opportunities of the Bardo: 'Whether you want to drink the nectar of the gods or the molten bronze of the hells, whether you wish to attain Buddhahood or wander in infernal realms: the choice is in your hands.'

Transcending birth and death

Early Buddhist teachings speak of death as occurring in every moment, as one set of circumstances passes out of existence and another arises. Death in this sense is the inherent, ever-shifting, contingent nature of all phenomena, as is rebirth. Despite the fact that Buddhist doctrine views selfhood as a conceptual illusion – a belief shared by contemporary neuroscience that explains 'mind' as a byproduct of brain activity – it nonetheless posits causal continuity between successive lives in absence of a supporting metaphysical substrate. By the early centuries of the first millennium, Mahāyāna Buddhism articulated two distinct modes of rebirth: the involuntary rebirth of the unawakened, and the wilfully chosen rebirth of the Bodhisattva who, through the power of compassion, reincarnates in a form commensurate with leading all beings to enlightenment. In this sense, the original Buddhist agenda of escaping rebirth was overridden by a more encompassing, if Sisyphean, objective: to remain in Saṃsāra until all beings are free of suffering and the causes of suffering. For ordinary beings who, through lack of mastery over death and the mind, continue to die and return to life in another body, the Bardo represents a purgatorial rite of passage which, depending on one's mental choices during the disembodied state, determines the conditions of one's future rebirth. For the Bodhisattva, the shadow realms of the Bardo resolve naturally into pure luminosity, thus ensuring unobstructed passage to a wholly volitional, enlightened birth.

As an intermediary dimension between successive lives, the Bardo helps to account for rebirth within a philosophical system that denies the existence of a self. Some Buddhist teachers maintain that the Buddha's reported remembrance of myriad former lives in the period leading up to his awakening was more accurately a form of evolutionary empathy – recognizing that, in essence, we have been and are all things. Literal interpretation of the doctrine of rebirth nonetheless remains a prominent aspect of popular Buddhism. The cause of rebirth is upheld to be *karma*, the impelling force of past actions based on deluded perceptions of phenomena as intrinsically real. Although the Buddha himself never reincarnated, a tradition of identifying and legitimizing lineages of reincarnate lamas began in Tibet with Karmapa Pakshi. The resultant tradition of Tulku, or reincarnate Bodhisattva lama, consolidated monastic power and perpetuates practice lineages to this day. Tulkus' vows as Bodhisattvas ensure that they voluntarily reincarnate time and time again to fulfill the spiritual needs of human beings. The institution of Tulku presents challenges in the modern world. Supremely revered contemporary lamas such as Chatral Sangye Dorje Rinpoche left as their final testament explicit instructions not to seek their reincarnation, nor to mourn their loss.

What is it that moves between lives? If no memory remains, can rebirth be said to be in any way personal? And if there is no persisting personhood, can anything be said to be reborn? When we remove ourselves from the hope and fear of continuity, the totality of nature constitutes our being. Death brings new life, just as the mulch of leaves brings forth new shoots and seedlings. In the entangled continuum of life and death, the Buddha's radical empathy at the moment of his enlightenment is ever illuminating. From photons to stellar dust, to residual gills, to remnant tailbones, an evolutionary genealogy is charted within our bodies as the remembrance of all things. Abiding in the dynamic, creative potentiality and flow of life is the ultimate Bardo Yoga. If Powa, the Yoga of Transference evades the interior phenomena that arise during the process of dying, Bardo Yoga fully embraces dissolution as well as resurrection, while remaining equally committed to emerging from unconscious cycles of thought and behavior. In the context of modernity, Bardo Yoga can be partly understood as embracing the ambiguity and uncertainly that pervades all existence and recognizing it as an endless source of creativity and insight. As Chatral Sangye Dorje Rinpoche once advised, 'Don't cling to the Bardo as real or you will never exceed its reach; the Bardo is our ever-present, natural state.'

Bardo Being, a visionary painting by Alex Grey, evokes the consciousness expanding inter-dimensionality associated with Tibetan descriptions of the journey between death and rebirth, as well as the liminal states of dream, meditation and psychedelic experience.

Potent solutions

The yoga of entheogens and elixirs

Some are bound by renouncing things. Others by these same things gain unsurpassable enlightenment.

Mahāsiddha Saraha, 8th century

Biochemistry of awakening

Opposite **A yogin seated on a leopard skin** holds a skull cup filled with ambrosial substances, in a detail from a wall painting in Bhutan. The Buddhist Tantras take a nuanced approach to altered states of consciousness, recognizing that, under certain circumstances, psychoactive substances can assist in unveiling the ultimately altered yet natural state of enlightenment.

Early teachings attributed to the historical Sakyamuni Buddha counsel against the use of inebriating substances on the path to liberation from human suffering. Nonetheless, the *Pātañjalayogaśāstra*, which partly derives from Sakyamuni Buddha's Eight-Fold Path leading to Nirvāṇa, cites medicinal herbs (*auṣadhi*) as the second of five means for achieving yogic powers and spiritual emancipation (*mokṣa*). Precedents for the use of psychoactive substances within India's yogic traditions date to the Rig Veda, which invokes a compound elixir called soma as a means for participating in the immortal condition of the gods. The subsequent use of cannabis, Datura, and other mind-altering medicinal herbs within Śaivism is well attested, but is less well known within Tantric Buddhism. Nonetheless, inebriating substances have been ritually consumed within Vajrayāna, the 'adamantine way', for both physical and psychic refinement. As the Hevajra Tantra states, 'The one who knows the nature of poison dispels the poison utilizing the poison itself.' Archaeological evidence of ritual drug use in Vajrayāna has recently emerged at sites ranging from India's Konkan Coast to Somapura Mahāvihāra in contemporary Bangladesh, while early Tibetan Buddhist texts describe the use of Datura, *Peganum harmala*, codonopsis, *Ephedra sinica* and possibly psychoactive fungi for cultivating altered states of consciousness central to the tradition's emancipatory goals. Such use illuminates Tantric Buddhism's 'path of skillful means' (*upāyamarga*), whereby what is proscribed outwardly often features centrally at an esoteric level for achieving yoga's, and thereby life's, highest goals. Using the metaphor of a poisonous plant, Tibetan tradition relates three means by which to eradicate adverse mental habits: Theravāda Buddhism councils one to avoid the poison, Mahāyāna teaches one to antidote it with the view of emptiness, and Vajrayāna instructs one how to transform the poison into a medicine. Dzogchen, however, reveals intrinsic liberation through the peacock's legendary ability to convert deadly Himalayan wolfsbane (*Aconitum ferox*) into the shimmering display of its eye-embellished tail feathers, symbols in Dzogchen for the radiant luminescence of the awakened mind.

Below **A gilded Scythian bowl** from the 3rd century BC depicts sixty-four snakes rising sinuously from a cluster of eggs. Although the vessel's specific purpose remains obscure, its ophidian symbolism evokes the 'serpent power' of *kuṇḍalinī*, while also suggesting the ritual consumption of psychologically potent substances. Buckingham Collection.

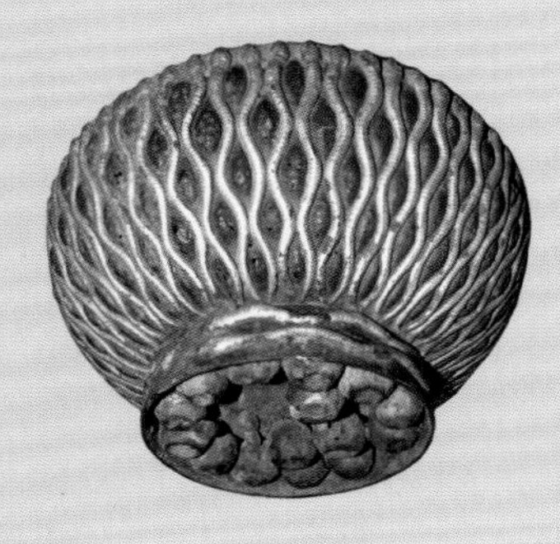

Negotiating power

Vajrayāna Buddhism was from the outset a transgressive tradition that challenged both the means and objectives of earlier forms of Buddhism. Its emancipatory goals often included psychophysical powers, called *siddhi*, which were understood as marks of spiritual attainment. One of the earliest listings of supranormal powers appears in the 8th-century Subāhuparipricchā Tantra, which describes 'delighting' deities through the practice of mantra, vanishing into palaces of the gods, and ingesting potent medicines derived from the five elements, as well as from human bodies, by which 'one lives a long time, without disease, and remains youthful with sharp faculties'. Other *siddhi* described in the text include skills such as flying through the sky, becoming invisible, running swiftly, and immediately comprehending the contents of any text. Later 8th-century accounts of 'great perfections' (*mahāsiddhi*) list ointments and drugs to be applied to the

Tantric mahāsiddhas are often depicted in states of intoxication, representing their inner transcendence of Saṃsāra and Nirvāṇa. The raised skull bowl brimming with immortal elixir, or *amṛta*, signifies the activation of the innate psycholytic, or 'mind-loosening', ambrosia located at the core of the brain that confers bliss and insight into the non-dual nature of reality. But more literal interpretations also apply. As Abhinavagupta wrote in Tantrāloka, 'Wine [*surā*] is pure by nature, it is light, bliss and consciousness, forever cherished by the gods; therefore the adept should always drink it!'

Right **The Tantric deity Yamāntaka**, in a contemporary painting by Luke Brown, with multiple eyes and a forebrain of crossed vajras, evokes the expanded vision and consciousness associated with the judicious, emancipatory use of mind-altering substances.

Below ***The Psychedelic Experience***: *A Manual based on the Tibetan Book of the Dead* provided the iconic lyrics for the Beatles' 1966 song 'Tomorrow Never Knows': 'Lay down all thoughts, surrender to the Void, it is shining, it is shining ... Love is all, and love is everyone, it is knowing, it is knowing.'

feet and eyes to achieve exceptional abilities. Various poisonous and hallucinogenic plants such as purple-flowered thorn apple (*Datura fastuosa*) and 'crazy Datura' (*unmattadhattūra*) were absorbed into the body as pastes or through the lungs in mind-altering fire ceremonies. Accounts of Datura can be found in numerous Buddhist Tantras. Highly toxic in comparison with other psychedelic substances, Datura has been widely used across cultures as a shamanic medicine associated with magical flight, although its value as a deliriant was mostly applied within Tantric Buddhism in rituals for rendering enemies powerless or insane. The 8th-century Cakrasaṃvara Tantra, for example, states that if one who is 'well-equipoised' immolates mustard seed oil, the wings of crows, and the name of one's intended victim in a fire of Datura, 'the person will immediately be driven away or die'.

States of consciousness elicited by hallucinogenic substances' interaction with serotonin receptors in the brain correspond with stages of the Bardo, the intermediate dimensions between living, dying, dreaming and rebirth. In describing how a distillate of Datura can be used in the eyes to heighten the visionary effects of Tögal practice, a Tibetan lama once stated that, 'If Powa, the Yoga of Transference, is Buddhahood without meditation, ingesting purified Datura is like experiencing the Bardo without having to die.' The simile was also apparent to Harvard psychology professors Timothy Leary, Ralph Metzner and Richard Alpert (Ram Dass) who, in 1964, published *The Psychedelic Experience: A Manual Based on the Tibetan Book of the Dead* as a guide to psychological death and rebirth in the context of 'mind-manifesting' experiences produced by LSD, mescaline and psilocybin mushrooms. As Ram Dass expressed it, 'When you extricate yourself from the solid identification with your body, you begin to have the spaciousness to allow for the possibility that death is a part of the process of life – rather than an end of life.' Consumption of such potent central nervous system stimulants within 21st-century Western Vajrayāna Buddhist communities indicates a nuanced approach to the use of psychoactive substances at negotiated boundaries between liberation and intoxication, as well as pharmacology and religion.

Tantric mahāsiddhas are customarily shown imbibing unspecified substances from human skull cups. On an outer level, such depictions indicate Vajrayāna Buddhism's co-evolution with Tantric Śaivism, as also indicated by the skull-piercing tridents common to both traditions. On an inner level, the hollow inverted cranium symbolizes the mind's intrinsic emptiness, freed from divisive thoughts and emotions. On a 'secret' level, the human skull cups are explained as brimming with ambrosial nectar, thus suggesting the release of endogenous mind-altering substances within the brain that are activated through Tantric Buddhist practices.

Entheopharmacology

The ritual use of Datura was not limited to the subjugation of external enemies, but was also applied to overcoming inhibiting mental states and gaining insight into the nature of reality. As expounded by Jamyang Khyentse Wangchuk (1524–68) in the context of the Sakya 'Path of Fruition' (*lamdré*), meditation on visionary phenomena produced by Datura establishes that, 'All phenomena of apparent existence, Saṃsāra and Nirvāṇa, do not exist outside of one's mind.' As a support for self-liberation in Dzogchen, the third Dodrup Chen Rinpoche (1865–1926) expounded cryptically on a method of imbibing a nectarous solution of Datura in order to activate the subtle body and attain 'excellent accomplishments'. Similarly, Padmasambhava is said to have plied Yeshe Tsogyal with a range of mind-altering substances in order to cultivate her ability to maintain clarity during expanded states of consciousness.

Vision inducing plants in Tibetan Buddhism are closely associated with the tradition of 'revealed treasures' (*terma*). A notable example occurs in a section of the 'Innermost Heart Essence of Vimalamitra', a compendium of Dzogchen pith instructions codified in the 11th and 12th century, which describes introducing a distillate of Datura into the eyes through the hollow quill of a vulture's feather in order to open the body's subtle energy channels and induce visions. An earlier noetic use of Datura is described in chapter twelve of the Mahākāla Tantra, which instructs practitioners to mix Datura and two other highly poisonous plants with honey and the bile of a black cat and to apply the resultant ointment to the eyes, after which 'one spins around and around like a bee', a simile later applied to the rising of *kuṇḍalinī.*

A 'nectar goddess' is shown hovering above a longevity elixir – indicted by the two black-legged cranes – in this detail from a contemporary wall painting in Gangteng Monastery in Bhutan. Mind-expanding substances used in Tantric Buddhism recall ancient Vedic rites in which propitiators of the fire-god Agni consumed a potent, psychoactive brew called soma, varyingly associated with cannabis (Tib. *somaradza*), *Ephedra sinica*, Syrian rue (*Peganum harmala*), the red and white-flecked fly agaric mushroom (*Amanita muscaria*), the sacred lotus (*Nelumbo nucifera*) and, most recently, with Psilocybin (*Stropharia cubensis*), based on clear depictions in an early first millennium BC textile panel discovered in 2009 in northern Mongolia.

A treasure text, or terma, entitled 'Luminous Web', attributed to Padmasambhava and revealed by the 18th-century adept Tertön Rigdzin Dorje Thokmé, describes 'five nectar-bestowing plants' ascribed with diverse physiological and psychic powers. As the text states, 'Whoever consumes the "excellent plant of miracles" will remain free of disease and attain miraculous powers. One's body will become youthful and capable of flying through the sky. Without abandoning the physical body, one can attain celestial realms ... Whoever eats the "plant of increasing bliss" experiences the inexhaustible union of bliss and emptiness ... Whoever partakes of the "plant of purification" dissolves all karmic obscurations and the eighty forms of habitual thought. They will recall countless past lives. Whoever eats the "plant that severs disturbing emotions" will never think of food or drink ... and meditative absorption will arise spontaneously.

The white bat lily (*Tacca integrifolia*) is used in traditional Asian medicine as both an aphrodisiac and a cure for cancer, but the plant also has esoteric applications as a psychoactive substance. Diverse plants at the interface of medicine and poison are used in yogic formulations for extending consciousness and activating subtle body processes.

These are the supreme plants of the realized adepts. Whoever consumes them will release all blockages of the inner energy channels and directly perceive the realms of the Buddhas.' Despite their overtly alluring qualities, the taxonomical descriptions of these five plants remain obscure, hindering positive identification. Nonetheless, traditional Tibetan and Bhutanese doctors have actively sought out the elusive, nectar-bearing plants in remote regions of the eastern Himalayas and used extracts of some of them during periods of meditative retreat.

Marijuana (*Cannabis sativa*) is a more readily accessible mind-altering plant in the Tibetan pharmacopeia and serves a magico-medicinal function in several major Buddhist Tantras. Its leaves and resin are included in 'perfect medicine' formulas of the Mahākāla Tantra, while the Cakrasaṃvara Tantra states that a mixture of compounds that include cannabis will help one to 'become a yogin who does what he pleases and can stay anywhere whatsoever.' The more obscure Tārā Tantra quotes the Buddha as saying that wine in absence of cannabis will not produce sufficient bliss to carry out the subtle energy yogas that the Tantra describes, an indirect acknowledgment of the brain's endogenous 'bliss molecule' anandamide, which binds to cannabinoid receptors.

Left **Dionysus, the primordial deity of divine intoxication**, as evoked on this 3rd-century gilded plate from India's northwest frontier, anticipates later images of Tantric mahāsiddhas; just as the earliest images of the Buddha derive from Greek depictions of philosopher sages. British Museum, London.

Opposite **Mahāsiddhas**, or 'realized adepts', were progenitors of Tibet's Tantric form of Buddhism. They are customarily depicted in states of ecstatic ease, representing freedom from social and emotional conditioning. Although these images from Pelkhor Chöde Monastery in Gyantse, Tibet, emphasize male adepts, some of the greatest mahāsiddhas were female. According to Tantric texts, the proffered skull cups contain the 'nectar of great bliss', referring to the cervical fluids that issue from a ḍākinī's 'secret place'. Such substances were mixed with water and alcohol ideally deriving from grapes.

༄། །སྨན་བླའི་དགོངས་རྒྱན་རྒྱུད་བཞིའི་གསལ་བྱེད་བཻ་ཌཱུར་སྔོན་པོ་ལས། མན་རྒྱུད་ལེའུ་དགུ་བཅུ་ཐམས་པ་གསོ་བའི་བཅུད་ལེན་ཆེན་པོ་དམིགས་སྐོར་དང་བཅས་པ་བཀོད་པའི་བྲིས་ཆ་སྟེང་གཉིས་པའོ།།

The alchemy of rejuvenation

The most prominent aspect of the Tibetan yoga of essences and elixirs is the tradition of Chulen, or 'essence extraction', which is used for purposes of rejuvenation, increasing vitality, extending the lifespan and enhancing meditative insight. Substances including plants, flowers, minerals and bodily fluids are compounded into empowering elixirs through the use of mantra and visualizations of Tantric deities such as Vajrayoginī and Amitāyus, the Buddha of Infinite Life. The rejuvenating substances are further enhanced when combined with specific dietary regimens, breathing practices and yogic exercises. Although nominally deriving from Indian traditions of Rasāyana, Chulen draws extensively from indigenous Tibetan medical culture as well as from Chinese Taoist practices of internal alchemy. The practice of Chulen is mentioned in the Four Medical Tantras (*Gyud Shi*) from the 11–12th century and was furthered by prominent Tertön, or 'treasure revealers', such as Ratna Lingpa (1403–79) and Tertön Pema Lingpa, who produced an influential treatise entitled 'Key to the Eight Principal Tantric Medicines'. Chulen remains a vital practice today, with prominent ingredients including the five-lobed tubers of the frog orchid (*Dactylorhiza viridis*), calcite and rock bitumen (*shilajit*). Accounts exist of past masters who subsisted entirely on pulverized stalagmites, while Milarepa is renowned for living for extended periods on a diet of stinging nettles. One of the more controversial components of many Chulen recipes is mercuric sulfide, derived from cinnabar. Although highly toxic in its crude state, mercury, once 'purified' through alchemical processes, is held by Tibetan medicine to be a powerful panacea. A mercury-based elixir called yogeshwar, 'lord of yoga', is prescribed within the tradition of the Caṇḍamahāroṣaṇa Tantra, the 'Fierce and Greatly Wrathful One', in order to enhance experiences of bliss and luminosity during sexual yoga. Yet, as with all ingredients used in Chulen, efficacy is held to derive as much from rituals of consecration as from the substances themselves.

One of the most esoteric practices within the Tibetan tradition of Chulen consists of ritually consuming human flesh, albeit in minute quantities. As attested in the Hevajra, Cakrasaṃvara and other Buddhist Tantras, 'flesh pills' compounded from the bodies of deceased Brahmin ascetics were reputedly ingested to eradicate subject–object duality, while reminding consumers of the transient nature of their own bodies. Although the specific ingredients are not specified, the life story of mahāsiddha Kṛṣṇācārya relates how, as soon as he put such ritually consecrated substances into his mouth, 'he was able to see the realms of the gods and the spirits of nature (*yaksha*) and could travel to those places in a flash if he so desired.'

Opposite **'The Greater Elixir of Rejuvenation'** is part of a series of 17th-century scroll paintings illustrating the Tibetan medical system. The central motif is a skull cup filled with potent substances for clearing energy channels, restoring vitality and conferring longevity. The Tantric deities that hover above the inverted bowl represent the transmuted essences of mind and body. Tibet's medical tradition drew from Indian, Chinese and indigenous Tibetan practices in formulating a system for optimizing human wellbeing. Studio of Romio Shrestha.

Below **A 1st-century Buddha figure**, from Gandhara made from zinc and solidified mercury and encircled by a cobra, recalls the Hindu god Śiva who engaged the 'serpent power' of *kuṇḍalinī* to consume a world-threatening poison and convert it into soma, the Vedic nectar of immortality. In non-dual Śaivism, the 'state of Śiva' is described as 'a luminous sea of subsiding waves.'

The inner essence

The ultimate elixirs invoked in Tibetan Buddhism are substances that flow from various glands within the human body during practices of yoga and meditation. These 'innermost essences' are more specifically male and female sexual secretions, possibly associated with related mood-elevating hormones such as dopamine, serotonin and oxytocin. The intensified flow of mind-altering neuro-chemicals resulting from yogic practice correlates with what Tantric texts describe as 'tasting the nectar' (*amṛtavādānam*). This inner experience is depicted symbolically in the transmission of Chulen by ḍākinī guardians who empower practitioners by pouring nectar into the interior of their bodies. A biography of Padmasambhava describes how he received the transmission of Chulen, or 'essence extraction', from a ḍākinī in a charnel ground. The text states that he then 'subsisted on wind and space, on five nectars and on sand,

Electrical activity in the brain correlates with levels of consciousness. The neural signature of high-amplitude gamma oscillations and increased functional connectivity seen among advanced meditators has also been observed in connection with the ritual use of psychedelic substances such as psilocybin. Science Photo Library, London.

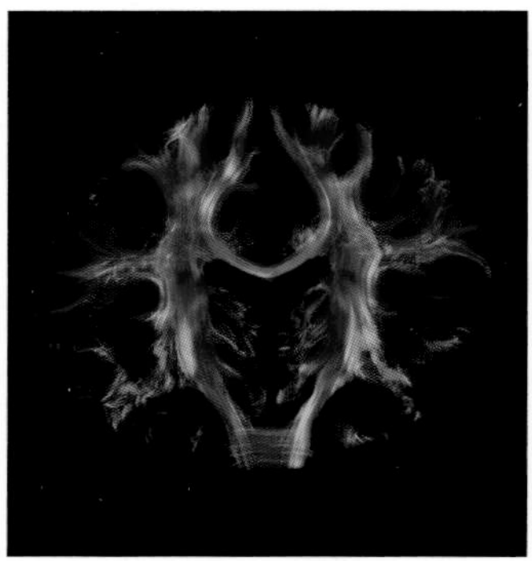

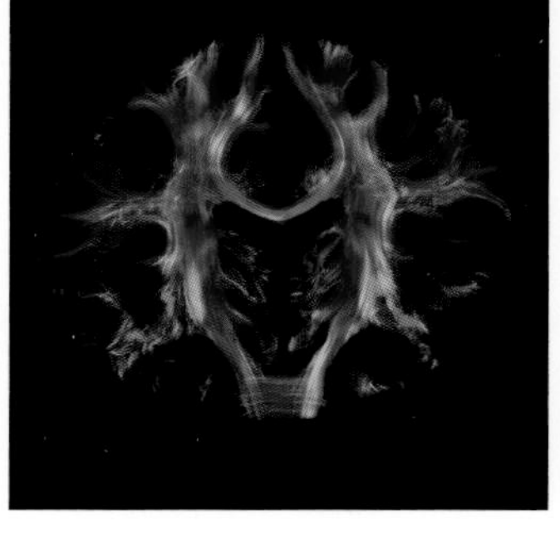

Right **A ḍākinī, or female embodiment of enlightenment**, pours an undisclosed elixir into the skull cup of mahāsiddha Kumaripa, signifying the awakening of intuitive wisdom. On an inner level, this image from a wall painting in the Lukhang temple represents the descent of nectar though the yogic body, possibly related to the release of psychoactive substances from the pineal gland during advanced forms of yogic practice.

Opposite left **A Harrapan-era bowl** depicts two extraterrestrial-looking beings raising elixir cups in a seeming toast. Buckingham Collection.

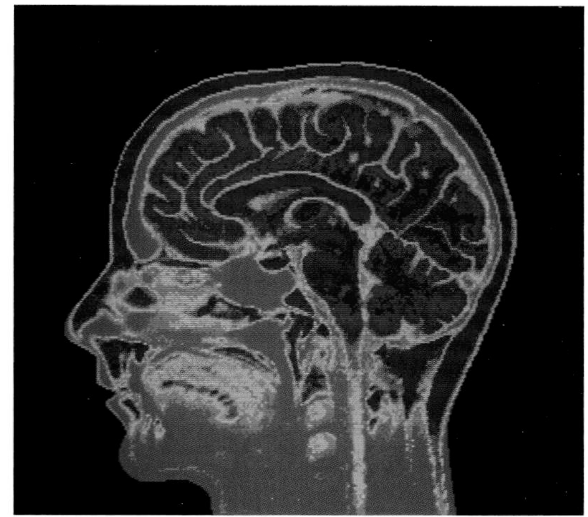

I once recited from the scriptures, 'Let there be success!'
But I drank the elixir and forgot the words.
There is now only one word that I know.
And that, my friend, is beyond all names.

Mahāsiddha Saraha, 'The Royal Song', 8th century

Above right **An MRI brain scan** reveals the ways in which unconstrained cognition, expanded awareness, and ego dissolution can be visually represented. But by privileging the brain, cranial imaging ignores the effects of contemplative practices on the equally involved neurons in heart tissue and the enteric nervous system of the viscera. Scientific research has shown that even single doses of psilocybin, the active ingredient in 'magic mushrooms', enhance brain connectivity and can lead to long term relief from depression, beyond that of placebo and patented pharmaceuticals. Science Photo Library, London.

as well as on various medicinal plants and poisons … He undertook austerities using shrubs, trees, and leaves, as well as lotus nectar [vaginal secretions] and the remaining five nectars [saliva, urine, menstrual blood, and feces] … He extracted the essence of rocks, flowers, fruit, horns, bones, and alcohol, and of an unimaginable number of other substances. As a result, he attained a deathless adamantine vajra body.' The vast array of transformative substances consumed by Padmasambhava represent the full spectrum of Chulen formulations that support inner awakening. Male and female sexual secretions remain core ingredients in the most potent forms of Chulen, such as *changsem kamar*, formulated from a dākinī's menstrual blood and a Bodhisattva's semen. There is also a specific form of Chulen for the Yoga of Inner Fire formulated from the deadly poison aconite, and one for sexual yoga made from Tibetan snow frogs. A Chulen recipe combining rock bitumen (*shilajit*), powdered nettle, wild ginseng and opium is named 'medicine horse' (*men ta*) because ingesting it reputedly transports one to any desired destination.

The secret alchemy

In *A History of Western Philosophy,* Bertrand Russell wrote that, 'In intoxication, physical or spiritual, the initiate recovers an intensity of feeling which prudence had destroyed; he finds the world full of delight and beauty, and his imagination is suddenly liberated from the prison of everyday preoccupations.' In the context of the Dionysian Mysteries, this exalted state resulted in 'enthusiasm'; literally the god (*theos*) entering and becoming one with the worshipper and, as such, evidence of a form of 'deity yoga' involving possession by the divine. Analogous rites in Tantric Buddhism include *gaṇacakra*, or 'gathering circles' involving sacramental feasts that formerly including substances and activities that were otherwise considered forbidden or taboo. Although contemporary Vajrayāna practice is generally less transgressive, the increasingly positive results of contemporary psychedelic research have led some practitioners to experiment with microdoses of psilocybin mushrooms and lysergic acid diethylamide (LSD) in the context of vision-based Dzogchen practices such as Lhundrup Tögal, 'leaping over the skull into spontaneous presence', and dark retreats. Other sacramental applications of psychedelics within contemporary Vajrayāna practice include the use of 5-MeO-N-Dimethyltryptamine, a naturally occurring psychedelic substance regarded as a powerful catalyst of ego dissolution and self-transcendent, empathic states of awareness. Although transient, the dimensions of consciousness revealed by another mind-expanding substance, MDMA, were described by Benedictine monk David Steindl-Rast as 'like climbing all day in the fog and then suddenly, briefly seeing the mountain peak for the first time. There are no shortcuts to the awakened attitude, and it takes daily work and effort. But the drug gives you a vision, a glimpse of what you are seeking.'

Above **The female adept Maṇibhadrā** is one of eighty-four canonized mahāsiddhas. Such realized adepts are often associated with magical flight, a sensation common to inebriation by *Amanita muscaria* mushrooms and Datura, the noetic use of which is described in several Buddhist Tantras. As stated in the Mahāmāyā Tantra: 'By consuming such substances one may see as many Buddhas as there are grains of sand in the Ganges River.'

Above **Great Perfection practices** based on illuminating mind and body are vividly depicted on the walls of Tibet's Lukhang temple. One yogi lies on his back and gazes at the rays of the sun to induce visions of rainbow-coloured light. The mural also displays an orange-petalled opium poppy (*Papaver somniferum*), the psychoactive, vision-producing alkaloids of which were widely known in Tibet. An 11th-century Tibetan Buddhist text refers to using a distillate of the highly psychoactive Datura plant to enhance the visions that unfold through Tögal practice.

Opposite **Tibetan adepts performing supranormal feats**, such as extracting nectar from solid rock and flying through the sky, recall the statement by Dr Albert Hoffman – the discoverer of LSD – that psychedelic, literally 'mind-manifesting', experiences 'can take us into the deepest depths or onto the highest heights, to the frontiers of which humankind is capable of experiencing.'

In 'manifesting the mind', psychedelic substances can free consciousness from limiting patterns of thought and engender new perspectives. But engaging those fluent depths without sufficient preparation can be more harrowing than enlightening. Psychedelic inebriation typically dissolves boundaries between the experiencing ego and the outer world, and can result in profound panic as well as ecstatic unity. While revealing the scientific truth, equally held by Buddhism, that what we perceive as an outer reality exists within our own consciousness, such potent substances are, like the legendary 'snow lion's milk' of Tibetan legend, best approached with judicious caution. Nonetheless, in a supportive context, they can enlarge the scope and capacity of the mind, while the numinous phenomena they invoke have led to their reclassification as entheogens, releasers of the god within. After years of experimentation with such substances, scientist Dr John Lilly observed that, 'What one believes to be true is true or becomes true, within certain limits to be found experientially and experimentally. These limits are further beliefs to be transcended. In the province of the mind there are no limits.' This was not advocacy for uninhibited forays into ecstatic states, but an insistence on open-minded and empathic scientific enquiry. It recalls the words attributed to Padmasambhava that, 'One's view may be as wide as the sky, but one's actions should be as as refined as grains of flour.'

ཕྱིག་ལེར་སྐུ་དང་ཞིང་
མས་དཔག་མེད་
ར་བ།
ཨོ། །རྗེ་ཞར་ཞར་ཀྱི
གཟིགས་སུ་ལྟ་བ།

Primal radiance

The yoga of innate perfection

The pith essence of the Great Perfection is to dwell in the natural radiance of all that occurs, at one with actions, energies, and thoughts and beyond all contrived boundaries of view and meditation; at ease in the naked clarity of the present moment.

Rigdzin Jigme Lingpa (18th century)

Unsurpassable yoga

Opposite **The view of Dzogchen** transcends conventional concepts of mindfulness and meditation by integrating Buddha Nature, or innate enlightenment, in all experience. This detail of a mural in the Lukhang temple shows a yogin gazing in the direction of the rising sun and 'leaping over the skull into spontaneous presence'.

Below **A circular mirror** is used in Dzogchen to point out the self-existing perfection of primordial awareness. As a mirror reflects whatever is placed in front of it, the mind's ultimate nature remains free of conditioning imprints while displaying infinite forms.

Dzogchen, the Great Perfection, is also known as Ati Yoga, or 'Ultimate Yoga'. Within Tibet's oldest school of Buddhism as well as in Bön, Dzogchen represents the culmination of the Creation Phase (Mahā Yoga) and the Completion Phase (Anu Yoga) of Vajrayāna Buddhism. Dzogchen differs from Vajrayāna as a whole in its presentation of Buddha Nature as an innately present wakefulness rather than an in-dwelling potential that needs to be deliberately cultivated in order to attain freedom from Saṃsāra, or conditioned existence. Dzogchen thus characteristically 'takes the end as the means' and dispenses with more gradual methods for realizing Buddhahood. Although practices based on the body's 'inner maṇḍala' of subtle energy channels are included in Dzogchen, such disciplines are traditionally viewed either as methods for removing psycho-physical obstacles or for intensifying realization of the mind's natural state of self-existing enlightenment. The intensely physical practices of Tsalung Trulkhor that developed in Tibet from the 11th century onwards also formed part of the Dzogchen Heart Essence transmission, but they were largely replaced by other physically and psychologically demanding practices that push body and mind towards a coalescent state of physical, psychological and spiritual illumination.

Dzogchen is presented in Tibetan Buddhism as 'beyond all mental concepts and free of both attachment and letting go; the essence of transcendent insight and the coalescence of meditation and non-meditation; perfected awareness free of all grasping.' While the unitary consciousness of Dzogchen can be directly realized without modifying the body or altering the mind in any way, its formal practice nonetheless traditionally begins with demanding physical exercises that culminate with held postures and associated breathing techniques that entrain consciousness towards an incisive realization of the primordial, self-perfected nature of enlightened awareness.

Preludes to perfection

Initiation in Dzogchen formally entails a lineage master pointing out the nature of *rigpa* (Skt. *vidyā*), the vivid, noetic condition of consciousness prior to thought and mentation, in an unelaborated ceremony called 'empowerment into the dynamic energy of awareness'. After receiving essential instructions, Dzogchen aspirants often undertake wilderness retreats to carry out a series of esoteric practices called Kordé Rushen that 'differentiate Saṃsāra from Nirvāṇa' until bounded consciousness and spontaneous self-liberating awareness arise indivisibly as 'one taste'. The practices of Kordé Rushen are divided sequentially into outer, inner, secret and 'ultrasecret' catagories.

In Outer Kordé Rushen, mind and body are pushed to unaccustomed extremes by acting out imaginary existences as animals, hell beings, demi-gods and whatever else the mind conceives, leading to the spontaneous recognition of the self-created, and thus mutable, nature of conditioned existence. When the capacity for physical and imaginative expression is exhausted, the practitioner enters a natural state of repose in a posture corresponding to an open-eyed 'corpse pose' (*śavāsana*) in Haṭha Yoga. The thought-free mental state is identified as the 'primordial purity' of the mind's essential and abiding nature in contrast with its transient and potentially deceptive expressions.

The physical exercises undertaken in Outer Kordé Rushen constitute a free-form version of Trulkhor, or 'magical movements' for deepening experience of the bodymind. The Tantra of Unimpeded Sound, the root text of Dzogchen's esoteric instruction cycle, counsels that one should 'perform the bodily yantras while twisting and turning and alternately while prone and moving. Stretch and bend the limbs and push the body beyond its accustomed limits. Physically act out the behavior of the six kinds of elemental beings.' A Dzogchen treatise entitled 'Flight of the Garuḍa' by Shabkar Tsokdruk Rangdrol instructs: 'With the conviction that Saṃsāra and Nirvāṇa are of one taste ... walk, sit, run and jump, talk and laugh, cry and sing. Alternately subdued and agitated, act like a mad person ... Beyond desire, be like a celestial eagle soaring through space ... free from the outset like bright clouds in the sky.' Rigdzin Jigme Lingpa reiterates in his 18th-century treatise 'Supreme Mastery of Wisdom Awareness' that one should 'run, jump, twist and turn, stretch and bend, and move your body in whatever way comes to mind, beyond purpose or design' and that, 'Finally you will be physically, energetically and mentally exhausted and thus totally relaxed.' Within this unbounded unitary sphere beyond the binary operations of

The 'outer' phase of Kordé Rushen, or 'distinguishing Saṃsāra from Nirvāṇa', recalls the creative and empowering dramatizations of psychic contents used in therapeutic modalities such as Psychodrama, defined by its founder Dr J. L. Monroe as 'the science that explores the truth by dramatic methods'.

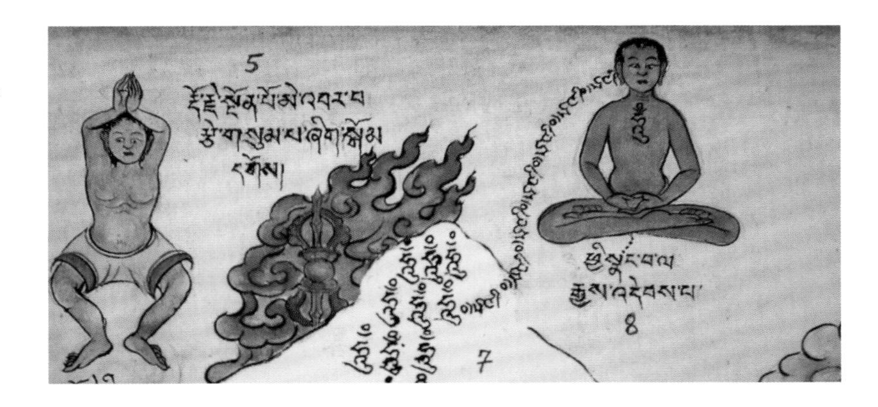

Right **A Bhutanese manuscript**, illustrating the 'Heart Essence of the Vast Expanse' (Longchen Nyingthik), depicts the 'secret' phase of Kordé Rushen in which the body, as shown at the left, is initially positioned in an isometric 'vajra posture' and the voice subsequently engaged in practices based on the seed-syllable *hūṃ*, as shown on the right.

thought, 'all spontaneous actions of body, speech and mind arise as the unity of Saṃsāra and Nirvāṇa, and thus as unobstructed Buddha-Body, Buddha-Speech and Buddha-Mind.'

As Jigme Lingpa clarifies, the exercises of Outer Kordé Rushen further engage the voice through 'chattering nonsensically or speaking in the tongues of imagined mythical beings'. Similarly, the mind is fully manifested by consciously invoking positive and negative thoughts that ultimately resolve into uncontrived, non-dual awareness. The subsequent Inner Kordé Rushen practices build on the cathartic dramatizations of Outer Kordé Rushen and focus proprioceptively on six seed-syllables along the body's central axis, associated with subconscious imprints of past actions. The practitioner clears each area in turn by visualizing white, red and blue light issuing from the antidotal seed-syllables, *oṃ*, *āḥ*, *hūṃ*, as consciousness shifts from identification with the body's materiality to direct experience of its energetic luminescent substratum (*nang sal*). As with Outer Kordé Rushen, sessions of practice alternate with motionless phases of concept-free awareness in which thoughts subside within the luminosity of primordial awareness, or *rigpa*.

Below **A Tibetan yogini** undertakes the practice of Outer Kordé Rushen at the sacred site of Gompo Né in Tibet's hiddenland of Pemakö.

Purifying the realms

In the practice of Inner Kordé Rushen, the seed-syllables *āḥ, su, nri, tri, pre* and *du* correlate with the forehead, throat, heart, navel, base of the trunk and soles of the feet which are energetically cleared with the radiant, all-encompassing mantra of body, speech and mind, *oṃ, āḥ, hūṃ*. Precise instructions for Kordé Rushen practices vary between different Dzogchen lineages. In some, the internal purification of the six lokas, or energetic realms of existence, is performed prior to the dramatizations of Outer Rushen. As with all aspects of Dzogchen, the key point is never technique but the end result: distinguishing the contents of consciousness from wakeful awareness and integrating that recognition of the mind's innermost, non-dual Buddha Nature within all experience.

Opposite **A Tibetan scroll painting** made from ground mineral pigments illustrates the ways in which phenomenal reality arises from psychoenergetic centres within the wisdom maṇḍala of the human body. Buddha figures emanate from sensory orifices, while erotically entangled Tantric deities radiate from the genitals, heart and the top of the head, multiplying into further forms. Surrounding the central figure are diverse psychological and existential states that can be transformed through yogic practice, as indicated by the Buddhas and Bön lineage teachers, who are depicted within each of the realms. Cosmic figure, 1900–59, Rubin Museum of Art, New York, C2002.30.1 (HAR 65194).

Right **A meditating yogin** on the walls of the Lukhang temple emanates spheres of light that signify the clarified essence of his psychophysical constituents, the basis of the Inner Kordé Rushen practice of 'purifying the six realms of existence'.

Transcending limits

Outer and Inner Kordé Rushen's clearing of physical and psychosomatic obstructions prepare the body and mind for the practices of Secret Rushen, which are divided into three progressive stages of Body, Voice and Mind. The Body phase begins with a highly strenuous isometric balancing posture – the 'posture of the vajra'. Standing with the heels together and the knees bent and stretched to the sides, the practitioner pulls his or her chin towards the larynx, straightens the spine, and places their palms together above the crown of the head while visualizing themself as an indestructible, blazing blue, vajra sceptre. Observing the flow of energy and sensation within the body, while pushing through barriers of exhaustion, pain and perceived futility, the practitioner maintains the position until his or her legs collapse and then continues in a modified posture while sitting on the ground until capable of resuming the standing position. At the end of the session one utters the seed-syllable *phaṭ* and lies down on the ground in a state of unconditional concept-free awareness 'like a corpse in a charnel ground'. When thoughts arise, one repeats the process in continuing cycles of effort and repose until the tenacious illusion of an abiding self yields to an all-pervasive, endorphin enriched awareness. As Jigme Lingpa explains in 'Supreme Mastery of Wisdom Awareness', 'exhausting the physical body exhausts the discursive tendencies of the mind' and leads ultimately to realization of one's innate, in-dwelling Buddha Nature.

The intensity of the Dzogchen vajra posture alters the flow of psychosomatic energies and encourages the emergence of adaptive mental and physical capacities as consciousness disengages from adventitious mental states and recovers its innate bliss, lucidity and non-conceptual awareness. Secret Kordé Rushen then continues with Voice practices of sound and vibration based on visualizations and intonations of the seed-syllable *hūṃ* to enter into direct experience of the pure potentiality, or 'emptiness' which underlies perception and both signifies and expresses the ultimate nature of mind and body.

The vajra posture is illustrated on the walls of the Lukhang temple, Tibet, in connection with the first of three phases of Secret Kordé Rushen. Pushing the body beyond perceived limits activates latent capacities of the mind. On an outer level, the vajra posture embodies the Dzogchen view of finding ease in extremity: one holds the position until one no longer can, and then rests until one can resume it; urging mind and body beyond perceived limitations.

Opposite **The vajra posture** relates to the biological phenomenon of hormesis, whereby deliberate exposure to therapeutic stress potentiates beneficial mental and physiological effects, such as increased strength, resilience, growth and longevity.

Dissolving appearances

Below **The Secret Rushen of the Voice** involves a series of meditative exercises using the mantric syllable *hūṃ* to alter reality's expression. As illustrated in these instructional vignettes, practitioners intone *hūṃ* to overlay consensual appearances with phonic symbols of the mind's ultimate nature of luminosity. The yogin at the right sends out blue, luminescent *hūṃs* to whatever appears in his field of perception, such as trees, houses and bridges, and dissolves them into radiant light.

In the Voice phase of Secret Rushen, the practitioner visualizes and intones blue seed-syllable *hūṃs* that imaginatively encompass the entire universe. The vibrating syllables then fill one's body and propel it imaginatively through space. The conjured *hūṃs* function like razors, lacerating outer appearances and, when turned inwards, all traces of one's physical self. At the end of the session one lies down, as at the conclusion of the Body phase, and remains in vivid open presence. When thoughts arise, one begins the practice anew, using the primal energy represented by the seed-syllable *hūṃ* to alter habitual perceptions and attachment to consensually appearing forms. By dissolving all appearances into effulgent light, the practitioner remains in luminous cognition, beyond conventional conceptions of time and space and unconditioned by external appearances or events.

Left **A folio from a Dzogchen manual** illustrates sequential practices of body, voice and mind connected with the 'secret' phase of 'distinguishing Saṃsāra from Nirvāṇa'.

Opposite, below left **One Voice practices** of Secret Rushen involves imaginatively winding and unwinding a chain of *hūṃs* around a stick so as to expand the mind's cognitive and perceptual capacities. Royal Danish Library, Copenhagen.

Below **Mantric syllables,** such as *hūṃ*, are often carved into rocks, as shown in this photograph of the glacial lake of Yilung Lhatso in eastern Tibet where a yogin sits in meditation. The Voice practice of Secret Rushen also integrates breath and visualization to reveal the luminous substrate of both mind and perceived reality.

The world we see is a painting
Born from the brush of discursive thought.
Within or upon it nothing truly existent can be found.
Knowing this one knows reality;
Seeing this one sees what is true.

Gedun Gyatso, the Second Dalai Lama, 16th century

Divine laughter

Secret Rushen culminates in ludic emulation of a wrathfully laughing Tantric deity, expressive of the mind and body's resolute freedom from confining limitations. The practitioner's hands form horned *mudrās* as she extends her limbs and consciousness to embrace pure possibility. As the grand finale of Secret Rushen, such daemonic laughter reveals the essential role of play in transcending limiting conceptions of reality.

Since everything is but an apparition
Perfect in being what it is,
Having nothing to do with good or bad,
Acceptance or rejection,
One might as well burst out laughing!

Longchen Rabjampa Drimé Özer, 14th century

The culminating 'ultrasecret' phase of Kordé Rushen dynamically unifies Body, Voice and Mind 'in order to free what has been stabilized'. In a dramatically embodied enactment of the Deity Yoga associated with Vajrayāna's Creative Phase, the practitioner manifests as a rampant Tantric deity, representing the creative mutability of sensation, thought and emotion. As Dzogchen texts and oral tradition prescribe, the practitioner stands with hands formed into horned *mudrās* while pivoting from left to right on heels rooted in the earth. With eyes rolling in the sky, one emits loud thought-subduing laughter from the core of one's being, filling all of space with the syllables, sounds and vibrations of *ha* and *hi*. As in all of the Kordé Rushen practices that proceed Dzogchen's more widely known and practised contemplative techniques of Kadak Trekchö, 'cutting through to primordial purity', and Lhündrup Tögal, 'leaping over the skull into spontaneous presence', the body is used to its fullest capacity to facilitate lucid, all-pervading awareness and altruistic freedom within all experience. However, as the great 14th-century Dzogchen master Longchenpa cautioned, no ultimate release can be obtained through contrived, conceptually-driven actions: 'If we aspire to the ultimate state we should cast aside all childish games that fetter and exhaust body, speech and mind … and realize the uncontrived unity inherent in every experience.' Nonetheless, as indicated by Longchenpa's remark on the opposite page concerning liberating laughter, non-dual mirth and cachinnation can serve spiritual functions that recall the essential role of play and humour in authentic religious life. The loss of appreciation of make-believe in adult life is prefigured in the loss of the original meaning of the English word 'silly', which in its earliest iteration 'sely' once meant 'holy'. Within the yoga tradition, foremost yoga teacher B. K. S. Iyengar, spoke of laughter and good humour as his most essential practice.

Above **A tigerskin-skirted Tantric deity** with a brimming skull cup embodies fundamental dynamics of mind and body at the heart of Dzogchen. Primordial noetic awareness (*rigpa*) arises vibrantly in response to physiology and perception pushed beyond their accustomed limits. As Dzogchen's source text, 'The All-Creative King' (Kunjé Gyalpo) states, 'Primordial enlightenment is self-existing; it does not need to be sought … Realize the perfect meaning that does not exist as words.' Ogyen Choling Manor.

Right **A Tantric initiation card** showing a dancing, animal-headed emanation of the intermediate dimension of the Bardo recalls what the Tantra of Unimpeded Sound calls the unbound 'self-radiance beyond all distinctions of Saṃsāra and Nirvāṇa'. Private collection.

Primordial purity

The ultimate purpose of physically enacted practices in Dzogchen is to harmonize the body's psychosomatic 'winds' so that the non-dual nature of awareness can directly manifest through the Dzogchen Heart Essence contemplative techniques of Kadak Trekchö and Lhündrup Tögal which, in essence, substitute for and supercede the Creation and Completion Phases fundamental to Vajrayāna Buddhist practice. After completing the cycles of Kordé Rushen, the practitioner relaxes into naturalness, savouring the continuity of body, breath and mind within all experience. In place of Mahāyāna Buddhism's emphasis on 'emptiness', Dzogchen presents the ultimate nature of reality as Kadak, or 'primordial purity' which while empty of essence is pervaded by luminous wakefulness and thus more accurately evokes the experiental state of Great Perfection.

Posture, breathing and positioning of the eyes all assist in making primordial purity fully conscious though Dzogchen's signature meditation practices of Kadak Trekchö, 'cutting through [mental activity] to primordial purity' and Lhündrup Tögal, 'leaping over the skull into spontaneous presence'. Although both practices equally unveil the non-dual nature of mind and reality, Trekchö emphasizes the 'empty' aspect of awareness while Tögal focuses on ephemeral appearances, just as waves and particles are distinguished in physics depending on how the same phenomenon are observed.

The Himalayan peak of Machapuchare, in morning mist, evokes the Dzogchen adage that thoughts and emotions are like transcient clouds that never alter the fundamental space in which they arise and dissolve. Dzogchen is sometimes referred to as Sky Yoga, in reference to merging awareness with the unbound outer, inner and secret sky of one's ultimate nature.

Trekchö, which literally means 'cutting through', fuses the concentrated attention of mindfulness-based meditation with the circumferential clarity of open presence, resulting in the 'great perfection' of non-dual noetic awareness. Trekchö is often described as transcending the bounds of what is normally considered meditation. Nor can Trekchö be accurately characterized as contemplation as non-dual awareness holds no object.

In distinction to the nasal breathing favoured in most forms of meditation, Trekchö practice typically involves extended and almost imperceptible exhalations through the mouth, with the lips and teeth slightly parted and the body maintained in alert repose. In the visionary practice of Tögal, exhalation and inhalation are naturally suspended as in the Haṭha Yoga technique of *kevala kumbhaka* in which both breathing and mentation are spontaneously stilled. Breathing in this way diminishes the amount of oxygen circulating in the lungs and is held to free consciousness from its conditioned 'karmic winds' so as to more effectively reveal the postulated 'wisdom wind' at the heart, through which consciousness is held to ultimately transcend the physical body.

Posture in Dzogchen practice often begins with the 'sevenfold position of Vairocana' in which the legs are enfolded like a lotus, the hands held in a gesture of equanimity, the spine straightened like a wishfulfilling tree, the eyes lowered towards the tip of the nose, the tongue touching the upper palette, the shoulders open like the wings of a vulture, and the neck drawn back 'like a perfect horse'. But prescribed postures shift in Tögal practice so as to open subtle energy channels that connect the eyes and the heart, thus entraining awareness towards naturally arising visionary states of consciousness. A core Dzogchen meditation instruction is to maintain the body like a mountain, the eyes like the ocean, and the mind like the sky.

'Sky breathing' involves blending the mind with space as inner and outer air merge as a single continuum. The 17th-century Dzogchen master Tsele Natsok Rangdröl stated that for ultimate realization of the nature of mind, 'you must mingle every moment of walking, sitting, eating, lying down and thinking with meditation. It is therefore not necessary to always maintain a specific posture or gaze.'

Leaping over the skull

In an extension of the Heart Sūtra axiom that 'form is emptiness and emptiness no other than form', Dzogchen presents experience as Primordial Purity inseparable from Spontaneous Presence. While the practice of Trekchö dissolves form into emptiness, Dzogchen's visionary method of Lhündrup Tögal – literally 'leaping over the skull into spontaneous presence' – focuses on the phenomenology of noumenal perception. The combined approach, 'like two wings of a bird', reveals the non-duality of emptiness and appearance.

Dzogchen actualizes the primordial unity of form and emptiness through meditation on the seed-syllable *āḥ*, the first vowel in the Sanskrit alphabet. Signifying the primary, alpha state of consciousness, contemplation of the mantric phoneme *āḥ* is also foundational to Shingon, a form of Vajrayāna Buddhism that was brought from China to Japan in 806 AD by the polymath adept Kūkai, also known as Kōbō-Daishi. In Dzogchen, *āḥ*'s noetic resonance entrains the mind to a naturally present if normally subconscious dimension of 'sound, light, and rays'. The Dzogchen practice of Tögal, or 'leaping over the skull', represents a form of integral perception that inverts the foundational Haṭha Yoga technique of sensory withdrawal (*pratyāhāra*) in which sense consciousness is turned resolutely inward. In the practice of Tögal, sensory awareness is instead extended outwards, 'leaping over' the conventional divisions of inner and outer to unite experientially with a field of self-manifesting visions that derive initially from phosphenes and related phenomena that arise within the eye in conjunction with specific secondary conditions.

Dzogchen's signature technique of 'leaping over the skull into a spontaneous state of perfection' builds on contemplation of the seed-syllable *āḥ*, which appears in the upper right corner of this mural detail from the Lukhang temple, Tibet. Whereas Trekchö, or 'cutting through', is associated with the emptiness and wisdom aspects of the mind, Tögal is associated with appearance and skilfull means. In Trekchö, fixated mental activity is severed so as to abide in a non-dual state of presence. In Tögal, awareness is integrated with spontaneously appearing visions that reveal the seamless totality of inner and outer reality.

The visions of Tögal develop through the application of 'key points' of posture, breath, and awareness. In distinction to the kinetic yogas of Tsalung Trulkhor, Tögal practice is performed while maintaining 'threefold motionlessness of body, eyes and consciousness'. 'Garland of Pearls', an 11th-century Dzogchen Tantra, emphasizes the importance of three body positions described as 'the postures of lion, elephant, and sage', corresponding to the Dharmakāya, Sambhogakāya and Nirmāṇakāya, and, by association, with emptiness, clarity and sensation. The Dzogchen master Rigdzin Jigme Lingpa points out in 'Supreme Mastery of Wisdom Awareness' that there are many other additional postures suitable for Tögal, but that 'for the innumerable heirs of Tantra who prefer simplicity, the three described here are sufficient.'

Above **The primary Tögal postures of lion, elephant and sage** are illustrated on the western mural of the Lukhang temple, Tibet. The seed-syllable *āḥ* in a rainbow-encircled sphere symbolizes the mind's primordially empty 'alpha' state and its natural disposition of manifestation. As a Buddhist Sūtra proclaims: 'The empty essence of this *āḥ* is itself the luminous nature of mind; it utterly transcends all limitations such as the permanence of being concrete or the discontinuance of being inconcrete.' The Vedic text *Aitareya Aranyaka* also mentions *āḥ* as the essence of all speech and identical to Brahman, or the creative principle of ultimate reality.

Right **The Tibetan *naljorma* Ani Rigsang** demonstrates a meditation posture used in Dzogchen to open channels of awareness within the yogic body. Tögal practice combines quiescent body postures, subtle breathing techniques, and focused gazes to activate the self-existing enlightenment that is held to be the ultimate nature of mind and body. Ideologically, the practice culminates at the time of death in the transfiguration of the physical body into radiant, all-pervading light.

Illuminating body, voice and mind

Trulkhor and Kordé Rushen are based on the principle that somatic states – from fluent postures to spontaneous movements – can influence cognition and alter not only the contents of consciousness but its fundamental expression. The three specified body postures and associated breathing techniques used for 'leaping over the skull' recalibrate visual perception and alter subjective representations of reality towards more inclusive and expanded states of awareness.

In the Dharmakāya posture of a seated lion, a variant of which is pictured below, practitioners hold their torso upright to allow energy to flow freely, with the soles of the feet placed together and the hands behind the heels in vajra fists, with the tips of the thumbs touching the base of the ring fingers. The upper body is extended upwards with the chin tucked slightly inwards to suppress discursive thought and the spine and back of the neck are straightened so as to allow allow vital energy to pervade the cranial arteries and associated 'light channels' connecting the heart and eyes. With the breath extended outwards through gently parted teeth and lips and the abdomen pulled slightly inwards, the eyes are rolled inwards and upwards past an imagined protuberance at the crown of the head into the limitless expanse of inner and outer sky.

In the Sambhogakāya posture of a recumbent elephant, the knees are drawn towards the chest to increase metabolic heat, with the feet pointing backwards and the elbows placed on the ground with the hands either positioned in front

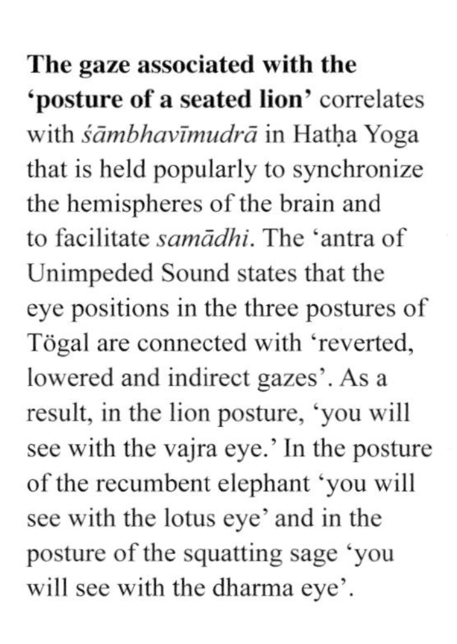

The gaze associated with the 'posture of a seated lion' correlates with *śāmbhavīmudrā* in Haṭha Yoga that is held popularly to synchronize the hemispheres of the brain and to facilitate *samādhi*. The 'antra of Unimpeded Sound states that the eye positions in the three postures of Tögal are connected with 'reverted, lowered and indirect gazes'. As a result, in the lion posture, 'you will see with the vajra eye.' In the posture of the recumbent elephant 'you will see with the lotus eye' and in the posture of the squatting sage 'you will see with the dharma eye'.

Below **The Tögal 'posture of a sage'** is similar to the 'six-sided stove posture' used in the Yoga of Inner Fire that involves pulling the knees against the chest to increase metabolic heat in the pelvic cavity. In the posture of a sage, the practitioner sits with uncrossed legs and normally adopts a slightly downwards gaze. In this instance, the yogini raises her eyes to the sky as in the posture of a seated lion.

Below right **The 'posture of a recumbant elephant'**, as demonstrated by a yogini in Bhutan, brings body, mind and respiration into a revitalized functional unity while entraining consciousness towards the pure perfect presence that, whether perceived or not, is held to be the mind's ever-present innermost nature.

as vajra fists or supporting the chin to inhibit coarse energy flow as the spine elongates and the eyes gaze with soft focus to the sides and ahead into visions that reflect the recursive activity of conscious perception.

In the Nirmāṇakāya posture of a sage (*ṛṣi*), one sits upright to open the channels and release the diaphragm, with the soles of the feet on the ground to suppress the water element, one's knees and ankles together, and the arms crossed in front with elbows resting on the knees, and the hands optionally tucked into the arm pits. As Jigme Lingpa clarifies in 'Supreme Mastery of Wisdom Awareness' (Tri Yeshé Lama), 'pulling the knees against the chest allows fire energy to blaze as luminous awareness. Slightly retracting the lower abdomen towards the spine inhibits discursive thought [presumably through the associated stimulation of the vagus nerve and parasympathetic nervous system] while ... placing the elbows on the knees with the hands in vajra fists and using them to support the throat equalizes heat and cold.' In the sage posture the gaze is normally directed slightly downwards through half-closed eyes to control the body's vital energies and still the mind, although the practitioner pictured below gazes upwards, as in the posture of the seated lion.

Rigdzin Jigme Lingpa further points out that there are many additional postures suitable for Tögal, but that 'for the innumerable heirs of Tantra who prefer simplicity, the three described here are sufficient'.

The three primary Tögal postures serve as gates for the body, voice and mind to enter into theophonic states. Jigme Lingpa points out in 'Supreme Mastery of Wisdom Awareness' that the sublime visions of Tögal bear

comparison with the 'empty forms' that arise as visual manifestations of consciousness during the practice of sense withdrawal in Kālacakra. Similarly, the Kālacakra Tantra refers to 'garlands of essences', which appear when gazing into the sky. The fact that the Kālacakra Tantra and the Seventeen Dzogchen Tantras seminal to Dzogchen's esoteric 'instruction cycle' both appeared in written form in the 11th century suggests that later Dzogchen doctrines may have been directly influenced by the Kālacakra's elucidation of visual forms that are neither wholly subjective nor wholly objective. As represented in the manuscript folio shown on this page, entoptic forms within the eye initially appear as abstract geometrical shapes that gradually transfigure into Buddhas, vajras and Tantric deities. In Dzogchen, such forms are understood as 'non-dual' appearances that illuminate the process of perception itself. By engaging such imagery in active contemplation, practitioners pass through four phases of self-illumination that culminate ideologically in the attainment of a 'rainbow body', a term originally used in the 7th-century Mahāvairocana Tantra to refer to an illusory light body that travels to Buddhist pure realms during the clear light of sleep.

Below **A folio from a Tögal manuscript** depicts visionary phenomena that arise when prescribed body postures are combined with subtle breathing and fixed gazes. The abstract geometrical shapes reflect the mind's essential nature as a seamless continuum of perceiver, perceived and the act of perception that culminates in an illuminated body of light. Royal Danish Library, Copenhagen.

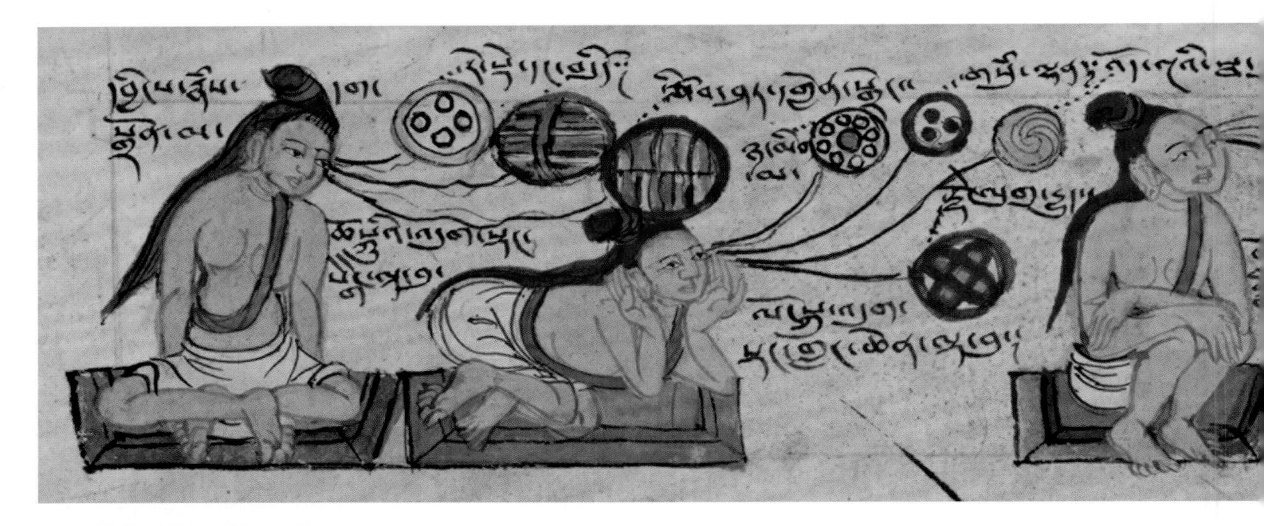

Opposite bottom left **Samantabhadra Buddha**, the 'All Good', symbolizes the self-existing enlightenment that is the base, path and fruition of Dzogchen and the primordial essence of human consciousness. Private collection.

Right **The postures of lion, elephant and sage** appear as line drawings in a Tibetan Dzogchen manual from eastern Tibet. Applying the postures, breathing techniques and gazes of Tögal alters habitual patterns of perception and leads to a series of visions that are described as spontaneous expressions of self-existing enlightened awareness.

The Tögal posture of a seated lion supports reflexive awareness of a unitary dimension transcendent of ordinary experience. The yogi merges his consciousness with the sky in self-illuminating non-dual cognition. As stated in an 8th-century Bön text entitled 'The Six Lamps', 'The basis of everything is like the clear light of the sky, the wisdom of awareness is like the quintessence of the sun, and the manifestations of mind are like the sun's luminescent rays.'

The anatomy of light

Tögal gazing techniques differ from the well-known Haṭha Yoga practice of *trāṭaka* in which a practitioner stares unblinkingly at an external object. In Tögal, the adept turns attention to an intermediate dimension of perception that is based initially on visual phenomena within the eye. Visions arise in conjunction with specific gazes and on the basis of posited 'channels of light' within the body, through which the heart centre's innate luminescence is perceived outwardly in progressively self-illuminating visions. In a chapter of the Khandro Nyingthik entitled 'The Hidden Oral Instruction of the Ḍākinī', Padmasambhava declares: 'Other teachings differentiate between channels, energy and subtle essences; [in the 'heart essence' teachings] these three are indivisible.' Padmasambhava goes on to describe the human body as a Buddha Field infused by luminescent wisdom in the same way that 'oil [pervades] a sesame seed'. Oral instructions in Dzogchen further clarify how, in the practice of Tögal, the body's elemental constituents manifest as five lights and four illuminating lamps representing purified and expanded expressions of Buddhahood. Through the specific postures, breathing methods and gazing techniques of Tögal, the body's inner luminescence projects outwards into the field of vision as spontaneously forming optical maṇḍalas and optic yantras inseparable from innate enlightenment. As Padmasambhava summarizes: 'The nature of one's body is radiant light.' Rising from the heart is the 'great golden *kati* channel' through which the five lights of one's essential nature radiate outwards as five-fold wisdom and four successive visions leading ultimately to the body's transfiguration at the time of death into rainbow-coloured light.

Dwell undistractedly in the mind's innate luminosity.
Your own mind, unadulterated, is the ultimate body of enlightenment ...
When you don't grasp at appearances,
all that arises is spontaneously free ...
In the great equanimity of the infinite expanse of reality,
There is nothing to cling to or reject, no meditation or non-meditation.

Mahāsiddha Niguma, 11th century

A yogin in the posture of a sage, depicted on a mural in Tibet's Lukhang temple, contemplates the 'vajra chain' which manifests here as a backlit 'string of pearls'. The visionary practices of Tögal are performed with the support of sunlight as well as total darkness. The apparitional forms are recognized as spontaneously arising manifestations of pure awareness. They gradually evolve into complex maṇḍalas and ultimately dissolve into imageless clear light.

Opposite **A contemporary painting** by Rolf Kluenter evokes the essence of both space and embodied experience, in the form of an ultimately dimensionless circular blue sphere, or *bindu* representing consciousness's encounter with infinitude.

Right **A yogini in Bhutan** uses a meditation belt for support as she merges her mind with the 'outer, inner and secret sky' of her ultimate nature.

Below **Yogins on the wall of the Lukhang temple** integrate their awareness with spontaneously arising visions that include fan-shaped rainbow lights, grid patterns, gossamer strings, peacock feathers and a disembodied eye.

Natural radiance

Just as Dzogchen essentializes Tantric physiology into a network of psychosomatic light, the creative visualization fundamental to Vajrayāna's Creation Phase is recast in Dzogchen as incisive attention to an intermediary dimension of perception, which arises in synchrony with naturally occurring enoptic phenomena within the eye. The visionary experiences are said to arise due to an interior 'luminescent wind' connected with the pristine 'awareness wind' located within the heart. As the 15th-century treasure revealer Tertön Pema Lingpa points out in his 'Secret Key to the Channels and Winds', the visions are physiologically based and they occur because of bodily practices, 'just as the limbs of a snake become apparent only when it is squeezed.'

The naturally arising visions of Tögal are held to reflect the channels, winds and vital essences of the human body in their subtler expression as primordial purity, spontaneous presence and radiant compassion. These three qualities are also aspects of Buddha Nature, or intrinsic enlightenment. The visions of Tögal are thus held to reflect the luminescent self-awareness of reality itself, as experienced by 'leaping over the skull' into the conscious coalescence of perceiver, perceived, and the act of perception that is reality's natural, undivided state. In less noumenal terms, the visions of Tögal reflect electrical signals within the visual cortex that are projected as images into the external field of vision. But the ontological and psychological correlates of the visions definitively transcend the bounds of optical science.

Opposite **Tögal visions** gradually encompass the 'three bodies' of Dharmakāya, Sambhogakāya and Nirmāṇakāya, referring, in Dzogchen, to Buddha Nature's inconceivable totality, luminous clarity and spontaneous creativity. The images shown here are from the Lukhang murals and display visionary phenomena ranging from seed-syllables, grids and elemental maṇḍalas to a fully manifest Buddha in a sphere of light.

A Tibetan yogini uses the support of sunrays in a window to illuminate an intermediary dimension of perception. As a practice of recursive vision and integral presence, Tögal can be considered a form of *sāmarasya* – the simultaneous practice of *dhāraṇā* (focused concentration), *dhyāna* (contemplative meditation) and *samādhi* (conscious absorption) – associated with self-transcendent identification with spontaneously arising noumenal forms. From a Dzogchen perspective, the unfolding visions are considered an autonomous perceptual process reflective of the non-duality of subtle physiology and awareness and leading to liberation from conditioned perception and cognition.

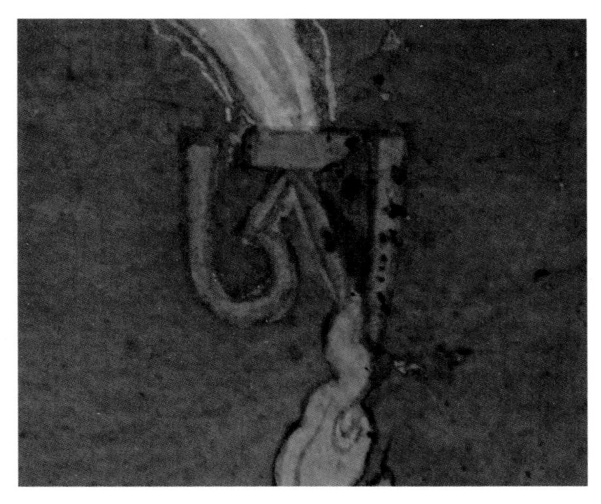

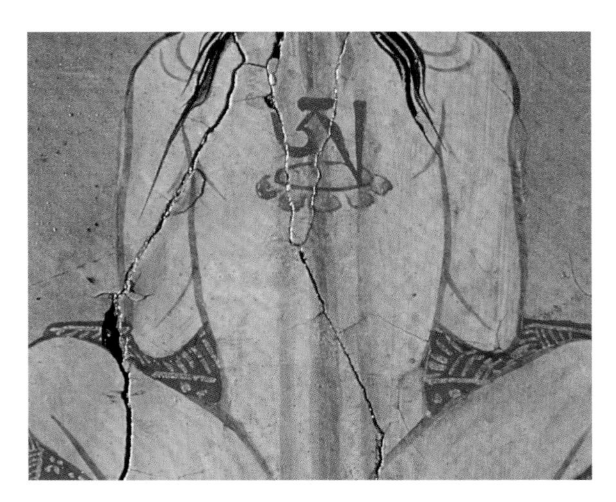

The initial visionary appearances associated with Tögal practice are vividly described by the Dzogchen master Dudjom Lingpa (1835–1904) in his 'mind treasure' entitled 'The Vajra Essence: A Tantra on the Self-Originating Nature of Existence': 'At the beginning stage, the lights of awareness, called vajra-strands, no broader than a hair's width, radiant like the sheen of gold, appear to move to and fro, never at rest, like hairs moving in the breeze ... Then as you become more accustomed to the practice, they appear like strung pearls, and they slowly circle around the peripheries of the *bindus* of the absolute nature, like bees circling flowers. Their clear and lustrous appearance is an indication of the efflorence of awareness. Their fine, wavy shapes indicate liberation based on the channels, and their moving to and fro indicates liberation based on the vital energies.'

Dudjom Lingpa clarifies that, as a result of continued practice, the visions gradually stabilize and 'appear in the forms of lattices and half-lattices, transparent like crystal, radiant like gold, and like necklaces of medium-sized strung crystals.' Once the beginner's phase has passed, Dudjom Lingpa continues, 'the visions of the absolute nature become beautiful, clear, and stable, and take on various divine forms.' As described in oral tradition and in early Dzogchen texts such as the 11th-century Vima Nyingthik, if the visions do not arise naturally they can be induced with psychotropic decoctions of Datura, boiled in goat's milk, the final

distillate to be introduced directly into the eyes using the hollow quill of a vulture's feather.

The visions of Tögal can be compared with blue field entoptic phenomena identified in 1924 by the German ophthalmologist Richard Scheerer and described as the appearance of bright dots flowing along wave-like lines in the visual field when looking into bright blue light, such as the sky. Ophthalmologically, the dots appear as a result of leukocytes, or white blood cells, flowing through the macular, retinal capillaries of the eyes in synchrony with the cardiac cycle between the beginning of one heartbeat and the onset of the next. In a convergence of science and traditional accounts, the luminous orbs that appear before one's eyes are manifestations of the cellular structure of one's own blood, or 'heart essence'. The blue field entoptic phenomena are distinct from other entoptic phenomena such as 'floaters' (*muscae volitantes*) that result from debris floating on the eye's vitreous humour. In the context of Tögal, subjective entoptic phenomena and associated hypnogogic imagery serve as affective entry points into liberative non-dual states of consciousness.

Opposite above **The human retina** is referred to in Dzogchen as the 'all-encompassing watery eye lamp'. An extension of the optic nerve, the retina consists of photosensitive cells that translate light energy into nervous impulses. Tögal visions derive in part from optical phenomena such as myodesopsia, the perception within the eye of gossamer like 'floaters', and subjective appearances of translucent orbs due to white blood cells transiting through retinal capillaries.

Opposite below left **The maṇḍala of the 'Five Buddha Families'** that manifests in Tögal visions is analogous to the naturalistic phenomena of 'Haidinger's brush', which can appear in the visual field due to the circular geometry of foveal cones within the retina and the eye's response to polarized light.

Below left and opposite below right **Tögal visions** are said to originate in the heart, as illustrated in a privately owned 14th-century meditation manual. The visions appear most readily when gazing into a deep blue sky, as also practised among Aborigines in Australia where elders retire to the mountains to merge their consciousness with the infinitude of the sky.

Below right **The human brain** mediates perception through the visual cortex. As the poet Emily Dickinson wrote: 'The brain is wider than the sky, / For, put them side by side,/ The one the other will include/ With ease, and you beside.' Science Photo Library, London.

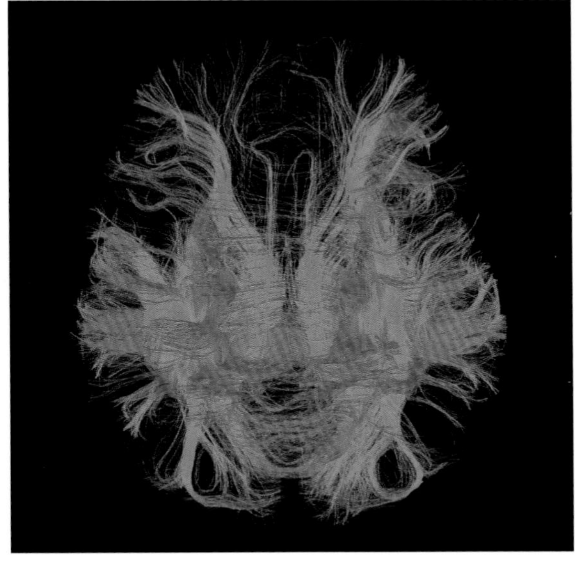

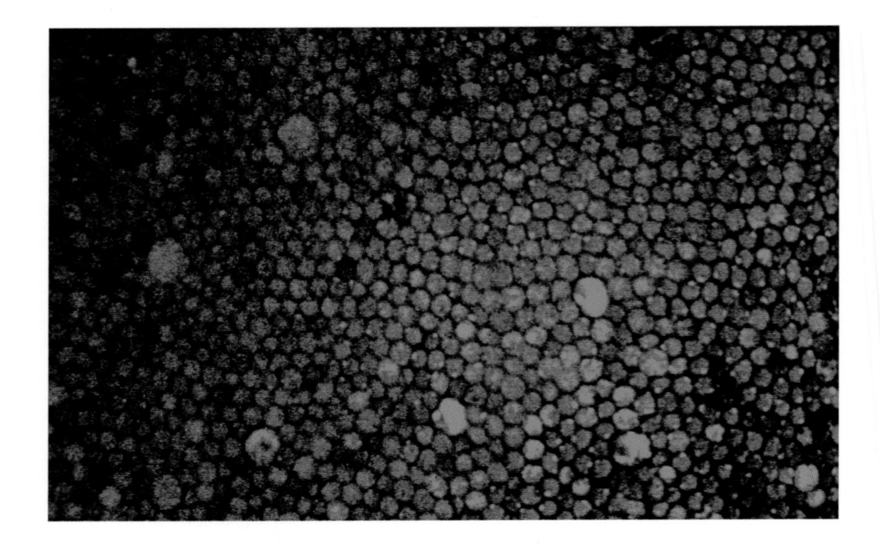

Photoreceptors in the eye, known as rods and cones, line the retina and communicate with the brain through the optic nerve. Mentally imagined imagery activates the same areas of the brain as visual perception and can profoundly influence neural processes and functions, as well as thoughts and emotions. Hightened states of perception, such as are associated with Tögal practice and maṇḍala visualization, may lead to expanded cognition, in which internally generated visual imagery can be projected eidetically so as to 'co-create' reality. Research further suggests that conscious awareness alters as a result of structural modifications of the anterior cingulate in the brain that occur as a consequence of interoceptive perception, or the supraliminal perception of autonomic physiological processes – the hallmark of 'leaping over the skull.' Science Photo Library, London.

Right **Tögal is often practised in total darkness**. The absence of external light quickens the appearance of visionary phenomena, which neuroscience describes as being based on phosphenes that originate within the eye and brain, either spontaneously through prolonged visual deprivation or intentionally as a result of direct stimulation of the retinal ganglion cells. Inwardly experienced luminosity in Tögal practice may also correlate with elevated levels of neurotransmitters such as oxytocin, an endorphin-based hormone produced in the hypothalamus and secreted from the posterior lobe of the pituitary gland.

Ecstatic perception

The combination of physical postures, breathing techniques and gazes in the practice of Tögal are said to lead to four progressive visions of the 'natural state' of existence, parallelling stages of manifestation and dissolution in near-death and posited postmortem experiences. The Four Visions integral to Tögal practice occur sequentially and are said to arise from the heart as visible manifestations of the innate dynamism of primordial awareness. The four successive phases are described as the Direct Perception of the Ultimate Nature, the Vision of Increasing Experience, the Perfection of Intrinsic Awareness and the Dissolution [of Phenomena] into the Ultimate Nature.

The first vision arises as a result of turning one's attention to naturally occurring phenomena within the 'watery lamp' of the eye, as described above by Dudjom Lingpa (see page 268). Although the garlands of pearls, gossamer threads, adamantine chains and transiting orbs that initially appear within one's field of vision may have naturalistic explanations as eye 'floaters' and magnified red and white blood cells transiting through retinal capillaries, the entoptic events nonetheless focus awareness towards normally overlooked phenomenological processes and illuminate the ways in which a shift in perspective, or change in the way one views things, can fundamentally alter subjective experience. Central to this process is what Rigdzin Jigme Lingpa clarifies as 'inner spaciousness shining visibly outwards' within a coalescent awareness in which boundaries between internal and external phenomena naturally dissolve.

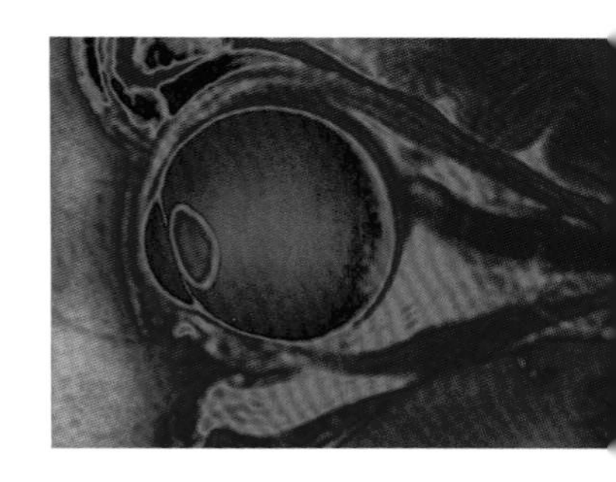

Right **A magnetic resonance image of the human eye** reveals the complex neurophysiology of vision in which photoreceptor cells interface with the primary visual cortex to produce images that reflect both external and internal visual input. Visionary forms of meditation such as Tögal bring conscious attention to subliminal perceptual events that are normally below the threshold of conscious awareness. Science Photo Library, London.

The visions of the heart's innate radiance gradually develop as shape-shifting phosphenes and optical symmetries that manifest ultimately as synergetic male and female Buddhas within spheres of rainbow-coloured light. Penultimately, the visions resolve into four illuminated spheres expressing the photonic essence of the four primary elemental processes within the human body. A larger orb that encompasses the four spheres signifies 'space', or boundless potentiality. The central circle dilates through steady foveal gaze, expanding beyond circumference or periphery as a sign of the luminescent wake-fulness of innate awareness. Practised in environments of total darkness and expansive light, the visionary methods of Tögal transcend ordinary sensory perception and lead ultimately to the posited awakening of all-encompassing luminescent and spontaneously compassionate awareness, or Buddha Mind.

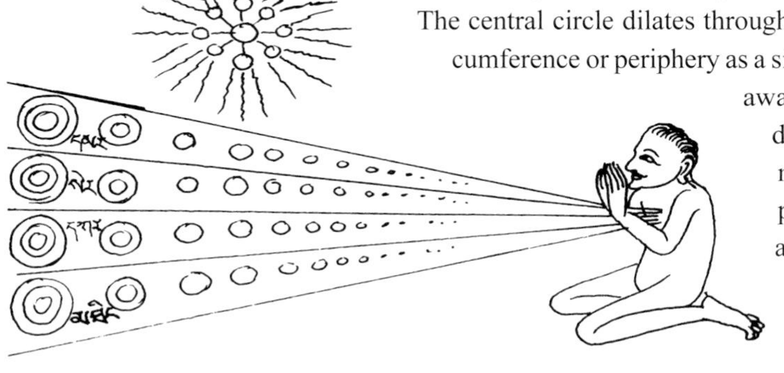

Below **A Tibetan line drawing** from a treatise on Dzogchen indicates that the visions of Tögal are held to ultimately arise from the heart, rather than the eyes or brain.

Yogas of darkness and light

When you look at mind,
there is nothing to be seen.
In this very not seeing,
you see the definitive meaning.

Machig Labdron, 11th century

Above **A yogin sits in a curtained chamber** with circular mirrors and peacock feathers placed on window ledges at each of the four sides. As indicated by the accompanying mural inscription, sunrays reflecting off the mirrors give rise to optical phenomena such as grids and strings of lights that the practitioner uses as a basis for 'leaping over the skull into spontaneous presence'.

Meditating in darkness, often for months on end, is a signature aspect of Dzogchen training and rapidly accelerates the unfolding of visions. As Lopön Tenzin Namdak explains, 'By remaining in darkness, we discover the radiance of the natural state. If we take that as the basis of practice, we will quickly attain Buddhahood. The wisdom eye opens and we will be able to see everything in the three worlds.' Prolonged exposure to total darkness stimulates endogenous production of the vision-inducing neurochemical Dimenthyltryptamine (DMT) and is thus associated with dreamlike phenomena during the waking state as well as modes of perception independent of the optic nerve.

Below **A yogini in a cave** gazes alternately into sunrays and empty space so as integrate her awareness with spontaneously manifesting luminous appearances in a state of non-dual open presence.

Right **Meditation caves in Lubrak, Nepal,** are traditionally used for *muntri*, or 'dark retreat' in which practitioners seal themselves in total darkness in order to awaken to the inner light of their self-transcendent Buddha Nature. As the 11th-century adept Padampa Sangye advised, 'In meditation beyond thought and without distraction, abandon the watcher.'

Integral presence

The word *haṭhayoga* first appears in the Guhyasamāja Tantra where it serves as an adjunct practice for facilitating visionary experience. Although the specific method of that initial Haṭha Yoga technique remains obscure, its stated optical intention relates it with the recursive visionary practices of Tögal.

As with Indian Haṭha Yoga, the somatic practices of Vajrayāna Buddhism use dynamic means to harmonize polarized modes of consciousness through the symbolic medium of the body's central energetic channel, or *madhyanāḍi*. In Dzogchen, body-based yoga evolves into a reorientation of physiological and attentional processes and an awakening of the heart's posited potential as an organ of recursive perception. By directing attention to what is commonly overlooked the mind becomes increasingly aware of normally subconscious processes and thereby develops insight, clarity and adaptability, which contribute to an openness of being and expanded experience of human embodiment. Yoga in Vajrayāna and Dzogchen ultimately transcends its cultural context and points towards the awakening of collective human capacities. Forceful Haṭha Yoga-like practices ultimately matter less in the optimization of the human condition than the integral consciousness represented by 'leaping over the skull'.

As a deeply embodied form of yoga, Tögal recalibrates physiological processes through changing the way they are perceived, leading to creative synergy within all experience. The liberating reorientation of consciousness at the heart of Tögal is expressed concisely in the Tantra of the All-Creative

Right **The Dzogchen posture of the soaring garuda** opens subtle energy channels within the body so as to reveal the self-existing, innately pure and expanded consciousness that is inseparable from enlightenment.

Opposite above **Dance in Tantric Buddhism** takes various forms, from the iconography of deities to choreographed monastic displays. As a yogic practice, Tantric dance expresses emotion through posture, gesture, facial expression, and attire. As mahāsiddha Nāropā stated, 'The human emotions are the great wisdom ... they are the yogin's allies.'

King, one of Dzogchen's earliest texts: 'With no need of transformation or purification, pure presence [within the body] is perfected in itself.' Rigdzin Jigme Lingpa reaffirmed this view in the 18th century by stating that, 'The pith essence of the Great Perfection is to dwell in the natural radiance of all that occurs, at one with actions, energies, and thoughts and beyond all contrived boundaries of view and meditation; at ease in the naked clarity of the present moment.'

Beyond the tradition of Vajrayāna Buddhism, the 18th-century poet William Blake, who first introduced the influential phrase 'doors of perception', expressed the essence of the self-transcendent and liberating vision of Tögal in a resonant line in his poem 'The Mental Traveller'. As Blake evocatively wrote: 'The Eye altering alters all.' Applying that perceptual meme to the persistent illusion of an 'I' and awakening to transpersonal dimensions of consciousness absent of cognitive and emotional strife lies at heart of Tibetan yoga, a process that involves altering ('making other') our embodied experience and, in so doing, promoting alternate forms of awareness that transcend perennially limiting perspectives and preoccupations. The fruition of Tibetan yoga, and by extension life itself, is thus the unveiling of the pure ecstatic presence that sees through the eyes of the heart into a world that is forever renewed by our synergetic perceptions and interactions.

Left **Mahāsiddha Karnapa and his consort** dance in intimate union. In Tantra and Dzogchen, powerful emotions become portals into pure awareness united with presence and compassion. Dzogchen and Mahāmudra are related to Sahajiya, which literally means 'born together' and signifies the co-creative nature of reality and human experience. Like Dzogchen, Sahajiya is also described as a 'state of non-dual unity free of existence and non-existence', the implicit meaning of Śūnyatā, or emptiness. Realized adepts of all denominations composed spontaneous ecstatic songs to express their insight, joy and compassion.

A Newar Cārya dancer merges with her chosen diety (*ishtadevata*), signifying transcendence of catagories and divisions, so as to realize enlightenment in all experience. In Tantric Buddhist yoga, the psychophysical aggregates of the body – form, sensation, perception, mental formation, and consciousness – are revered as 'self-illuminating lamps' that reveal that all that exists are moments of consciousness without substance or duration, subject or object, birth or death.

The yogin must always sing and dance.

Hevajra Tantra, 8th century

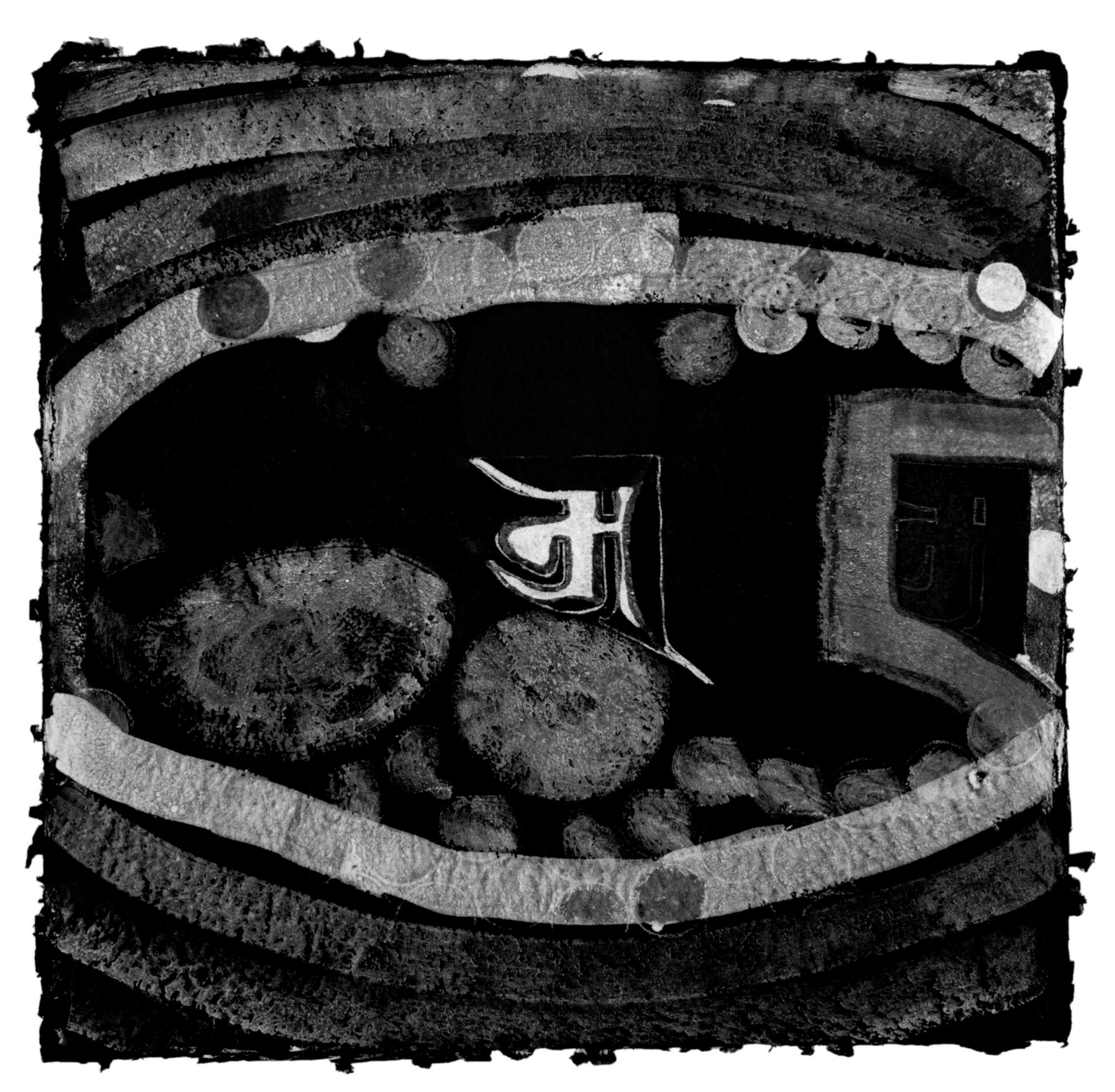

Above **The primordial seed-syllable *āḥ*,** in 'perfected' Siddhaṃ script, manifests within the eye of space as the radiant source of all apparent form and emptiness; *āḥ* symbolizes the primordial state of pure being, the ultimate nature of the mind, the indivisibility of syllable and sound, and the unity of emptiness and appearance.

Overleaf **A yogin in an uncurtained meditation chamber** gazes at grids and rainbow lights that reveal the mind and body's essential nature as radiant, all-pervading luminosity. As the Dzogchen master Padampa Sangye proclaimed, 'Pure awareness is without fixation, like a rainbow in the sky.'

From any of the four times and ten directions
the perfect Buddha will not be found.
Mind, in its essence, is the perfect Buddha.
Do not search for the Buddha elsewhere.

Guhyagarbha Tantra, 'Womb of Secrets', 8th century

Afterword

Tibetan yoga in the West

Until recently, Tibet's geographical isolation meant that only small amounts of information about its culture reached Europe. Its seclusion lent the country an aura of mystery and magic. For this reason, Tibet offered itself as a screen upon which Western fantasies could be projected.

Dagyab Kyabgön Rinpoche, 'Buddhism in the West and the Image of Tibet', *2001*

Like the Six Yogas that the mahāsiddha Tilopā transmitted to Nāropā on the banks of the Ganges River nearly a thousand years ago, the core techniques of Haṭha Yoga forgo external ritual and present innate psycho-physiological processes as the most effective means of existential liberation. The Amṛtasiddhi Tantra, 'Perfection of Immortal Nectar', which developed at the intersection of Vajrayāna Buddhism and Śaivism at the end of the first millennium AD is widely upheld as the first Indic text to describe physical methods for directing psychoenergetic currents (*nādi*) at the core of the body towards the realization of a divine state of being that 'is made of everything, composed of all elements, and always dwelling in omniscience'. Translated into Tibetan in the 12th century as Düdtsidrupa, the Amṛtasiddhi explicitly states that its integral practice of dynamic yoga poses, expansive breathing, and ambrosial visualization ensures 'liberation while living' (*jīvanmukti*) and is recommended to all, without preconditions and irrespective of social context or religious affiliation.

A dancing ḍākinī with a treasure vase appears on a mural on the outer wall of Tibet's Lukhang temple. Ḍākinīs symbolize the numinous potentiality within every moment. Like the depictions of angels by poet Rainer Maria Rilke, they 'break you open, out of who you are.'

Although the Tibetan practice of Tsalung Trulkhor, or 'magical movements of channels and winds', shares a common etiology with Vajrayāna-based Haṭha Yoga, the secrecy with which Trulkhor has traditionally been transmitted is at odds with the productive openness in which physical postures, breathing practices and meditation have been taught within Haṭha Yoga, including its currently recognized source text, the Amṛtasiddhi. Whereas unrestricted access in Haṭha Yoga led directly to Haṭha Yoga's globalization, institutionalized constraints within Tibetan Buddhism have progressively marginalized Vajrayāna's most dynamic psychophysical practices. In the 12th century, the Tibetan master Drakpa Gyaltsen (1147–1216) composed 'Yogic Exercises of Thirty-Two Actions', connected with the Hevajra Tantra, in which he indicated that the bodily manoeuvres (*yantra*) remove obstacles to spiritual realization and 'are suitable for beginners as well as for advanced students'. Monastic institutions have nonetheless remained constitutionally wary of Trulkhor, as the energies

Mahāsiddha Jālandhara, the 'Net Holder', demonstrates the fluidity and flexibility of being that is integral to the practice of Tantric yoga. Jālandhara renounced his former life to meditate in a charnel ground, where a ḍākinī initiated him into the Hevajra Tantra. As the Hevajra Tantra states; 'When joy arises let the yogin dance with full attention . . . for the liberation of all beings'. Scroll painting. Gyandrak Monastery, Tibet.

that deeply embodied Tantric practices awaken are not always consonant with monastic ways of life. As Dzogchen Ponlop Rinpoche explains, 'the Tantric path is meant primarily for lay practitioners . . . Of course we can be monastic yogis, but in many ways these methods are more suitable for lay practitioners, lay yogis and yoginis.' This view is explicit in the Buddhist Tantras themselves which typically begin with a king, such as Indrabhūti, beseeching the Buddha to reveal a method of liberation that does not entail renouncing the world and encompasses socio-political responsibilities as well as life's transient delights.

Many of the issues that currently vex Vajrayāna Buddhism in the West stem from the discordance of embodied Tantric practices with monastic orientations, and subsequent institutional concerns with 'secrecy'. Such historical preoccupations also led to textual reinterpretations that sought to reconcile challenging imperatives in the Buddhist Tantras with monastic codes of conduct. The ritual substitutions that have proliferated within Vajrayāna Buddhism, although well intended, have often caused confusion within Tantric Buddhist communities through implicit institutional support for virtual over visceral experience.

In the 8th century, the renowned mahāsiddha Saraha proclaimed in ecstatic verse that, 'I have visited many shrines and temples, but none are as joyous as my own body.' Saraha's song clearly indicates Tantric Buddhism's exaltation of embodied experience and the mahāsiddhas' wariness of institutionalized religion. Although Tantric disciplines promoted by the mahāsiddhas were held to reveal enlightenment in every moment, the conjugal rites and existential dispensation of the Buddhist Tantras were clearly not viable for anyone bound by monastic regulations. Because of this institutional dissonance, Tantric practices such as the Haṭha Yoga-like disciplines of Tsalung Trulkhor continue to be transmitted with caution and equivocation.

In contrast with the historic reticence in teaching Completion Phase Tantric practices such as Tsalung Trulkhor, the once equally hidden Great Perfection teachings of Dzogchen have been transmitted by contemporary Tibetan masters such as the late Tulku Urgyen Rinpoche and Chögyal Namkhai Norbu as liberating introductions to the fluent, spontaneously adaptive, heart-centered awareness that is the innermost nature of human consciousness and the essence of the Vajrayāna teachings. The physical practices that ground and empower Dzogchen's 'pure and perfect presence' – as explored in the final chapter of this book – have nonetheless remained largely concealed within conventions of secrecy. This situation has recently begun to change, in part due to demands by Western disciples for more embodied practices and the simultaneous ubiquity and tangible benefits of Haṭha Yoga and Qi Gong.

The convergence of Haṭha Yoga and Vajrayāna Buddhism in the West arguably began with Theos Bernard, the self-proclaimed 'white lama' who travelled to Tibet in 1936 at the invitation of the Tibetan government. Although the American anthropologist Walter Evans-Wentz had authored four

The Tibetan yogi Milarepa eschewed institutional religion: 'Let others go to monasteries to light lamps', he sang; 'I will stay here and light the butter lamp in my heart.' 18th-century Tibetan scroll painting, Rubin Museum of Art, New York.

seminal works on Vajrayāna Buddhism for Oxford University Press, including a 1927 translation of the Bardo Thödel entitled *The Tibetan Book of the Dead* and a translation of Tibetan treatises on the Six Yogas of Nāropā in 1935 entitled *Tibetan Yoga and Secret Doctrines,* Theos Bernard actively promoted Tibetan yoga through the American Institute of Yoga, which he established in 1939. A Tibetan hermit had reputedly presented Bernard with an illustrated Trulkhor manuscript, with line drawings of its characteristic sequenced movements performed while retaining and controlling the breath. Bernard's writings and radio interviews in the United States established a firm link between the physical culture of Haṭha Yoga and the Vajrayāna Buddhism of Tibet, but his premature death in a riot in India in 1947 delayed the transmission of physically based Tibetan yoga in Europe and North America by several decades.

Western interest and awareness of Tibetan Buddhism escalated during the 1960s, resulting in influential publications such as the 1964 adaptation of *The Tibetan Book of the Dead* by former Harvard professors Timothy Leary, Ralph Metzner and Richard Alpert as a guide to psychedelic experience. Tantric Buddhism's popular import into Western society has been problematic, however, as attested by widely publicized altercations within Western Buddhist institutions. Many idealistic Western Buddhists have been dismayed as anachronistic Tibetan power structures collide with 21st-century ideologies of equality, transparency and disclosure. The end result is that the Vajrayāna Buddhism evident in the colourful, if antinomian lives of the Tantric mahāsiddhas is transforming in response to the increasingly restrictive social values and egalitarian ideals of the early 21st century. Sex between teachers and students is deemed inherently abusive, even though consensual union was originally central to Vajrayāna Buddhist empowerments. Many teachers, such as Dzongsar Khyentse Rinpoche, have debated whether Vajrayāna Buddhism's existential commitment to critically questioning the nature of experience can survive within categorical prohibitions against non-normative behaviour. In this regard, he advised Western students to investigate root texts such as the Vajracheddikā and Hevajra Tantra to determine whether or not one actually feels constitutionally suited for the Vajrayāna path, as 'other forms of Buddhist practice may be less physically, emotionally and intellectually demanding.'

Top **A Bhutanese yogi** – his identity concealed behind a mask of Milarepa – demonstrates the vigorous practice of Trulkhor which was vital to Milarepa's success in Tummo, the yoga of inner fire.

Above **Ani Rigsang**, a yogini in Terdrom, Tibet, spent nine years in solitary retreat perfecting the inner yogas of the Nyingma and Drigung Kagyu traditions. Her red and white Tantric shawl symbolizes the dynamic polarity of male and female energies within the yogic body.

Others concern themselves with the demands of *samaya* (Tib. *damsig*), the existential commitments intrinsic to Tantric initiation. Yet as Chökyi Nima Rinpoche has clarified, 'all the hundreds of thousands of *samayas*' are maintained by experiencing 'the actuality that all sights, sound and awareness are visible emptiness, audible emptiness and aware emptiness.' A thousand years earlier, Mahāsiddha Tilopā stated the matter pithily in his 'Song of Mahāmudrā': 'The real vow of *samaya* is broken by thinking in terms of precepts, and it is maintained with the cessation of fixed ideas. Let thoughts rise and subside like ocean waves. If you neither dwell, perceive, nor stray from the ultimate meaning, the Tantric precepts are automatically upheld, like a lamp which illuminates darkness.'

Despite such clarifying statements, Vajrayāna in the West has often succumbed to archaic notions of unquestioning submission to a spiritual preceptor, rather than to the wisdom and compassion that a particular teacher may or may not embody. Many suspect that a more vital form of Western Vajrayāna, and thus of Tantric yoga, may emerge from Vajrayāna's productive convergence with contemplative neuroscience. One of the first initiatives in this regard was Dr Herbert Benson's 1982 study of Tibetan practitioners of Tummo, or 'fierce heat', the foundational practice of Vajrayāna's Completion Phase. More recent studies among female Tummo practitioners at Gebchak Nunnery in eastern Tibet have shown that regulating the breath with mental focus productively stimulates the sympathetic nervous system, leading to enhanced bodymind synchronization and cognitive abilities.

Tantric Yoga is not reducible, however, to neurobiological coordinates or to physical and psychological resilience, as it cannot be separated from the integral vision of human flourishing from which it arose. In this respect, the existential coalescence of Saṃsāra and Nirvāṇa that is Vajrayāna's distinguishing characteristic is furthered as much by poetry and aesthetics as it is by science. The life-enhancing ethos of Tibetan yoga is vividly expressed in Tantric Buddhist art, in which revered adepts such as Padmasambhava, the 'second Buddha', supersede mundane human limits and illuminate the world with Dionysian self-abandonment. Similarly, the Amṛtasiddhi Tantra is originally associated with the Tantric deity Chinnamastā, 'she whose head has been cut off'. The vivid iconography of the headless goddess assaults all instincts for self-preservation while empowering self-transformation. Yet, as many past and present masters caution, the vitalizing path of Tantric yoga is not for the faint of heart. It may, after all, be as Chögyam Trungpa once famously warned: 'like licking honey from a razor blade', a nourishing if fundamentally dangerous pursuit that nonetheless expands the parameters of human possibility and, at its best, frees both oneself and others from self-limiting attitudes and beliefs.

Acknowledgments

Semo Saraswati is the daughter and lineage holder of the legendary Dzogchen master Chatral Sangye Dorje Rinpoche. She is also the granddaughter of Tertön Tulshuk Lingpa and the recognized reincarnation of the female treasure revealer Sera Khandro Dewa Dorje, one of Chatral Rinpoche's principal preceptors of Tantric yoga and Dzogchen. She is pictured here in the hiddenland of Beyul Yolmo, in 1987.

This book draws on decades of immersion and research within the Tantric Buddhist tradition, as well as from the scholarly insights of innumerable individuals. I am particularly grateful to Chatral Sangye Dorje Rinpoche for his personal guidance on the path of Dzogchen and his example of compassionate presence in every moment. I would also like to acknowledge the individual instruction that I have received from Dudjom Jigdral Yeshe Dorje, Kyabjé Dungse Thinley Norbu, Bhakha Tulku Pema Tenzin, Tulku Urgyen, Dilgo Khyentse Rinpoche, Chögyal Namkhai Norbu and many other great Tibetan and Bhutanese teachers. Any errors of understanding and interpretation that appear in the book are solely my own.

For the contemporary artwork that appears in this book, I am primarily indebted to Rolf Kluenter, whose numinous paintings on handmade Himalayan paper invoke Tantric yoga in visual form. I am also grateful for the visionary artwork provided by Robert Powell, Alex Grey and Luke Brown. I am also very thankful to the Beijing Palace Museum, the Royal Danish Library, Copenhagen, the Rubin Museum of Art, New York, the Newark Museum of Art, New Jersey, the Metropolitan Museum of Art, New York, the Musée Guimet, Paris, the British Museum, London, the Wellcome Collection, London, and several private collectors for historical artworks featured in the book.

For support in Bhutan, I am particularly grateful to Dasho Karma Ura and other staff at the Centre for Bhutan Studies & GNH Research, Dzongsar Khyentse Rinpoche, Gangteng Tulku Rinpoche, Karma Lhatrul Rinpoche, Tulku Tenzin Rabgye, Lama Tashi Tenzin, Amchi Sherab Tenzin, Naljorma Tseyang Ösel, Ashi Kunzang Choden, Tshering Tashi, Kuenga Wangmo, Dechen Choden, Pema Yuden, Namgay Zam, Tshetem Norbu and Laxmi Sherpa. I am also highly indebted to Ani Rigsang, Pasang Lhamo and Semo Saraswati.

Others who have contributed to this book in notable ways include the Dowager Countess Angelika Cawdor, Alak Zenkar Rinpoche, Hon Wai Wai, Tanika Pook Panyarachun, Jeff Watt, David Salmon, Maya Klat, David Christensen, Ruth Garde, James Peto, Durga Martin, Ampinee Suwunsawet, Sanya Tugwun, Lana Oh, Shiang Ying Chan, Somananda, Joshua Kinney, Susan Richardson, David Pritzker, Megan Frasheski, Naldjor, Meghan Lambert, Imma Ramos, Joseph Wagner, Hamid Sardar, Elena Antonova, William Bushell, Eli Jellenc, Robert Parenteau, Thomas Laird, Dr James Mallinson, Dr Mark Singleton, David Verdesi, Dr Nida Chenagtsang, Laurent Solomon, Naljor Jinpa, Laurence Brahm, Jiayi Li, Akarpa Lobsang Rinpoche and Lama Lar Short.

Lastly I would like to thank all those at Thames & Hudson whose patience and persistence made this book a reality, namely Jamie Camplin, Sophy Thompson, Johanna Neurath, Ilona de Nemethy Sanigar and Karolina Prymaka.

Notes and resources

The opening chapter of this book 'Outer, inner, secret' provides an overview of Tibet's Vajrayāna, or Tantric form of Buddhism. Further readings on this subject include *Religions of Tibet in Practice*, edited by Donald S. Lopez Jr. (Princeton University Press, 1997), Geoffrey Samuel's *Origins of Yoga and Tantra: Indic Religions to the Thirteenth Century* (Cambridge University Press, 2008), John H. Crook's and James Low's *The Yogins of Ladakh: A Pilgrimage Among the Hermits of the Buddhist Himalayas* (Motilal Banarsidass, [1997], 2007), Matthew Kapstein's *The Tibetans* (Blackwell Publishing, 2006), Ronald Davidson's *Indian Esoteric Buddhism: A Social History of the Tantric Movement* (Columbia University Press, 2002) and *Tibetan Renaissance: Tantric Buddhism in the Rebirth of Tibetan Culture* (Columbia University Press, 2005), Christian K. Wedemeyer's *Making Sense of Tantric Buddhism: History, Semiology, and Transgression in the Indian Traditions* (Columbia University Press, 2013) and Miranda Shaw's *Passionate Enlightenment: Women in Tantric Buddhism* (Princeton University Press, 1994). With regard to yogic practice in Tibetan Buddhism, Tsangnyön Heruka's *The Life of Milarepa*, translated by Andrew Quintman (Penguin Books, 2010) provides a valuable starting point, while Glenn Mullin's *The Six Yogas of Naropa* (Snow Lion Publications, [1996] 2005) and *The Practice of the Six Yogas of Naropa* (Snow Lion Publications, [1997] 2006) offer important historical overviews. Keith Dowman's *Masters of Mahamudra: Songs and Histories of the Eighty-Four Buddhist Siddhas* (State University of New York Press, 1985), Sarah Harding's *Niguma: Lady of Illusion* (Snow Lion Press, 2011) and *The Roots of Tantra*, edited by Katherine Anne Harper and Robert L. Brown (State University of New York Press, 2002) illuminate the original ethos, poetics and non-monastic practice of the Buddhist Tantras. Further elucidations of the yoga of pilgrimage can be found in Ian A. Baker's *The Heart of the World: A Journey to Tibet's Lost Paradise* (Penguin Press, 2004) and in Toni Huber's *The Holy Land Reborn: Pilgrimage and the Tibetan Reinvention of Buddhist India* (University of Chicago Press, 2008). The chapter 'Elemental wisdom' offers an overview of Buddhist meditation with its culmination in the non-referential, open presence of Dzogchen. Incisive contemporary accounts of Buddhist meditation can be found in David L. McMahan's and Erik Braun's edited volume *Meditation, Buddhism, and Science* (Oxford University Press, 2017). The chapter 'Immaculate perception' outlines the Tantric Buddhist Creation Phase in which imagination is engaged as a vehicle of self-transformation. Jamgön Kongtrül Lodrö Thayé's and Elio Guarisco's *Creative Vision and Inner Reality* (Shang Shung Publications, 2012) provides a highly instructive overview. Illuminating perspectives on the wider Asian phenomenon of 'deity yoga' can be found in Michael J. Puett's *To Become a God: Cosmology, Sacrifice, and Self-Divinization in Early China* (Harvard University Asia Center, 2002) and Frederick M. Smith's *The Self Possessed: Deity and Spirit Possession in South Asian Literature and Civilization* (Columbia University Press, 2006). The nature of Tantric deities is further explored in John C. Huntington's and Dina Bangdel's *The Circle of Bliss: Buddhist Meditational Art* (Serindia Publications, 2003). 'Enlightened anatomy' introduces Tantric physiology as well as internal energy techniques (Tsalung) based on intangible structures and processes in the yogic body. Valuable works on this subject include Gyalwa Yangönpa's *Secret Map of the Body: Visions of the Human Energy Structure* (Shang Shung Publications, 2017), Geoffrey Samuel's and Jay Johnston's *Religion and the Subtle Body in Asia and the West: Between Mind and Body* (Routledge, 2013), James Mallinson and Mark Singleton's *Roots of Yoga: A Sourcebook of Indic Traditions* (Penguin Classics, 2017) and David Gordon White's *The Alchemical Body: Siddha Traditions in Medieval India* (University of Chicago Press, 1996). Also useful is Will Johnson's *Breathing through the Whole Body: The Buddha's Instructions on Integrating Mind, Body, and Breath* (Inner Traditions, 2012). 'Flowing wholeness' explores the evolution of Haṭha Yoga-like practices in Vajrayāna Buddhism. Further elucidations of Lujong, 'body training' and Trulkhor, or 'magical movements', in Tibetan culture include Chögyal Namkhai Norbu's *Yantra Yoga: The Tibetan Yoga of Movement* (Snow Lion Publications, 2008) and *Tibetan Yoga of Movement: The Art and Practice of Yantra Yoga* by Chögyal Namkhai Norbu and Fabio Andrico (Shang Shung Publications, 2013). Yantra yoga represents a highly accessible form of Trulkhor, which focuses on integrated breath and movement rather than Trulkhor's signature acrobatic 'falls' (*beb*). Further reading on Yantra yoga and Lujong includes Tenzin Wangyal's *Awakening the Sacred Body: Tibetan Yogas of Breath and Movement* (Hay House, 2011). Tummo, or 'fierce heat', arises from Trulkhor and is the subject of the chapter 'Incandescence'. A highly accessible introduction to Tummo can be found in Lama Thubten Yeshe's *The Bliss of Inner Fire: Heart Practice of the Six Yogas of Naropa* (Wisdom Publications, 1998). An academic and scientific perspective is provided by Maria Kozhevnikov, James Elliot, Jennifer Shephard and Klaus Gramann in an article entitled 'Neurocognitive and Somatic Components of Temperature Increases during g-Tummo Meditation: Legend and Reality' (PLOS ONE, 29 March 2013). Contemporary, non-traditional forms of 'inner fire' practice are currently being advanced globally as the 'Wim Hof Method' and its various offshoots. The chapter 'Numinous passion' contextualizes sexual practices in Vajrayāna Buddhism. Valuable resources in this field include Jamgön Kongtrül Lodrö Thayé's *Treasury of Knowledge: Book Eight, Part Four: Esoteric Methods* (Snow Lion, 2007), Lama Thubten Yeshe's and Jonathan Landaw's *Introduction to Tantra: The Transformation of Desire* (Wisdom Publications, 2001), David Gordon White's *Kiss of the Yogini: 'Tantric Sex' in its South Asian Contexts* (University of Chicago Press, 2006) and Dr Nida Chenagtsang's highly informative *Karmamudrā: The Yoga of Bliss* (Sky Press, 2018), which illuminates sexuality from the perspective of Tibetan Buddhist medicine. Also very valuable are Gendun Chopel's *The Passion Book: A Tibetan Guide to Love and Sex* (University of Chicago Press, 2018) and Robert Hans Van Gulik's *Sexual Life in Ancient China: A Preliminary Survey of Chinese Sex and Society from ca. 1500 B.C.*

till 1644 A.D (Brill, [1961] 2002), which claims evidence that Karmamudrā practice and sexual yoga came to India from ancient China. The chapter 'Noetic light' elucidates the luminescent state of consciousness that is accessed through Tantric yoga. Further readings include Matthew Kapstein's *The Presence of Light: Divine Radiance and Religious Experience* (University of Chicago Press, 2004). Highly valuable resources for dream yoga, as discussed in the chapter 'Dreamtime', include Namkhai Norbu's *Dream Yoga and the Practice of Natural Light* (Snow Lion, 1992), Tenzin Wangyal Rinpoche's *The Tibetan Yogas of Dream and Sleep* (Snow Lion, 1998), Andrew Holecek's *Dream Yoga: Illuminating Your Life Through Lucid Dreaming and the Tibetan Yogas of Sleep* (Sounds True, 2013) and Charlie Morley's *Dreams of Awakening: Lucid Dreaming and Mindfulness of Dream and Sleep* (Hay House, 2013). For additional perspectives on the practice of consciousness transference at the time of death, as explored in the chapter 'Exit strategies', see Peter Fenwick and Elizabeth Fenwick's *The Art of Dying: A Journey to Elsewhere* (Continuum, 2008) and Francis V. Tiso's *Rainbow Body and Resurrection* (North Atlantic Books, 2016). For further accounts of the intermediate state between death and rebirth, as discussed in the chapter 'Liminality', Donald Lopez Jr's *The Tibetan Book of the Dead: A Biography* (Princeton University Press, 2011) provides a valuable historic overview, while Elio Guarisco's *The Tibetan Book of the Dead: Awakening Upon Dying* (Shang Shung Publications, 2013), with an introductory commentary by Dzogchen master Chögyal Namkhai Norbu, offers an insightful translation of the original 14th-century text. *Tibetan Shamanism: Ecstasy and Healing* (North Atlantic Books, 2016), by Larry Peters, offers insight into the interface of shamanism and Tantric Buddhism. For further inquiry into the role of psychoactive substances in Tantric Buddhism, as discussed in the chapter 'Potent solutions', see *Entheogens and the Future Religion*, edited by Robert Forte (Park Street Press, 1997), *Zig Zag Zen: Buddhism and Psychedelics*, edited by Allan Badiner and Alex Grey (Synergetic Press, 2015), Douglas Osto's *Altered States: Buddhism and Psychedelic Spirituality in America* (Columbia University Press, 2016), Michael Pollan's *How to Change Your Mind: What the New Science of Psychedelics Teaches Us About Consciousness, Dying, Addiction, Depression, and Transcendence* (Penguin Press, 2018) and forthcoming scientific reports by the Beckley Foundation in Oxford. For further readings on Dzogchen, as presented in the chapter 'Primal radiance', see Samten G. Karmay's *The Great Perfection (rDzogs chen): A Philosophical and Meditative Teaching of Tibetan Buddhism* (Brill, [1988] 2007), Chögyal Namkhai Norbu's *The Mirror: Advice on Presence and Awareness* (Shang Shung Editions, 1983) and *The Supreme Source: The Fundamental Tantra of the Dzogchen Semde,* co-authored with Adriano Clemente (Snow Lion Publications, 1999). Other valuable perspectives on Dzogchen can be found in Christopher Hatchell's *Naked Seeing: The Great Perfection, the Wheel of Time, and Visionary Buddhism in Renaissance Tibet* (Oxford University Press, 2014) and Nida Chenagtsang's *Mirror of Light: A Commentary on Yuthok's Ati Yoga* (Sky Press, 2016). For Dzogchen's parallels with non-dual Śaivism, see Paul Eduardo Muller-Ortega's *The Triadic Heart of Śiva: Kaula Tantricism of Abhinavagupta in the Non-Dual Shaivism of Kashmir* (State University of New York Press, 1989). For a unified vision of Buddhism and Taoism, see *Awakening to the Tao* by Liu I-Ming (Shambhala, 1998). For background on the evolution of Dzogchen and Mahāmudrā, see Per Kvaerne 'On the Concept of Sahaja in Indian Buddhist Tantric Literature' (Temenos, 1976). For Tibetan yoga's introduction in the West, as discussed in the Afterword, see Donald S. Lopez Jr's *Prisoners of Shangri-La: Tibetan Buddhism and the West* (University of Chicago Press, 1998), *Imagining Tibet: Perceptions, Projections, and Fantasies,* edited by Thierry Dodin and Heinz Räther (Wisdom, 2001), 'When the Iron Bird Flies: Tibetan Buddhism Arrives in the West' (DVD, 2014) and Hugh B. Urban's *Tantra: Sex, Secrecy, Politics, and Power in the Study of Religion* (University of California Press, 2003). See also *The Eye of Revelation: The Ancient Tibetan Rites of Rejuvenation* by Peter Kelder (Booklocker [1939], 2008) for an account of a highly popular, if apocryphal, form of Tibetan yoga first revealed in the 1930s. For the wider interface of Buddhism and Western intellectual tradition, see *Critical Terms for the Study of Buddhism*, edited by Donald S. Lopez, Jr. (University of Chicago Press, 2005). See also *Yoga in Transformation: History and Contemporary Perspectives on a Global Phenomenon*, eds Karl Baier, Philipp A. Maas and Karin Preisendanz (University of Vienna Press, 2017). Additional references in the Afterword include James Mallinson's 'The Tantric Buddhist Roots of Haṭha Yoga' (*Advaya Magazine*, Issue One: Origins, 2017), Dzogchen Ponlop Rinpoche (*Lions Roar* Forum on Tantra, 2016) and *White Lama: The Life of Tantric Yogi Theos Bernard, Tibet's Lost Emissary to the New World* by Douglas Veenhof (Harmony, 2011). For science's convergence with Tantric Buddhism, see *Where Buddhism Meets Neuroscience: Conversations with the Dalai Lama on the Spiritual and Scientific Views of Our Minds,* edited by Zara Houshmand, Robert B. Livingston and B. Alan Wallace (Shambhala Publications, 2018). See also *Longevity and Optimal Health: Integrating Eastern and Western Perspectives* (Wiley-Blackwell, 2009), edited by William C. Bushell, Erin L. Olivio and Neil D. Theise. For insights into the inner processes involved in Tantric yoga, see Mihaly Csikszentmihalyi's *Flow: The Psychology of Optimal Experience* (Harper & Row, 1990). For Tantric yoga's portrayal in modern museums, see *The Museum on Roof of the World: Art, Politics, and the Representation of Tibet* by Claire Harris (University of Chicago Press, 2012) and Debra Diamond's and Molly Emma Aitken's *Yoga: The Art of Transformation* (Smithsonian Books, 2013). For practical adaptations of ancient Tantric practices in the modern world and their antecedents in Western tradition, see Ian A. Baker's *Yogas of Fire and Light: Vajrayāna in the Modern World* (forthcoming). See also proceedings of the Centre for Bhutan Studies & GNH Research in connection with annual international conferences in Bhutan on tradition and innovation in Vajrayāna Buddhism. For a condensed, academic overview of the contents of this book, see Ian A. Baker, 'Tibetan Yoga: Somatic Practice in Vajrayāna Buddhism and Dzogchen', in *Yoga in Transformation: Historical and Contemporary Perspectives* (V&R unipress, 2018). It is perhaps not out of place to end with a quotation from the 15th-century Haṭhayoga Pradīpikā that, like the Six Yogas taught by Tilopā, claims to represent the distilled essence of pre-existing Tantric texts and practices: 'Success comes to one who engages in practice . . . Merely reading books on Yoga will never bring success!'

Picture credits

Unless otherwise indicated, all photographs in this book are by Ian A. Baker. A photograph by Megan Frasheski appears on page 67. The photograph on page 161 is by Susan Richardson. The photograph on page 181 is courtesy of Hamid Sardar. The photographs of 'flying' yogis on pages 10, 139, 140–41 and 283 are courtesy of Dasho Karma Ura.

The contemporary artwork featured on pages 2, 74, 106, 150, 159, 176, 190, 195, 220, 257, 264 and 277 are with the kind permission of the artist Rolf Kluenter. The paintings on pages 116–17 and the detail on page 7 are courtesy of the artist Robert Powell. Luke Brown kindly permitted the reproduction of his painting of Yamāntaka on page 231. Alex Grey generously contributed the *Bardo Being* painting that appears on page 227. Details of Tibetan medical paintings that appear on pages 93, 109 and 236 are with the kind permission of Romio Shrestha. The painting of Trulkhor exercises on pages 114–15 is courtesy of Akarpa Lobsang Rinpoche, who is also featured in a photograph on page 154.

Historical artwork featured in this book derives from multiple sources. The folios and folio details that appear on pages 4, 14, 121, 188, 250 and 260–61 are courtesy of the Royal Danish Library in Copenhagen, while those on pages 32, 52, 75 (above), 120, 127, 158, 178, 185 and 197 are with the permission of the Beijing Palace Museum. The Tibetan thangka paintings, with related details, which appear on pages 13, 31, 90, 95, 152, 164, 168, 169, 205, 209, 246, 282 and 287 were provided by the Rubin Museum of Art in New York. The Cakrasaṃvara painting featured on page 50 is with the kind permission of the Metropolitan Museum of Art in New York. The Newark Museum of Art in New Jersey provided the image of Milarepa in a mountain on page 65. The Musée Guimet in Paris provided the image of Mahāsiddha Dārikapa that appears on page 18 and on the back cover. The image of Silenus, the teacher of Dionysus, on page 234 is courtesy of the British Museum in London. The thermography image of Akarpa Rinpoche on page 17 was provided by the Wellcome Library in London, as was the MRI scan on page 15 and the Vajrayoginī maṇḍala on page 73. The images on pages 84, 139, 188, 238, 239, 269, 270 and 271 are courtesy of the Science Photo Library in London.

The mural details from Ogyen Choling Manor in Central Bhutan that feature on pages 30, 81, 103, 121, 136, 210, 213, 216 and 253 are included with the kind permission of Ashi Kunzang Choden. The mural details shown on pages 112, 194 and 233 are with the kind permission of Gangteng Tulku Rinpoche. The images of the vajra body and *cakras* that appear on pages 88 and 94 are courtesy of Lama Tinley and Naljor Jinpa. David Pritzker kindly allowed the reproduction of the *cakra* diagrams that appear on page 86 and on page 118. The images of the 14th-century Tögal manuscript on pages 99, 222, 225 and 269 are from a private collection, as are the paintings on pages 118, 133,149,166 and 253. Laurent Solomon provided the image of mahāsiddha Virūpā shown on page 105. Tashi Tshering provided the image of Tārā on page 78. Naldjor provided the images that appear in the margins of pages 48 and 117. The images on pages 102, 229, 237 and 239 are courtesy of the Buckingham Collection. The Tibetan calligraphy that augments the book's chapter headings is by Karma Lhatrul Rinpoche.

Above **Padmasambhava and Eight Mahāsiddhas.** Kham Province, Eastern Tibet; 19th century. Pigments on cloth. Rubin Museum of Art, New York. (See details on pages 31 and 169.)

Index

Page numbers in *italics* refer to illustrations

Ian A. Baker is an anthropologist and cultural historian and the author of several books on Tibetan Buddhism and Himalayan art and culture, including *The Dalai Lama's Secret Temple* and *The Tibetan Art of Healing* (both published by Thames & Hudson). He was joint curator of the 2016 exhibition 'Tibet's Secret Temple: Body, Mind and Meditation in Tantric Buddhism' at the Wellcome Collection, London. He leads travel seminars in Tibet and Bhutan and was named by the National Geographic Society as one of seven 'Explorers for the Millennium' for his ground-breaking field research in Tibet's Tsangpo Gorges.

First published in the United Kingdom by Thames & Hudson Ltd,
181A High Holborn, London WC1V 7QX

Designed by Karolina Prymaka

British Library Cataloguing-in-Publication Data
A catalogue record for this book is available from the British Library

ISBN 978-0-500-51926-4

Printed in China by Reliance Printing (Shenzhen) Co. Ltd

To find out about all our publications, please visit **www.thamesandhudson.com.** There you can subscribe to our e-newsletter, browse or download our current catalogue, and buy any titles that are in print.